FREEMASONRY
AND ITS ANCIENT
MYSTIC RITES

C. W. Leadbeater, 1926

FREEMASONRY AND ITS ANCIENT MYSTIC RITES

C. W. LEADBEATER

GRAMERCY BOOKS
New York

This 1998 edition is published by Gramercy Books,
a division of Random House Value Publishing, Inc.,
201 East 50th Street, New York, New York 10022,
by arrangement with the Theosophical Publishing House and Quest
Books.

Gramercy Books® and design are registered trademarks of
Random House Value Publishing, Inc.

Random House
New York • Toronto • London • Sydney • Auckland
http://www.randomhouse.com/

Printed and bound in the United States of America

Library of Congress Cataloging-in-Publication Data
Leadbeater, C. W. (Charles Webster), 1847-1934.
    [Glimpses of Masonic history]
    Freemasonry and its ancient mystic rites / C.W. Leadbeater.
        p.   cm.
    Originally published as: Glimpses of Masonic history, 1926.
    ISBN 0-517-20267-0
    1. Freemasonry—History.   I. Title.
HS403.L4 1998
366'.1'09—dc21   98-10836
                                                                   CIP

Previously published as *Glimpses of Masonic History* (1926) and
Ancient Mystic Rites (1986)

8 7 6 5 4 3 2 1

Publisher's Note. This republication of the 1926 edition of C. W.
Leadbeater's *Glimpses of Masonic History* neither promotes nor endorses
the philosophical and religious beliefs contained in the original book.

Contents

PREFACE TO THIS EDITION ix
AUTHOR'S PREFACE xi

CHAPTER I

SCHOOLS OF MASONIC THOUGHT

The Origins of Masonry. The Authentic School. The Anthropological School. The Mystical School. The Occult School. The Knowledge of the Occultist. The Occult Records. The Sacramental Power. The Form and the Life. Orthodoxy and Heresy   1

CHAPTER II

THE EGYPTIAN MYSTERIES

The Message of the World-Teacher. The Gods of Egypt. Isis and Osiris. Animal Deities. The Practice of Embalming. Other Deities. The Brothers of Horus. Consecration. The Purpose of the Mysteries. The Degrees of the Mysteries. The Mysteries of Isis. The Preliminary Trials. The Mystery Language. The Duality of each Degree. The Inner Mysteries of Isis. The Mysteries of Serapis. The Inner Degree of Serapis. The Mysteries of Osiris. The Legend of Osiris. The Meaning of the Story. The Inner Mysteries of Osiris. The Office of Master. The Higher

Grades of the Mysteries. Red Masonry in the Mysteries. Black Masonry in the Mysteries. White Masonry in the Mysteries. The Stages of the Occult Path. The First Three Initiations. The Fourth Initiation. The Fifth Initiation and Beyond 15

CHAPTER III

THE CRETAN MYSTERIES

The Unity of the Mysteries. Life in Ancient Crete. The Cretan Race. Recent Discoveries in Crete. Worship in Crete. The Throne Room. The Three Columns. Models of Shrines. The Altar Objects. Various Symbols. The Statuettes........ 50

CHAPTER IV

THE JEWISH MYSTERIES

The Jewish Line of Descent. The Jewish Migrations. The Prophets. The Builders of K. S. T. The Recasting of the Rituals. The Mingling of Traditions. The Transmission of the New Rites. The Essenes and the Christ. Kabbalism. The Spiritualization of the Temple. The Loss of the Divine Name............................... 63

CHAPTER V

THE GREEK MYSTERIES

The Eleusinian Mysteries. The Origin of the Greek Mysteries. The Gods of Greece. The Officials. The Lesser Mysteries. The Greater Mysteries. The Myths of the Greater Mysteries. The Magic of the Greater Mysteries. The Hidden Mysteries. The School of Pythagoras. The Three Degrees. Other Greek Mysteries............ 78

CHAPTER VI

THE MITHRAIC MYSTERIES

Zarathustra and Mithraism. Mithraism among the Romans. The Mithraic Rites. The Roman Collegia. The Work of King Numa. The Colleges and the Legions. The Introduction of the Jewish Form. The Transition to the Operatives   103

CHAPTER VII

CRAFT MASONRY IN MEDIAEVAL TIMES

Evolutionary Methods. The Withdrawal of the Mysteries. The Christian Mysteries. The Repression of the Mysteries. The Crossing of Traditions. The Two Lines of Descent. The Culdees. Celtic Christianity in Britain. The Druidic Mysteries. The Holy Grail. Heredom   112

CHAPTER VIII

OPERATIVE MASONRY IN THE MIDDLE AGES

The Temporary Custodians. Decline of the Collegia. The Comacini. The Comacine Lodges. Other Survivals of the Collegia. The Compagnonnage. The Stonemasons of Germany. The English Guilds. The Rise of Gothic Architecture. The Old Charges   125

CHAPTER IX

THE TRANSITION FROM OPERATIVE TO SPECULATIVE

The Reformation. The Reappearance of Speculative Masonry. The First Minutes. Scottish Minutes. English Minutes. Irish Minutes. The Grand Lodge of England. The Recomposition of the Rituals. Two and Three Degrees.

Opposition. The Succession of I.M.s. The Grand Lodges
of York, Ireland and Scotland. The "Ancients". The Holy
Royal Arch. The United Grand Lodge. Craft Masonry
in Other Countries   140

CHAPTER X

OTHER LINES OF MASONIC TRADITION

The Stream of Secret Societies. The Knights Templars. The
Suppression of the Templars. The Preservation of the
Templars' Tradition. The Royal Order of Scotland. The
Brothers of the Rosy Cross. The Literature of Rosicru-
cianism. The Traditional History of the Rosicrucians.
The History of the Order   160

CHAPTER XI

THE SCOTTISH RITE

Origin of the Rite. The Jacobite Movement. The Oration of
Ramsay. The Chapter of Clermont. The Council of
Emperors. Stephen Morin. Frederick the Great. The
Charleston Transformation. The Spread of the Scottish
Rite   178

CHAPTER XII

THE CO-MASONIC ORDER

The Restoration of an Ancient Landmark. The Succession
of Co-Masonry. The Co-Masonic Rituals. The Future
of Masonry   191

APPENDIX I. Degrees of the Rite of Perfection   197
          II. Principal Masonic Events from 1717   201
INDEX   221

Preface to This Edition

In this classic work, C. W. Leadbeater shows the kinship between Freemasonry and some ancient Mystery Rites, as well as some more recent movements. The history that he presents is based on extensive research into Masonic documents and on his own clairvoyant investigations. Clairvoyant findings cannot be verified by ordinary means, of course, but Leadbeater was known to use meticulous care in observing superphysical phenomena and was one of the most distinguished clairvoyants of his day. This edition was edited only very slightly to remove some untimely material. The book is reprinted as a historical document that may reveal fresh meaning in the ancient mysteries and in Freemasonry.

EDITOR

About the Author

Charles W. Leadbeater (1847 to 1934) was among the clergy of the Church of England as a young man. He became a Theosophist in 1883 and went to India to help Helen P. Blavatsky, the spiritual head of the movement. In India he also worked with Col. H.S. Olcott, President of the Theosophical Society, in revitalizing Buddhism in Southeast Asia and in founding Buddhist schools. His clairvoyant powers were opened while he was in India, and he became a teacher and lecturer for the Society. He is well known for the meticulous care he took in observing and reporting on superphysical phenomena.

Leadbeater is author of many books on Theosophy and on his clairvoyant investigations, including *Man Visible and Invisible* and *The Chakras,* and he co-authored books such as *Thought Forms* with Annie Besant, who was President of the Society after Col. Olcott's death. Leadbeater was a 32nd degree Mason and, in addition to this book, wrote *The Hidden Side of Freemasonry.*

Author's Preface

WHEN I wrote *The Hidden Life in Freemasonry,* it was at first my intention to devote my second chapter to a brief outline of Masonic history. I soon found that that plan was impractical. The most compressed account that would be of any use would occupy far more space than I could spare, and would entirely overweight the book with what is after all only one department of its subject. The obvious alternative is to publish the historical sketch separately; hence this book, which is really but a second volume of the other.

The keynote of both volumes, and indeed the only reason for their publication, is to explain precisely what the title indicates—the hidden life in Freemasonry—the mighty force in the background, always at work yet always out of sight, which has guided the transmission of the Masonic tradition through all the vicissitudes of its stormy history, and still inspires the utmost enthusiasm and devotion among the Brn. of the Craft to-day.

The existence and the work of the Head of all true Freemasons is the one and sufficient reason for the virility and power of this most wonderful Organization. If we understand His relation to it and what He wishes to make of it, we shall also understand that it embodies one of the finest schemes ever invented for the helping of the world and for the outpouring of spiritual force.

Many of our Brn. have been for many years unconsciously taking part in this magnificent altruistic work; if they can be brought to comprehend what it is that they are doing and why, they will continue the great work more happily and more intelligently, throwing into it the whole strength of their nature both bodily and spiritual, and enjoying the fruit of their labours far more definitely than ever before.

1

Schools of Masonic Thought

A HISTORY of Freemasonry would be a colossal undertaking, needing encyclopaedic knowledge and many years of research. I have no pretension to the possession of the qualities and the erudition required for the production of such a work; all I can hope to do is to throw a little light upon some of the dark spots in that history, and to bridge over to some extent some of the more obvious gaps between the sections of it which are already well known.

THE ORIGINS OF MASONRY

The actual origins of Freemasonry, as I have said in a previous book, are lost in the mists of antiquity. Masonic writers of the eighteenth century speculated uncritically upon its history, basing their views upon a literal belief in the history and chronology of the Old Testament, and upon the curious legends of the Craft handed down from operative times in the Old Charges. Thus it was put forward in all seriousness by Dr. Anderson in his first *Book of Constitutions* that "Adam, our first parent, created after the Image of God, the *great Architect of the Universe,* must have had the Liberal Sciences, particularly *Geometry,* written on his Heart," while others, less fanciful, have attributed its origin to Abraham, Moses, or Solomon. Dr. Oliver, writing as late as the first part of the nineteenth century, held that Masonry, as we have it to-day, is the only true relic of the faith of the patriarchs before the flood, while the ancient Mysteries of Egypt and other countries, which so closely resembled it, were but human corruptions of the one primitive and pure tradition.

As scientific and historical knowledge progressed in other fields of research, and especially in the criticism of the Scriptures, scientific methods were gradually applied to the study of Masonry, so that to-day there exists a vast body of fairly accurate and most interesting information upon the history of the Craft. In consequence of this and other lines of investigation there are four main schools or tendencies of Masonic thought, not in any way necessarily defined or organized as schools, but grouped according to their relation to four important departments of knowledge lying primarily outside the Masonic field. Each has its own characteristic approach towards Freemasonry; each has its own canons of interpretation of Masonic symbols and ceremonies, although it is clear that many modern writers are influenced by more than one school.

THE AUTHENTIC SCHOOL

We may consider first what is sometimes called the Authentic School, which arose in the latter half of the nineteenth century in response to the growth of critical knowledge in other fields. The old traditions of the Craft were minutely examined in the light of authentic records within reach of the historian. An enormous amount of research was undertaken into Lodge minutes, documents of all kinds bearing upon Masonry past and present, records of municipalities and boroughs, legal and judicial enactments; in fact, whatever written records were available were consulted and classified. In this field all Masons are greatly indebted to R. F. Gould, the great Masonic historian; W. J. Hughan; G. W. Speth; David Murray-Lyon, the historian of Scottish Masonry; Dr. Chetwode Crawley, whose work upon the early Irish Craft is in its way a classic; and others of the Inner Circle of the famous Lodge *Quattuor Coronati,* No. 2076, the fascinating Transactions of which are a precious mine of historical and archaeological lore. Two great names in Germany are J. F. Findel, the historian, and Dr. Wilhelm Begemann, who made the most minute and painstaking researches into the Old Charges of the operative Craft. A vast amount of material which will be of permanent value to students of our Craft has become available through the labours of the scholars of the Authentic School.

This school, however, has limitations which are the outcome of its very method of approach. In a society as secret as Masonry there must be much that has never been written down, but only transmitted orally in the Lodges, so that documents and records are but of partial value. The written records of speculative Masonry hardly antedate the revival in 1717, while the earliest extant minutes of any operative Lodge belong to the year 1598.[1] The tendency of this school, therefore, is quite naturally to derive Masonry from the operative Lodges and Guilds of the Middle Ages, and to suppose that speculative elements were later grafted upon the operative stock—this hypothesis being in no way contradicted by existing records. Bro. R. F. Gould affirms that if we can assume the symbolism (or ceremonial) of Masonry to be older than 1717, there is practically no limit whatever to the age that can be assigned to it[2]; but many other writers look for the origin of our Mysteries no further back than the mediaeval builders.

Amongst this school there is a tendency, also very natural when such a theory of origin is held, to deny the validity of the higher degrees, and to declare, in accordance with the Solemn Act of Union between the two Grand Lodges of the Freemasons of England, in December, 1813, that "pure Antient Masonry consists of three degrees and no more, *viz.*, those of the Entered Apprentice, the Fellow Craft, and the Master Mason, including the Supreme Order of the Holy Royal Arch."[3] All other degrees and rites are, among the more rigid followers of this school, looked upon as Continental innovations and are accordingly rejected as "spurious" Masonry.

As far as interpretation goes, the authentics have ventured but little further than a moralization upon the symbols and ceremonies of Masonry as an adjunct to Anglican Christianity.

THE ANTHROPOLOGICAL SCHOOL

A second school, still only in process of development, is applying the discoveries of anthropology to a study of Masonic history, with remarkable results. A vast amount of information upon the religious and initiatory customs of many peoples, both ancient and modern, has been gathered by anthropologists; and Masonic students in this

---

[1] *History of the Lodge of Edinburgh,* by D. Murray-Lyon, p. 9.

[2] *Concise History of Freemasonry,* by R. F. Gould, p. 55.

[3] *Book of Constitutions, 1884,* p. 16.

field have found many of our signs and symbols, both of the Craft and higher degrees, in the wall-paintings, carvings, sculpture and buildings of the principal races of the world. The Anthropological School, therefore, allows a far greater degree of antiquity to Masonry than the Authentics have ever ventured to do, and traces striking analogies with the ancient Mysteries of many nations, which clearly possessed our symbols and signs, and in all probability ceremonies analogous to those worked in Masonic Lodges to-day.

The Anthropologists do not confine their studies to the past alone, but have investigated the initiatory rites of many existing tribes, both in Africa and Australia, and have found them to possess signs and gestures still in use among Masons. Striking analogies to our Masonic rites have also been found among the inhabitants of India and Syria, interwoven with their religious philosophy in a way which renders entirely impossible the idea that they were copied from European sources. Masonic scholars have by no means exhausted the facts which may be discovered in this most interesting field of research, but even with our present knowledge it is clear that rites analogous to those we call Masonic are among the most ancient on earth, and may be found in some form or other in almost all parts of the world. Our signs exist in Egypt and Mexico, in China and India, in Greece and Rome, upon the temples of Burma and the cathedrals of mediaeval Europe; and there are said to be shrines in Southern India where the same secrets are taught under binding pledges as are communicated to us in the Craft and high grades in modern Europe and America.

Among pioneers in this field we should mention Bro. Albert Churchward, the author of several interesting books on the Egyptian origin of Masonry, although it may be that he is not always quite sufficiently critical; Bro. J. S. M. Ward, the author of *Freemasonry and the Ancient Gods, Who was Hiram Abiff?* and a number of other works, who looks to Syria as the source of Masonry, though he has compiled a mass of valuable information from many other lands; and Mr. Bernard H. Springett, author of *Secret Sects of Syria and Lebanon,* who has collected much material bearing upon Masonic rites among the Arabs.

To the work of the Anthropological School is due a clear revelation of the immense antiquity and diffusion of what we now call Masonic symbolism. It tends, however, to find the origin of the ancient Mysteries in the initiatory customs of savage tribes which, although admittedly of incalculable antiquity, are often neither dignified nor spiritual.

Another important work which has been accomplished by its efforts is the justification of many of the higher degrees to be considered "pure Antient Masonry"; for in spite of the pronouncement of the Grand Lodge of England quoted above, there is just as much evidence for the extreme antiquity of Rose-Croix as of Craft and Arch signs and symbols, and the same may be said of the signs of many other degrees as well. It is quite clear from the researches of anthropologists that, whatever may be the precise links in the chain of descent, we in Masonry are the inheritors of a very ancient tradition, which has for countless ages been associated with the most sacred mysteries of religious worship.

THE MYSTICAL SCHOOL

A third school of Masonic thought, which we may call the Mystical, approaches the mysteries of the Craft from another standpoint altogether, seeing in them a plan of man's spiritual awakening and inner development. Thinkers of this school, on the record of their own spiritual experiences, declare that the degrees of the Order are symbolical of certain states of consciousness which must be awakened in the individual initiate if he aspires to win the treasures of the spirit. They give testimony of another and far higher nature upon the validity of our Masonic rites—a testimony that belongs to religion rather than to science. The goal of the mystic is conscious union with God, and to a Mason of this school the Craft is intended to portray the path to that goal, to offer a map, as it were, to guide the feet of the seeker after God.

Such students are often more interested in interpretation than in historical research. They are not primarily concerned in tracing an exact line of descent from the past, but rather in so living the life indicated by the symbols of the Order that they may attain to the spiritual reality of which those symbols are the shadows. They hold, however, that Masonry is at least akin to the ancient Mysteries, which were intended for precisely the same purpose—that of offering to man a path by which he might find God; and they deplore the fact that the majority of our modern Brn. have so far forgotten the glory of their Masonic heritage that they have allowed the ancient rites to become little more than empty forms. One well-known representative of this school is Bro. A. E. Waite, one of the finest Masonic scholars of the day, and an authority upon the history of the higher degrees. Another is Bro. W. L. Wilmshurst, who has given some beautiful and deeply spiritual interpretations of Masonic symbolism. This school is doing much to spiritualize masculine Masonry, and the deeper reverence for our mysteries that is becoming more and more apparent is without doubt one of the marks of its influence.

THE OCCULT SCHOOL

The fourth school of thought is represented by an evergrowing body of students in the Co-Masonic Order, and is gradually attracting adherents in masculine Masonry also. Since one of its chief and distinctive tenets is the sacramental efficacy of Masonic ceremonial when duly and lawfully performed, we may perhaps not improperly term it the sacramental or occult school. The term occultism has been much misunderstood; it may be defined as the study and knowledge of the hidden side of nature by means of powers which exist in all men, but are still unawakened in the majority—powers which may be aroused and trained in the occult student by means of long and careful discipline and meditation.

The goal of the occultist, no less than that of the mystic, is conscious union with God; but the methods of approach are different. The aim of the occultist is to attain that union by means of knowledge and of will, to train the whole nature, physical, emotional and mental, until it becomes a perfect expression of the divine spirit within, and can be employed as an efficient instrument in the great plan which God has made for the evolution of mankind, which is typified in Masonry by the building of the holy temple. The mystic, on the other hand, rather aspires to ecstatic union with that level of the divine consciousness which his stage of evolution permits him to touch.

The way of the occultist lies through a graded series of steps, a pathway of Initiations conferring successive expansions of consciousness and degrees of sacramental power; that of the mystic is often more individual in character, a "flight of the alone to the Alone," as Plotinus so beautifully expressed it. To the occultist the exact observance of a form is of great importance, and through the use of ceremonial magic he creates a vehicle through which the divine light may be drawn down and spread abroad for the helping of the world, calling to his aid the assistance of Angels, nature-spirits and other inhabitants of the invisible worlds. The method of the mystic, on the other hand, is through prayer and orison; he cares nothing for forms and, though by his union therewith he too is a channel of the divine Life, he seems to me to lose the enormous advantage of the collective effort made by the occultist, which is so greatly strengthened by the help of the higher Beings whose presence he invokes. Both these paths lead to God; to some of us the first will appeal irresistibly, to others the second; it is largely a matter of the Ray to which we belong. The one is more outward-turned in service and sacrifice; the other more inward-turned in contemplation and love.

THE KNOWLEDGE OF THE OCCULTIST

The student of occultism, therefore, learns to awaken and train for scientific use the powers latent within him, and by their means he is able to see far more of the real meaning of life than the man whose vision is limited by the physical senses. He learns that each man is in essence divine, a veritable spark of God's fire, gradually evolving towards a future of glory and splendour culminating in union with God; that the method of his progress is by successive descents into earthly bodies for the sake of experience, and withdrawals into worlds or planes which are invisible to physical eyes. He finds that this progress is governed by a law of eternal justice, which renders to each man the fruit of that which he sows, joy for good and suffering for evil.

He learns, too, that the world is ruled, under the will of T. M. H., by a Brotherhood of Adepts, who have Themselves attained divine union, but remain on earth to guide humanity; that all the great religions of the world were founded by Them, according to the needs of the races for which they were intended, and that within these religions there have been schools of the Mysteries to offer to those who are ready a swifter path of unfoldment, with greater knowledge and opportunities for service; that this Path is divided into steps and degrees: the probationary Path, or the Lower Mysteries, wherein the candidates are prepared for discipleship, and the Path proper, or the Greater Mysteries, in which are conferred within the Great White Lodge itself five great Initiations, which lead the disciple from the life of earth to the life of adeptship in God, to become "a living flame," as it is said, "for the lighting of the world." He is taught that God, both in the universe and in man, shows Himself as a Trinity of Wisdom, Strength and Beauty, and that these Three Aspects are represented in the Great White Lodge in the Persons of its three chief Officers, through whom the mighty power of God descends to men.

THE OCCULT RECORDS

It will be seen that this occult knowledge depends no more upon the study of books and records than do the experiences of the mystics; both belong to a higher order of consciousness, the existence of which cannot be satisfactorily demonstrated on the physical plane. Nevertheless, the study of the physical-plane records of the past is of value in confirming the historical researches of the trained occultist, who is able to read what are sometimes called the akashic records, and so to acquire an accurate knowledge of the past. This subject is so little understood that it may perhaps be useful if at this point I quote somewhat at length from a book entitled *Clairvoyance* which I wrote many years ago:

On the mental plane (the records) have two widely different aspects. When the visitor to that plane is not thinking specially of them in any way, these records simply form a background to whatever is going on, just as the reflections in a pier-glass at the end of a room might form a background to the life of the people in it. It must always be borne in mind that under these conditions they are really merely reflections from the ceaseless activity of a great Consciousness upon a far higher plane. . . .

But if the trained investigator turns his attention specially to any one scene, or wishes to call it up before him, an extraordinary change at once takes place, for this is the plane of thought, and to think of anything is to bring it instantaneously before you. For example, if a man wills to see the record of the landing of Julius Caesar in England, he finds himself in a moment. . .standing on the shore among the legionaries, with the whole scene being enacted around him, precisely in every respect as he would have seen it if he had stood there in the flesh on that autumn morning in the year 55 B.C. Since what he sees is but a reflection, the actors are of course entirely unconscious of him, nor can any effort of his change the course of their action in the smallest degree, except only that he can control the rate at which the drama shall pass before him—can have the events of a whole year rehearsed before his eyes in a single hour, or can at any moment stop the movement altogether, and hold any particular scene in view as a picture as long as he chooses.

In truth he observes not only what he would have seen if he had been there at the time in the flesh, but much more. He hears and understands all that the people say, and he is conscious of all their thoughts and motives; and one of the most interesting of the many possibilities which open up before one who has learnt to read the records is the study of the thought of ages long past—the thought of the cave-men and the lake-dwellers as well as that which ruled the mighty civilizations of Atlantis, of Egypt or Chaldaea. What splendid possibilities open up before the man who is in full possession of this power may easily be imagined. He has before him a field of historical research of most entrancing interest. Not only can he review at his leisure all history with which we are acquainted, correcting as he examines it the many errors and misconceptions which have crept into the accounts handed down to us; he can also range at will over the whole story of the world from its very beginning, watching the slow development of intellect in man, the descent of the Lords of the Flame, and the growth of the mighty civilizations which They founded.

Nor is his study confined to the progress of humanity alone; he has before him, as in a museum, all the strange animal and vegetable forms which occupied the stage in days when the world was young; he can follow all the wonderful geological changes which have taken place, and watch the course of the great cataclysms which have altered the whole face of the earth again and again.

In one especial case an even closer sympathy with the past is possible to the reader of the records. If in the course of his inquiries he has to look upon some scene in which he himself has in a former birth taken part, he may deal with it in two ways; he can either regard it in the usual manner as a spectator (though always, be it remembered, as a spectator whose insight and sympathy are perfect), or he may once more identify himself with that long-dead personality of his—may throw himself back for the time into that life of long ago, and absolutely experience over again the thoughts and the emotions, the pleasures and the pains of a prehistoric past.

In the light of this occult knowledge (which is within the reach of the inner sight) Masonry is seen to be far greater and holier than its initiates appear generally to realize. As tradition has always indicated, it is found to be a direct descendant of the Mysteries of Egypt (once the heart of that splendid faith whose wisdom and power were the glory of the ancient world—those Mysteries which were the parent and prototype of the secret schools of other neighbouring lands), and its purpose is still to serve as a gateway to the true Mysteries of the Great White Lodge. It offers to its initiates far more than a mere moralization upon building tools, and yet it is "founded upon the purest principles of piety and virtue," for without the practice of morality and the living of the ethical life no true spiritual progress is possible.

The ceremonies of Freemasonry (those at least of its higher degrees) are dramatizations, as it were, of sections of the invisible worlds, through which the candidate must pass after death in the ordinary course of nature—which also he must enter in full consciousness during the rites of initiation into those true Mysteries of which Masonry is a reflection. Each degree relates to a different plane of nature, or to an aspect of a plane, and possesses layer after layer of meaning applicable to the consciousness of T. G. A. O. T. U., the constitution of the universe, and the principles in man, according to the occult law formulated by Hermes Trismegistus and adopted by Rosicrucians, alchemists and students of the Kabbala in later ages: "As above, so below." The Masonic rites are thus rites of the probationary Path, intended to be a preparation for true Initiation, to be a school for training the Brn. for the far greater knowledge of the Path proper.

THE SACRAMENTAL POWER

To the occult student Masonry has also another aspect, of the greatest importance, concerning which I have written in *The Hidden Life in Freemasonry*. It is not only a wonderful and intricate system of occult symbols enshrining the secrets of the invisible worlds; it has also a sacramental aspect which is of the utmost beauty and value not only to its initiates but to the world at large. The performance of the ritual of each degree is intended to call down spiritual power, first to assist the Bro. upon whom the degree is conferred to awaken within himself that aspect of consciousness which corresponds to the symbolism of the degree, as far as it can be awakened; secondly to aid in the evolution of the members present; and thirdly and most important of all, to pour out a flood of spiritual power intended to uplift, strengthen and encourage all members of the Craft.

Some years ago I undertook an investigation into the hidden side of the sacraments of the Catholic Church, and published the results of that investigation in a book called *The Science of the Sacraments*. Those who have read that book will remember that the shedding abroad of spiritual power is one great object of the celebration of the Holy Eucharist, and of other services of the Church, and that it is attained by the invocation of an Angel to build a spiritual temple in the inner worlds with the aid of the forces generated by the love and devotion of the people, and the charging of that temple with the enormous power called down at the consecration of the Sacred Elements. A somewhat similar result is achieved during the ceremonies performed by the Masonic Lodge, although the plan is not exactly the same, being indeed far older; and each of our rituals, when properly carried out, likewise builds a temple in the inner worlds, through which the spiritual power called down at the initiation of the candidate is stored and radiated. Thus Masonry is seen, in the sacramental sense as well as the mystical, to be "an art of building spiritualized," and every Masonic Lodge ought to be a channel of no mean order for the shedding of spiritual blessing over the district in which it labours.

Sometimes orders and rites which were once channels of great force have admitted, as the years passed by, Brn. less worthy than their predecessors—Brn. who thought more of their own gain than of service to the world. In such cases the spiritual powers associated with those grades were either entirely withdrawn by the H.O.A.T.F.,[4] to be introduced later into some other and more suitable group, or allowed to remain dormant until more fitting candidates should be found to hold them worthily—the bare succession passing down and transmitting, as it were, the seeds of the power, although the power itself was largely in abeyance.

On the other hand, there have been cases in which a rite or grade has been manufactured by a student who wished to throw some great truth into ceremonial form, but knew little of all this inner side of Masonry; if such a degree or rite were doing useful work and attracting suitable candidates, sacramental powers fitted for that rite or grade were sometimes introduced into it, either by some Bro. on the physical plane who possessed one of the lines of succession mentioned above, which was then adapted by the H.O.A.T.F. for the work, or by a direct and non-physical interference from behind.

Furthermore, the inner effect of a given degree, even in a rite that may be fully valid, may vary greatly with the degree of advancement and general attitude of the Bro. upon whom it is conferred; so that in one case, let us say, the 33° would confer stupendous spiritual power, and in another, less worthy, the powers given would be much smaller, because of the candidate's incapacity to respond fully to them. In such cases a fuller degree of power will manifest itself as greater advancement is made in the development of character. It also appears to be possible for power to be temporarily withdrawn in cases of evil-doing by one of the Brn., and to be restored later when the evil-doing has ceased.

All this may seem a little bewildering to the student of the form

---

[4]See *The Hidden Life in Freemasonry*, pp. 15, 185.

side of Masonry; and indeed it is a fact that there is but little means on the physical plane of judging the inner effect of a given degree without reference to those who may be working it. It may however be generally stated that the chief lines of Masonic tradition—those which are of the greatest inner or spiritual value—are the Craft degrees, upon which all other grades are superimposed, the Mark and the Arch degrees, and the chief degrees of the Ancient and Accepted Scottish Rite, the 18°, 30° and 33°. Other degrees that are worked have their own peculiar powers, and these are often valuable; but the grades which I have mentioned are those which are considered by the H.O.A.T.F. to be of the greatest value to our present generation, and they are therefore those which are worked at present in the Co-Masonic Order. Another line of great interest, though very different from any other degrees existing among us, is that of the rites of Memphis and Mizraim, which are relics in their occult power, although not in their form, of perhaps the very oldest Mysteries existing upon earth. These too have their part to play in the future, as in the past, and they have therefore been preserved and transmitted to us in the present day.

The Form and the Life

In all cases we must realize that the form of the degrees of Masonry and their life are two very different things, although of course in a perfect system, as in that of the ancient Mysteries at the height of their glory, they would correspond perfectly. Masonry is yet in a transitional stage, and is but emerging from the ignorance of the Dark Ages. The rites of Memphis and Mizraim are an example of this discrepancy. These colossal systems of 96° and 90° respectively are a mass of artificially-manufactured ceremonies, of but little value to a Masonic student except as a record of high-grade Masonic invention in France at the end of the eighteenth century. Most of the degrees have little occult power, and have simply been inserted into the rites by Brn. who could have known nothing of their real purpose; but behind the rites and quite independent of the form side of the tradition a line of succession has been handed down from a past even more ancient than that of the Scottish Rite itself. Even in the Scottish Rite many of the intermediate degrees are of but little occult value.

The whole position will be best understood if it can be realized that the plan of Masonry is in the hands of the H. O. A. T. F., who rules His mighty Order with perfect justice and the most marvellous skill, so that all that can be done is done for the greatest good of all. The powers that stand behind Freemasonry are great and holy, and it is but right that they should be conferred in their fullness only upon those who are likely to use them as they should be used and to treat them with the reverence they deserve. There is a great and glorious reality in the background all the time, ever pressing towards realization, and employing whatever channels are available for its manifestation. Whatever can be used is always used to the very fullest extent, and none need fear that he is overlooked. It is obvious, however, that where the Brn. think more of gratifying their own vanity than of the Hidden Work, where they spend their time in banqueting and revelry and curtail the sacred ritual in order that they may adjourn as quickly as possible to the South, they are less worthy channels of the Divine Glory than those more spiritual Brn. who are willing to study and to understand. All the time the H. O. A. T. F. is watching; He sees the slightest endeavor of the Craftsmen to serve, and He will pour forth His wondrous power just in so far as the Brn. become worthy of it.

ORTHODOXY AND HERESY

Another point which arises in connection with the transmission of Masonic degrees will be developed more fully as we proceed. We must realize that in Masonic ritual it is not a case of one orthodoxy, and a number of heresies and schisms; it is rather that there are as many lines of tradition in form as there are types of succession in inner power. The Mysteries worked in the different countries of the ancient world varied considerably in the details of their form and legend, and vestiges of these differences remain in the various workings now in use among us. Many equally valid streams of tradition have crossed and recrossed one another throughout the ages, and have influenced each other to a greater or less degree. The seating of the principal officers in a Craft Lodge, for instance, differs in English and Continental Masonry. English Masonry follows the old Egyptian method of arranging them, while Continental Masonry follows the Chaldaean plan and seats them in an isosceles triangle.

The powers of the succession of I. M.s in these two systems are in essence the same, but since in the Continental Lodges the ceremony of Installation is reduced to the merest vestige, only the minimum of power necessary for the actual transmission of the degrees is conferred, and very much less is done for the R.W.M. than under the English plan. But this is a question of imperfection of form rather than of absence of power. The spiritual powers behind Masonry work through the different forms according to the value of the form and the will of the H.O.A.T.F. behind, who is the only judge of the much-argued difference between genuine and spurious Masonry. In the light of this view of the Masonic succession, it will be seen that genuine rites are those which possess and transmit spiritual power, whereas spurious Masonry is the working of a form from which for one reason or another the life has been withdrawn, or to which it has never been linked.

In the following chapters I shall endeavour to trace the descent of the Masonic tradition from the Egyptian Mysteries to the present day, not in any way attempting to delineate each separate link in the chain of succession, for that would be the work of a life-time and would not be of any fuller value to the student, but touching rather upon important periods of Masonic history, as revealed by the inner sight, and confirmed in the writings of Masonic scholars.

2

The Egyptian Mysteries

In *The Hidden Life in Freemasonry* I have described to some extent
the form and meaning of Freemasonry as I knew it in Egypt about
six thousand years ago. That form was largely due to the birth of the
World-Teacher among the Egyptian people about 40,000 B.C. when
He taught them the doctrine of the Hidden Light. It may be well to
sketch briefly the history of the nation from that period up to
13,500 B.C., where I took it up in the previous book.

The authentic history of Egypt, as determined by modern scholars,
begins with the First Dynasty, which was founded by Mena or Manu
about 5,000 B.C.—the dates are variously given. It is considered that
the pyramids of Gizeh, which played so great a part in the hidden side
of Egyptian worship, were built by the Kings of the Fourth Dynasty,
Khufu (Cheops), Khafra (Chephren) and Menkaura (Mycerinus), during the fourth millennium B.C. But the inner history of Egypt and its
pyramids extends back further than this, into ages upon which even
tradition is almost silent, although some echoes of the reigns of the
Divine Kings of the Atlantean Dynasties, who ruled Egypt for many
thousands of years, appear in the Egyptian and Greek myths of the
gods and demigods who are said to have reigned before the coming
of Manu.

According to Manetho, the Egyptian historian of the Ptolemaic period, whose works are now lost (except for certain fragments preserved in quotations), the gods and demigods reigned for 12,843 years. After these came the *Nekyes* or *Manes,* who are said to have reigned for 5,813 years; and some of these may perhaps be identified with the *Shemsu Heru,* or Followers of Horus, who are frequently mentioned in Egyptian texts.[1] Diodorus Siculus, who visited Egypt about 57 B.C., tells us that it was traditionally believed that the gods and heroes had reigned over Egypt for a little less than eighteen thousand years before the time of Mena.[2] The book *Man: Whence, How and Whither* carries us much further into the past, and gives us the following facts.

The Atlantean conquest of Egypt took place over one hundred and fifty thousand years ago, and the first great Egyptian empire lasted until the catastrophe of 75,025 B.C., when the two great islands Ruta and Daitya were whelmed beneath the ocean, and only the island of Poseidonis remained.[3] It was during the dominance of that empire that the three pyramids were built in accordance with the astronomical and mathematical lore of the Atlantean priests;[4] and it is to this age also that we look for the origin of those Mysteries which have been handed down to us in the ceremonies of Freemasonry. Even then the ceremonies were ancient, and we must search a still more remote past for their ultimate source. In the great catastrophe of 75,025 B.C. the whole land of Egypt was flooded, and nothing remained of all its glory save the three pyramids rising above the waters.[5] After this, when the swamps had become habitable, there came a negroid domination; and then the land was again colonized by the Atlanteans, who restored the splendour of the Egyptian temples and established once more the hidden Mysteries which had been celebrated in the great pyramid. This empire lasted up to the time of the Aryanization of Egypt in 13,500 B.C.; it was ruled by a great dynasty of divine kings, among whom were

---

[1] Sir E. A. Wallis Budge. *The Nile,* p. 26

[2] Diod. Sic., *Hist.,* Bk. I., xliv.

[3] *Op. cit.,* pp. 119 and 132, and *The Story of Atlantis,* by Scott Elliott.

[4] See *The Hidden Life in Freemasonry,* p. 229.

[5] *Man: Whence, How and Whither,* pp. 242 and 283.

many of the heroes whom Greece later regarded as demigods, such as Herakles of the twelve labours, whose tradition was handed on to classical times.

It was to this people about 40,000 B.C. that the World-Teacher came forth from the White Lodge, bearing the name of Tehuti or Thoth, called later by the Greeks Hermes; He founded the outer cult of the Egyptian Gods and restored the Mysteries to the splendour of byegone days.

He came to teach the great doctrine of the 'Inner Light' to the priests of the Temples, to the powerful sacerdotal hierarchy of Egypt, headed by its Pharaoh. In the inner court of the chief Temple He taught them of 'the Light that lighteth every man that cometh into the world'—a phrase of His that was handed down through the ages, and was echoed in the fourth Gospel in its early Egyptian-coloured words. He taught them that the Light was universal, and that that Light, which was God, dwelt in the heart of every man: "I am that Light," He bade them repeat, "That Light am I". "That Light," He said, "is the true man, although men may not recognize it, although they neglect it. Osiris is Light; He came forth from the Light; He dwells in the Light; He is the Light. The Light is hidden everywhere; it is in every rock and in every stone. When a man becomes one with Osiris the Light, then he becomes one with the whole of which he was part, and then he can see the Light in everyone, however thickly veiled, pressed down, and shut away. All the rest is not; but the Light is. The Light is the life of men. To every man—though there are glorious ceremonies, though there are many duties for the priest to do, and many ways in which he should help men—that Light is nearer than aught else, within his very heart. For every man the Reality is nearer than any ceremony, for he has only to turn inwards, and then will he see the Light. That is the object of every ceremony, and ceremonies should not be done away with, for I come not to destroy but to fulfil. When a man knows, he goes beyond the ceremony, he goes to Osiris, he goes to the Light, the Light Amen-Ra, from which all came forth, to which all shall return.

"Osiris is in the heavens, but Osiris is also in the very heart of men. When Osiris in the heart knows Osiris in the heavens, then man becomes God, and Osiris, once rent into fragments, again becomes one. But see! Osiris the Divine Spirit, Isis, the Eternal Mother, give life to Horus, who is Man, Man born of both, yet one with Osiris. Horus is merged in Osiris, and Isis, who had been Matter, becomes through him the Queen of Life and Wisdom. And Osiris, Isis, and Horus are all born of the Light.

"Two are the births of Horus. He is born of Isis, the God born into humanity, taking flesh of the Mother Eternal, Matter, the Ever-Virgin. He is born again into Osiris, redeeming his Mother from her long search for the fragments of her husband scattered over the earth. He is born into Osiris when Osiris in the heart sees Osiris in the heavens, and knows that the twain are one."

So taught He, and the wise among the priests were glad.

To Pharaoh, the Monarch, He gave the motto: "Look for the Light"; He said that only as a King saw the Light in the heart of each could he rule well. And to the people He gave as a motto: "Thou art the Light. Let that Light shine." And He set that motto round the pylon in a great Temple, running up one pillar, and across the bar, and down the other pillar. And this was inscribed over the doors of houses, and little models were made of the pylon on which He had inscribed it, models in precious metals, and also in baked clay, so that the poorest could buy little blue clay models, with brown veins running through them, and glazed. Another favourite motto was: "Follow the Light," and this became later: "Follow the King," and this spread westward and became the motto of the Round Table. And the people learned to say of their dead: "He has gone to the Light."

And the joyous civilization of Egypt grew yet more joyous, because He had dwelt among them, the embodied Light. The priests whom He had taught handed on His teachings and His secret instructions, which they enshrined in their Mysteries, and students came from all nations to learn the Wisdom of the Egyptians, and the fame of the Schools of Egypt went abroad to all lands.[6]

THE GODS OF EGYPT

It will be seen from the above that the deities, or rather forms of Deity, Osiris, Isis and Horus were already familiar to the people, and the World-Teacher made it part of His work to draw their attention to the true meaning of the three Persons. At what time knowledge of these three Aspects of God was introduced into the land we do not know, but at the date of our experience they had their places in the symbology of the Mysteries.

ISIS AND OSIRIS

Isis, to whom the Lesser Mysteries were ascribed, was not only the universal feminine principle expressed in nature, but also a real and very lofty Being, just as the Christ is the universal Life, the Second Logos, and also a high Official of the Occult Hierarchy. She by virtue of her high development and office was able to represent the Feminine Aspect of the Deity to man. Isis was the Mother of all that lives, and wisdom and truth and power; upon her temple at Sais the inscription was written: "I am that which is, which hath been, and which shall

[6]*Man: Whence, How and Whither,* pp. 284-7.

be; and no man has ever lifted the veil that hides my Divinity from mortal eyes."[7] The moon was her symbol; and the influence which she outpoured upon her worshippers to the music of the shaken sistrum was of brilliant blue light veined with delicate silver, as of shimmering moonbeams, the very touch of which brought upliftment and ecstasy.

Osiris was the embodiment of God the Father in a mighty Planetary Spirit. His symbol was the sun, and the influence which He outpoured was a dazzling glory of light shot through with gold, like the rays of the sun caught upon the surface of a lake. The influence of Horus, who represented the divine Child, was the glowing rose and gold of the eternal love which is perfect wisdom.

ANIMAL DEITIES

The Egyptians also followed the ancient practice of regarding certain animals as mirroring various aspects of the divine, because of their outstanding qualities. Thus they took the intelligence of the ape, the clear-sightedness of the hawk, the strength of the bull, and so on, and attributed the quality to some particular aspect of the Deity. They carefully bred certain animals as perfect representatives of their species, and kept them apart as symbols of those divine qualities. Such were the Apis bulls, and the cats of Bast or Pasht. These animals were regarded not exactly as sacred, but as objectified examples of the qualities. In the beginning the creature was a mere symbol, but in later days the Egyptians had the idea that those which had been especially set apart came to be linked with the godhead, and so were to some extent a manifestation of the deity. They then embalmed the animals and laid up the mummies in their temples, with the intention of preserving the divine influence.

THE PRACTICE OF EMBALMING

In the same way the Pharaoh was embalmed with the idea that his power, his connection with the deity (which was a very close one as Pharaoh), would be preserved and would continue to radiate so long as the body remained. This resembled the later custom of preserving the relics of a saint. The strong love of the Egyptians for their country provided another reason for embalming their dead; they hoped to preserve a definite link on the physical plane which would operate

---

[7]Plutarch. *Moralia; De Iside et Osiride.*

to draw them back to rebirth among their own people. That it did so operate in many cases seems to have been a fact, although the will of the re-incarnating ego would doubtless have been sufficient to achieve the same result. The custom was not altogether a good one, because if the body of a man of evil life is embalmed, a good deal of additional power is thereby left to him after death; he may more easily materialize and operate on the physical plane in undesirable ways. It is on the whole fortunate that the practice has not persisted.

OTHER DEITIES

Many other deities were reverenced in ancient Egypt, in much the same way as numerous gods are adored to-day in India; and in every case the devotion addressed to the Supreme obtained its response through the particular channel chosen by the worshipper. Great Angels of different Orders and Rays were appointed to represent these various qualities of the Deity, and these were worshipped as gods in the older faiths. But so close is the union in these cases that devotion rendered to one of these was at the same time given to God Himself. Shri Krishna, speaking as the Supreme in the *Bhagavad Gita* says: "Even those who worship other Gods with devotion, full of faith—they also worship Me."[8]

Wherever devotion is offered through a particular form, we may be sure that there is an Intelligence behind that form who acts as a mediator or channel between the suppliant and the Deity behind. Hathor, for instance, was the goddess of love and beauty, while as we have seen, Isis was the Queen of Truth and the Mother of all things; yet both were representatives of the feminine aspect of the Deity, as also was Nephthys. Ptah was the Master Architect of the Universe, the Holy Spirit who is the Creative Fire of God; He was the celestial worker in metals, and the chief smelter, caster and sculptor of the Gods, the skilful Craftsman by whom the design for every part of the framework of the world was made.[9]

THE BROTHERS OF HORUS

Among the other deities who were especially connected with the Mysteries, who still play a most important part in the inner working

---

[8]*Op. cit.*, ix, 23.

[9]Sir E. A. Wallis Budge, *The Papyrus of Ani*, p. 170.

of our Masonic ceremonies to-day, are to be found the four children or brothers of Horus, who are depicted in the well-known judgment scene as standing on a lotus before the throne of Osiris. These represent the Gods of the four quarters, or of the cardinal points, who support the canopy of heaven at its four corners. The God of the north was Hapi, who bore the head of an ape; the God of the east was Tuamutef, who bore the head of a jackal; Amset or Kestha ruled the south, and had the head of a man; while the west was governed by Qebsennuf, whose head was that of a hawk.[10]

The truth underlying these strange deities is of the deepest interest when examined by the inner sight, for these four are the same as the four Devarajas of India—the Kings of the elements, earth, air, fire and water, who likewise preside over the cardinal points. They correspond also with the cherubim described by Ezekiel, and with the four beasts of the Revelation. S. John says of them:

And in the midst of the throne, and round about the throne, were four beasts full of eyes before and behind. And the first beast was like a lion, and the second beast like a calf, and the third beast had a face as a man, and the fourth beast was like a flying eagle. And the four beasts had each of them six wings about him; and they were full of eyes within: and they rest not day and night, saying, Holy, Holy, Holy, Lord God Almighty, which was and is, and is to come.[11]

Ezekiel describes them a little differently:

Their wings were joined one to another; they turned not when they went; they went every one straight forward. As for the likeness of their faces, they four had the face of a man, and the face of a lion on the right side: and they four had the face of an ox on the left side; they four also had the face of an eagle. As for the likeness of the living creatures, their appearance was like burning coals of fire, and like the appearance of lamps: it went up and down among the living creatures; and the fire was bright, and out of the fire went forth lightning. Now as I beheld the living creatures, behold one wheel upon the earth by the living creatures, with his four faces. The appearance of the wheels and their work was like unto the colour of a beryl: and they four had one likeness: and their appearance and their work was as it were a wheel in the middle of a wheel. When they went, they went upon their four sides: and

---

[10]Sir E. A. Wallis Budge, *The Nile*, p. 267, *Egyptian Ideas of the Future Life*, p. 107

[11]Rev., iv, 6-8.

they turned not when they went. As for their rings, they were so high that they were dreadful; and their rings were full of eyes round about them four.[12]

This symbolism is strange; but it has its meaning, and any investigator who has ever had the privilege of seeing the mighty Four will at once recognize that S. John and the prophet Ezekiel had seen them too, however inadequate are their descriptions. The beast with the face of a man stands for the physical body (earth); the ox or the bull (as in the case of the bull of Mithra and the Apis bull) typifies the emotional or astral body (water); the lion symbolizes the will or the mental aspect (air); and the soaring eagle is taken to indicate the spiritual side of man's nature (fire). The Egyptian forms were a little different; but the same four elements and their Rulers are depicted in that ancient symbolism, which indeed we find in all religions. There is a four-faced Brahma; there is the fourfold Jupiter, who is aerial, fulgurant, marine and terrestrial. And that leads us back to the reality behind all these symbols, the four great Angel-Rulers of the elements, the administrators of the great law, who are the gods or leaders of the hierarchies of Angels of earth, water, air and fire. Those are the mystical four; and they are full of eyes within, because they are the scribes, the recorders, the agents of the Lipika: they watch all that happens, all that is done, all that is written or spoken or thought in all the worlds.

In *The Light of Asia* they are described as the Rulers of the four points of the compass:

> ...the four Regents of the Earth, come down
> From Mount Sumeru—they who write men's deeds
> On brazen plates—the Angel of the East,
> Whose hosts are clad in silver robes, and bear
> Targets of pearl: the Angel of the South,
> Whose horsemen, the Kumbhandas, ride blue steeds,
> With sapphire shields: the Angel of the West,
> By Nagas followed, riding steeds blood-red,
> With coral shields: the Angel of the North,
> Environed by his Yakshas, all in gold,
> On yellow horses, bearing shields of gold.

This is a poetical Oriental description; yet it has a definite foundation. The form in which it is cast is obviously merely traditional; but

---

[12]*Ezekiel*, I, 9, 10, 13, 15-18.

always there is a fact behind. Those Great Ones are surrounded by, and in constant communication with, vast hosts of Angels and assistants, but these do not take the form of a guard of horsemen; yet the colours of the respective hosts are correctly given. These four most strange and wondrous beings are not exactly Angels, in the ordinary sense of the word, though they are often called so; under them are hierarchies of Angels who carry out their will in accordance with the Law, for they direct the whole tremendous machinery of divine justice and in their hands is the working of the law of karma. They are sometimes spoken of as the overseers who guard the gates and test the material for the building of the holy temple.

CONSECRATION

These beings are very closely connected with the inner working of the Mysteries, and therefore of Masonry which is derived therefrom. They represent the great building forces of the universe, the constructive powers of nature; and since in our Lodges we are engaged in building a universe in miniature, it is these who are invoked to assist us in our work. This invocation is performed at the consecration of every Lodge, however little the modern consecrating officer may know what he is really doing when he pours forth the traditional offerings of corn, wine, oil and salt, symbols which they themselves have chosen from time immemorial to represent their especial powers. This ancient piece of ritual, when performed by an I. M. duly commissioned to consecrate a Lodge, produces stupendous results in the inner worlds; for it amounts to a call made to the planetary spirits at the head of the four lines to recognize the new Lodge and to dedicate it to the service of T. G. A. O. T. U.

The call is answered. As the corn is scattered in the north, a great golden Angel of earth descends in majesty, followed by his Angel-train, some of whom are left behind to be the channels of the power of his hierarchy whenever the Lodge is opened in due and ancient form. The pouring of wine in the south invokes a great blue Angel of water, also attended by other Angels less great than he; similarly the offering of oil in the west calls upon a mighty crimson Angel of fire, who pours down into the Lodge the splendid rhythmic Power of that 'most terrible and lovely' of the elements. As the salt is strewn in the east, an Angel of the air flashes down from on high, he and his attendants being of a wonderful silver hue shot through with mother-of-pearl.

These four Great Ones, representing the four gods of the elements, the four children or brothers of Horus, solemnly consecrate the Lodge, binding the Brn. into a close unity in the inner worlds and linking with them Angels of their orders, who will act as their representatives at each Lodge meeting. The tradition of these four passed down to the mediaeval operative Craftsmen and became mingled with that of the four Crowned Martyrs who are the patron-saints of the Craft.

Let me warn my Brn. who may be called upon to act as consecrating officers to see that it *is* corn which is supplied to them for the ceremony—wheat, and not maize. Once, through an oversight, maize (which in America is called ''Indian corn'') was given to me on such an occasion, and as there was no time to send for wheat I used what was offered. The result was unanticipated, for there came a cloud of nature-spirits of a totally different type, who knew nothing whatever of the work expected of them, and were entirely unsuited for it. I had to repeat that part of the consecration afterwards with the proper material.

THE PURPOSE OF THE MYSTERIES

In *The Hidden Life in Freemasonry* I have already written briefly of the purpose of the Mysteries.[13] I said there:

The Mysteries were great public institutions, supported by the State, centres of national and religious life to which people of the better classes flocked in thousands; and they did their work exceedingly well, for one who had passed through their degrees—a process of many years—thereby became what we should now call a highly-educated and cultured man or woman, with, in addition to his knowledge of this world, a vivid realization of the future after death, of man's place in the scheme of things, and therefore of what was really worth doing and living for.

It should not be thought therefore that the Mysteries were secret societies, with all their affairs deliberately concealed from the ordinary public. It will be seen presently that thousands of people entered the ordinary degrees of Isis. The teaching and the training of the inner and higher degrees (as we may call them) certainly were concealed from those whom they did not concern, that is to say from those who were not sufficiently evolved to be fit to take part in them, but only as in a modern University the classes in which, let us say, conic sec-

---

[13]*Op. cit.*, p. 34.

tions are taught are closed to children who are as yet learning simple arithmetic.

Everyone in Egypt knew that there were Mysteries, and practically everyone knew that they were largely concerned with the life after death and the preparation for it. This teaching was, however, given to the initiates of the Mysteries under solemn and binding pledges of secrecy; and the results of certain lines of action in the world after death were shown in elaborate detail. The essential outline of this secret instruction was embodied in the rituals of Initiation, Passing, and Raising, and it is these rituals which have in part descended to us in the ceremonies of Freemasonry, which are still protected by oaths of secrecy as in the old days.

Every great nation has had its Mysteries, through which the great Teachers of mankind sought to instruct the people in matters of importance, inspired by the Great White Lodge which stands behind all religions alike. Among these the Egyptian Mysteries were pre-eminent among the western peoples of the ancient world, not only because of their immemorial age, but because of the fact that Egypt was one of the auxiliary centres of the White Lodge. The Great White Brotherhood has its headquarters in Central Asia, but it has at various times and for various purposes maintained subsidiary Lodges in different parts of the world.

The presence of this secret centre belonging to the White Brotherhood had much to do with Egypt's greatness throughout the ages; although the fact of its existence was not known to the outer world, that Lodge of the true Mysteries supervised the whole scheme of Egyptian initiation, and made it the prototype of the Mysteries of all the nations around. Egypt was thus the centre of spiritual illumination for the entire western world, and all those who sought the Great Initiations were attracted to it; and it is this fact which explains the reverence paid to the Egyptian Mysteries by learned Greeks in later times.

The principal centre for the public work of these Mysteries was the great pyramid, called in ancient Egypt Khut, "The Light". It was built on the most exact astronomical and mathematical calculations, and provided a veritable key in stone to the enigmas of the universe.[14]

The initiates of the Egyptian Mysteries were symbolically engaged

---

[14]See *The Hidden Life in Freemasonry,* pp. 228-30.

in the building of the pyramid, just as in our modern Masonry we are engaged in erecting the temple of King Solomon, both structures being intended to be emblematical of the building processes of nature. In the halls below the pyramid—those underground chambers which were mentioned by Herodotus as being contained in an island, fed by a channel from the Nile,[15]—certain of the ceremonies of the Mysteries were held. These and other halls in and near the great pyramid are still unknown to the explorer, though they may yet be opened "by the proper steps"—the secret doors turning upon pivots according to an elaborate system of counterpoises, and being set in motion by treading upon certain spots in the floor in a certain order.

The ceremonies of the Mysteries were also intended to portray the higher evolution of man, his return to the divine source whence he came, through the development of the higher part of his nature, which is not merely consequent upon practices of meditation and ceremonial, but even more upon the living out of the ethical precepts which were taught. Many people of our day imagine that we know ethical truths without being taught them, but that is not so; they seem to us quite natural now, but long ago they were discoveries or revelations somewhat analogous to the steps of advancement in material science and invention.

Each degree of the Mysteries was designed to reflect one or other of the great Initiations of the White Lodge, so that the initiates of this lower level might prepare themselves ultimately to enter the Path of Holiness and so strive after the fullness of union with Osiris, the Hidden Light. When we come to consider these degrees we shall see how this teaching was graded, and how those initiates who were properly prepared were enabled to reach the true knowledge which they were seeking. The whole scheme of initiation provided a complete chart of man's spiritual evolution, and it was for the individual candidate to endeavour to put the teachings into practice and to make real in his own consciousness that which was symbolized in the ritual.

The Degrees of the Mysteries

The Mysteries of Egypt were, as ever, divided into two main sections, the Lesser and the Greater. The Lesser Mysteries are typified to some extent by what we now know as the First Degree of Craft

---

[15]Her. Book ii, 124.

Masonry, while the Greater Mysteries were analogous to what we now call the Second and Third Degrees. Beyond these there was a ceremony corresponding to the degree of I. M., in which the succession of powers was guarded and transmitted from age to age; and still further in reserve there were the yet greater spiritual powers that are indicated, and even given to some extent, in the higher degrees of the Ancient and Accepted Scottish Rite. Behind the whole system of Masonic initiation was (and is) the White Lodge itself, conferring the five great Initiations which lead to human perfection and full union with God.

THE MYSTERIES OF ISIS

In the Lesser Mysteries the initiate was taught what lies on the other side of death, and the ceremony of initiation was a symbolical map of that intermediate world which is sometimes called the astral plane. Probably Apuleius refers to this degree when he describes the Mysteries of Isis as celebrated in Greece during the second century A.D., although he wrote at a time when they had fallen into considerable decay. After mentioning various purifications through which he passed, he goes on to relate something of what took place at his initiation:

Then, behold, the day approached when as the sacrifice of dedication should be done; and when the sun declined and evening came, there arrived on every coast a great multitude of priests, who according to their ancient order offered me many presents and gifts. Then was all the laity and profane people commanded to depart, and when they had put on my back a new linen robe, the priest took my hand and brought me to the most secret and sacred place of the temple. Thou wouldest peradventure demand, thou studious reader, what was said and done there: verily I would tell thee if it were lawful for me to tell, thou wouldst know if it were convenient for thee to hear; but both thy ears and my tongue should incur the like pain of rash curiosity. Howbeit I will not long torment thy mind, which peradventure is somewhat religious and given to some devotion; listen therefore, and believe it to be true. Thou shalt understand that I approached near unto hell, even to the gates of Proserpine, and after that I was ravished throughout all the elements, I returned to my proper place: about midnight I saw the sun brightly shine, I saw likewise the gods celestial and the gods infernal, before whom I presented myself and worshipped them. Behold now have I told thee, which although thou hast heard, yet it is necessary that thou conceal it; wherefore this only will I tell, which may be declared without offence for the understanding of the profane.

When morning came and that the solemnities were finished, I came forth sanctified with twelve stoles and in a religious habit, whereof I am not forbidden to speak, considering that many persons saw me at that time. There I was commanded to stand upon a pulpit of wood which stood in the middle of the temple, before the figure and remembrance of the goddess; my vestment was of fine linen, covered and embroidered with flowers; I had a precious cope upon my shoulders, hanging down behind me to the ground, whereon were beasts wrought of divers colours, as Indian dragons, and Hyperborean griffins, whom in form of birds the other part of the world doth engender: the priests commonly call such a habit an Olympian stole. In my right hand I carried a lighted torch, and a garland of flowers was upon my head, with white palm-leaves sprouting out on every side like rays; thus I was adorned like unto the sun, and made in fashion of an image, when the curtains were drawn aside and all the people compassed about to behold me. Then they began to solemnize the feast, the nativity of my holy order, with sumptuous banquets and pleasant meats: the third day was likewise celebrate with like ceremonies, with a religious dinner, and with all the consummation of the adept order.[16]

It is also reported that during the ceremony Isis said:

I am Nature—the parent of all things, the sovereign of the elements, the primary progeny of time.

THE PRELIMINARY TRIALS

The secrets communicated in the Mysteries have been well and loyally kept, and no details about them are available, though we occasionally find guarded hints which give us a slight idea of their character. There is a picturesque account of the preparation for them given in Mackey's *Lexicon of Freemasonry* which, although it does not appear to be substantiated by the records preserved in Greek and Latin authors, nevertheless contains some fragments of truth. I take the liberty to epitomize it as follows:

For some days before his initiation the candidate was expected to preserve perfect chastity, to confine himself to a light diet from which all animal food was excluded, and to purify himself by repeated ceremonial ablutions. When the time came he was conducted at midnight to the mouth of a low gallery along which he had to crawl on his hands and knees. Presently he came to the opening of a well which the guide directed him to descend. If he showed the slightest hesitation he was reconducted to the outer world, never again to become a candidate for initiation; if however he attempted to descend, the conductor pointed out to him a concealed ladder which enabled him to climb down safely. They then entered a narrow and winding gallery at the entrance of which was this inscription: ''The mortal who shall travel over this road

---

[16]Apul. *Met*, xi, 23, 24. tr. William Adlington A.D. 1566.

without hesitating or looking behind shall be purified by fire, by water, and by air, and if he can surmount the fear of death he shall emerge from the bosom of the earth; he shall revisit the light and claim the right of preparing his soul for the reception of the Mysteries of the great Goddess Isis.''

The conductor now left the aspirant, warning him that many dangers surrounded and awaited him, and exhorting him to continue unshaken. Heavy doors closed behind him, rendering his return impossible. Presently he entered a spacious hall filled with flames through which he had to rush with the greatest speed. Even when he had passed through this fiery furnace he came to another hall the floor of which was covered with a huge network of red-hot iron bars with very narrow interspaces between them. Having surmounted this difficulty he reached a wide and rapid channel across which he had to swim. On the other side he found a narrow landing place bounded by two high walls of brass, in each of which was an immense wheel of the same metal, and beyond them was an ivory door. He found no means of opening this door, but presently discovered two large rings, which he seized; but the only result was to set the brazen wheels revolving with a stunning noise and to cause the platform upon which he stood to sink from beneath him, so that he remained suspended by the rings over an apparently fathomless abyss, from which issued a cold wind which blew out the tiny flame of his lamp and left him in profound darkness. He was left hanging there for a short time, but soon the noise ceased, the platform returned to its former position and the ivory door opened itself. Through it he then entered a brilliantly lighted apartment in which he found a number of the priests of Isis dressed in the mystic insignia of their offices, who welcomed and congratulated him. On the walls he saw the various symbols of the Egyptian Mysteries, the signification of which was by degrees explained to him.

One cannot guarantee all the details of such an account, but it is true that severe tests more or less of the nature described were applied to candidates for the inner Mysteries. None of these trials were imposed on the man who wished to take merely the ordinary course of intensive culture; he might pass through the Lesser and the Greater without encountering anything more formidable than hard and long-continued study; and he would never even know that there was another stage (or rather a number of stages) lying altogether beyond those, in which he would have to face astral dangers of so serious a nature that it was considered necessary first to submit the candidate to severe trials of his courage and self-command.

In the early days of the Mysteries, living pictures were materialized by the priests before the eyes of the candidate, so that he was enabled to see for himself what lay on the other side of death. In later days, when there was less knowledge among the hierophants, elaborate mechanical devices were shown to him, representing the realities of the astral world as far as such resources would allow. Still later, the characteristic points of these pictures were reproduced in a system of symbolic ceremonies, the main outline of which has come down to us today in the initiation ceremony of Masonry, although in some Obediences only a mere vestige of the original procedure remains.

THE MYSTERY LANGUAGE

Besides the teaching upon the life after death—which was elaborated by countless stories of imaginary individuals, showing the results in the astral plane after death of certain courses of action during life—a fine course of education was also given to the initiates of the First degree, embracing what Masons term the seven liberal arts and sciences—grammar, logic, rhetoric, arithmetic, geometry, music and astronomy. By grammar the Egyptians meant the sacred hieroglyphic writing of the priests, which was taught to all the initiates of the Mysteries, but it also signified a kind of secret language, a way of speaking peculiar to the priesthood. In the secret language of the Mysteries it was not so much that different words were used, as that the familiar words had a different meaning. Those who have studied the translations of Egyptian texts will have noticed how widely these vary in the versions of the different scholars; I have sometimes wondered whether this is in any way due to that system of double meanings.

In ancient Egypt we were able to talk about the secrets of the inner life before crowds of people without letting them know what we meant; and we had quite a large vocabulary of such significant words, so that an entire conversation could be conducted seemingly about ordinary every-day affairs, but in reality upon the secrets of the Mysteries. Much instruction was given in this way; a lecture or address might be delivered publicly by one of the priests, bearing two entirely distinct meanings—the one ethical and intended for the helping of people who were not initiated, and the other esoteric, for the students of the Mysteries. The legend that Masonry possesses a universal language known only to the Brn. may be an echo of tradition about this ancient and secret tongue.

This secret tongue of the Initiates was also used in inscriptions, and in the hieroglyphic wall-paintings and papyri. Many of the inscriptions, telling of the victories of some great Pharaoh, could be read in a hidden sense, and they then conveyed spiritual instruction to those who had learnt the real meaning. This is certainly true of *The Book of the Dead*, which when translated into English by modern scholars seems often unintelligible and even grotesque. Yet in the interpretation of it taught in the Mysteries those same texts were full of inner illumination and gave much information about the realities of life and death.

It is perhaps necessary to repeat that in all this there was no desire on the part of the priests to mislead the people; their idea was simply to give instruction graded to suit the needs of the hearer and to guard important secrets from those who were not prepared to receive them. It was for the same reason that the interior arrangements of the great pyramid were confused. Some of the passages were not used at all in the scheme of initiation, the real passage having been obtainable in quite another way. This policy was dictated by wisdom. Would it not be well if in these present days we could devise some means by which new discoveries in science (which are now used for injury and destruction) could be preserved solely for the use of people who would be certain to employ them for the public good?

THE DUALITY OF EACH DEGREE

The ordinary Lesser Mysteries (which may be called the First Degree) were open to practically all who sought admission, provided that they were of good life and reasonably intelligent, that they were free, and that the t...o...g...r...had been heard in their favour. In due course they would pass on to the Greater Mysteries (the Second and Third Degrees). But in each of these degrees there were also inner Mysteries, as I have mentioned in connection with the preliminary trials.

THE INNER MYSTERIES OF ISIS

Within and behind the outer Mysteries of Isis there were inner circles of students carefully chosen by the priests, the very existence of which was kept utterly secret, even from most of the initiates themselves. In these circles the practical occult teaching was given that enabled the student to awaken and train his inner faculties, so that he could study at first hand the conditions of the astral plane, and thus know for himself what was but theoretical for the majority of the Brn. It was in these circles only that the severe tests which have been partially described were imposed upon the candidate, and he was definitely prepared by individual and personal instruction for the greater and holier Mysteries which lay behind the whole scheme of Egyptian initiation.

The candidate for these inner tests was required, after a preliminary bath (from which was derived the idea of Christian baptism), to attire himself in a white robe, emblematic of the purity which was expected of him, before being brought before a conclave of priest-initiates in a kind of vault or cavern. He was first formally tested as to his development of the clairvoyant faculty which he had been previously instructed how to awaken; for this purpose he had to read an inscription upon a brazen shield, of which the blank side was presented to his physical vision. Later he was left alone to keep a kind of vigil; certain *mantras*, or words of power, had been taught to him, which were supposed to be appropriate to control certain classes of entities; and during his vigil various appearances were projected before him, some of them of a terrifying and some of a seductive nature, so that it might be seen whether his courage and coolness remained perfect. He drove away all these appearances in turn, each by its own special sign and word; but at the end, all these combined bore down upon him at once, and in this final effort he was instructed to use the mightiest word of power, by which all possible evil could be vanquished. A course of instruction along these lines was given to those candidates whom the priests deemed suitable, so that at the end of their training they were thoroughly versed in the knowledge of the astral world, and able to wield its powers freely in waking consciousness.

THE MYSTERIES OF SERAPIS

The Second Degree of the Egyptian Mysteries corresponded somewhat closely with our degree of F. C.; these were termed the Greater Mysteries or in later days the Mysteries of Serapis. Apuleius gives us practically nothing in the way of description beyond the bare fact that he had passed the degree. The instruction in the Greater Mysteries was carried further and deeper as regards science and philosophy; a more advanced course of intellectual training was set before the students, which one might well call a research into "the more hidden paths of Nature and Science". At the same time the study of the life after death was extended to include the heaven-world, the m...c...into which all must go to receive their wages for the good deeds done on earth; much of this deeper knowledge of the mental plane was taught in the Greater Mysteries, in the same manner as the facts of the astral life had been taught in the First Degree—namely, by representation and drama. The purpose of the Mysteries of Serapis in the life of the individual initiate was the control of the mind[17] and the training of the mental body; and the sacramental powers invoked by the ceremonial had as their object the quickening of this mental development.

THE INNER DEGREE OF SERAPIS

Behind the outer mysteries in this degree there were also secret circles, quite unknown to those who had not been through the inner work of the First Degree; in these practical instruction was given on the development of the mental body, and the method of awakening accurate sight on the mental plane, so that the student was enabled to verify the teaching of the priests for himself.

In connection with this degree it may be of interest to mention that in the temple of Philae the body of Osiris is represented with stalks of corn springing from it which a priest waters from a vessel which he holds in his hand. An inscription sets forth that "this is the form of Him whom we may not name, Osiris of the Mysteries, who sprang from the returning waters"[18]—this symbolism referring among other things to the quickening of the inner life in response to the power poured down from on high. The s...n of the degree is often found in Egyptian paintings, and is exactly the same as is in use among Craftsmen to-day. As in the First Degree, an average of seven years was also spent in the Mysteries of Serapis, at the end of which candidates who had passed a far more searching examination, and had satisfied the Hierophants that they were ready for further teaching, were eligible for the Third Degree.

THE MYSTERIES OF OSIRIS

The Third Degree was called in Egypt the Mysteries of Osiris; it corresponds to the Degree of M. M. in our modern Craft system. Apuleius describes Osiris as: "The more powerful God of the great

---

[17]See *The Hidden Life in Freemasonry*, Ch. vii.

[18]Cheetham, *The Mysteries, Pagan and Christian*, p. 53.

Gods, the highest of the greater, the greatest of the highest, and the ruler of the greatest."[19] In the Egyptian ritual, which was much more complete and impressive than the traditional history preserved in modern Masonry, the candidate had to pass through a symbolical representation of the suffering, death and rising again of Osiris, which included his experiences between death and resurrection, when he entered the world of Amenta, and became the judge of the dead, who should decide for each soul what measure of felicity was due to him, and turn back to earthly incarnation those who needed further human development. The legend of the death and resurrection of Osiris was well known to all the people of Egypt, both initiates and profane, and there were great public ceremonies, corresponding to those of our Good Friday and Easter Day in Catholic countries, when these mystic events were celebrated with the utmost splendour and with the heartfelt devotion of the people.

The story of Osiris is nowhere found in a connected form in Egyptian literature, but in texts of all periods his life, sufferings, death and resurrection are accepted as facts universally admitted.[20] It would appear, however, that in ancient times it was not lawful to speak of the tradition in any detail, at least to strangers, for Herodotus says:

Also at Sais there is the burial place of Him whom I account it not pious to name in connection with such a matter, which is in the temple of Athene (Isis) behind the house of the goddess, stretching along the whole wall of it; and in the sacred enclosure stand great obelisks of stone, and near them is a lake adorned with an edging of stone, and fairly made in a circle, being in size, as it seemed to me, equal to that which is called the 'Round Pool' in Delos. On this lake they perform by night the show of His sufferings, and this the Egyptians call Mysteries. Of these things I know more fully in detail how they take place, but I shall leave this unspoken.[21]

Diodorus writes to the same effect:

In olden days according to received tradition the priests kept the manner of the death of Osiris as a secret; but in after times it came about through the indiscretion of some that that which had been hidden in silence among the few, was noised abroad among the many.[22]

---

[19] Apul. *Met.* Bk. xi, 30.

[20] Sir E. A. Wallis Budge, *The Papyrus of Ani*, p. 53.

[21] Her. Bk. ii, 170, 171.

[22] Diod, Sic. *Hist*. Bk. i, xxi.

THE LEGEND OF OSIRIS

The best exoteric account of the legend is preserved for us by Plutarch in his treatise *De Iside et Osiride,* written in Greek about the middle of the first century of our era, a large portion of which is substantiated by the Egyptian hieroglyphic texts which have been deciphered by scholars. It may be briefly summarized as follows:

Osiris was a wise king in Egypt who set himself to civilize the people and redeem them from their former states of barbarism. He taught them the cultivation of the earth, gave them a body of laws, and instructed them in the worship of the Gods. Having made his own land prosperous, he set out in like manner to teach the other nations of the world. During his absence the land of Egypt was so well ruled by his wife, Isis, that his jealous brother Typhon (Set), the personification of evil, as Osiris was the personification of good, could do no harm to his kingdom; but on the return of Osiris to Egypt Typhon made a conspiracy against him, persuading seventy-two other persons to join him, together with a certain Queen of Ethiopia named Aso, who chanced to be in Egypt at that time. He secretly measured the body of Osiris, and caused a beautiful chest to be made of exactly the same size. This he brought into his banqueting hall when Osiris was present as a guest, and promised, as it were in pleasantry, to give it to anyone whose body it might be found to fit.

All those present at the feast tried it, but since the box fitted none of them, Osiris at the last laid himself down in it, whereupon the conspirators at once fastened down the lid securely, sealing it with lead, and cast it into the Nile. The murder of Osiris is said to have taken place on the seventeenth day of the month Athyr (Hathor), when the sun was in Scorpio, Osiris being in the twenty-eighth year either of his reign or his age. (It will be noted that this date marks the beginning of winter, when the sun is mystically slain by the forces of darkness; and it was on this date, corresponding to the festival of All Souls in the Christian Church, that the land of Egypt mourned the death of Osiris, as we mourn the death of the body of Jesus on Good Friday.)

News was brought to Isis at Coptos of the tragedy which had occurred, whereupon she cut off a lock of her hair, arrayed herself in mourning apparel, and went forth in search of the body of Osiris. She learnt that the chest had been carried by the sea to Byblos—not the Byblos of Syria, but the papyrus swamps of the delta[23]—and that it had been caught in a tamarisk tree, which had so grown around the chest that nothing of it was to be seen; and furthermore that the King of the country, amazed at its unusual size, had cut the tree down and made of it a pillar to support the roof of his palace. Isis went to Byblos and became nurse to one of the king's sons. Each night she put the child in the fire to consume his mortal parts, changing herself into a swallow, and be-

---

[23]Sir E. A. Wallis Budge, *Egyptian Ideas of the Future Life,* p. 48, footnote.

moaning the loss of her husband. But the Queen happened to see her child in flames and cried out in fear, thereby depriving him of the immortality which would otherwise have been conferred upon him. The goddess revealed herself and begged for the pillar which supported the roof. This was granted to her, and she took the chest containing the body of Osiris back to Egypt, hiding it in a secret place while she sought her son, Horus. But Typhon, by an unlucky chance, found the chest while hunting in the light of the moon, and recognizing the body as that of Osiris, tore it into fourteen pieces, which he scattered up and down throughout the land. When Isis heard of this she made a boat of papyrus, and set out to collect the fragments of the body. Osiris returned from the other world and appeared to his son, Horus, instructing him to do battle with Typhon; this battle lasted many days, and at length Horus was victorious. Ultimately Osiris became the king of the underworld and the judge of the dead.

This story, like our own traditional history, has suffered from the materializing tendencies of those who did not understand; for there is no clear mention of a resurrection in the account given by Plutarch, but merely a vague return from the dead. This represents, however, a very late version of the tradition, one which is materialized and distorted almost beyond recognition; and in the Mysteries of Osiris the legend was much more in accordance with the real facts of the spiritual world. Even in the Egyptian inscriptions which have been deciphered there are clear indications of a resurrection. The main outline of the true legend was the death of Osiris at the hands of Set; the division of His body into twice seven parts, representing the coming forth of the seven rays, or types of manifestation, consequent upon the descent of the Logos into matter; the search of Isis and the finding of the various portions of the body; their reunion and the final raising of Osiris by the third of three successive attempts to triumphant immortality and eternal resurrection.

It was at this stage also that the function of Osiris as the judge of the dead was studied; and the vignette in the papyrus of Ani of the judgment of Osiris and the weighing of the heart of Ani against the feather of truth represents the judgment of the soul by the Lords of Karma. If the soul was utterly pure it was allowed to pass onwards into immortality; if it was not "true of voice" it was delivered over to the monster Amemit, "the devourer," and was swallowed up again in the cycle of generation, to be reborn on earth in another body. Although these symbols and legends were known in the outer world, their true inner meaning was explained only to initiates of the Third Degree.

THE MEANING OF THE STORY

It is often thought that the story of Osiris, like that of Mithra and the other sun-gods (among whom some writers include even Christ Himself), is simply an apotheosis of the processes of nature familiar to an agricultural people. Thus Plutarch says that Osiris was also regarded as Nilus, the river Nile, and Isis as the land of Egypt, periodically fertilized by his overflow.[24] Astronomically, Osiris was the sun, Isis the moon, and Typhon darkness and winter, who in his triumph destroyed the fertilizing powers of the sun, preventing him from giving his life to the world. It is the universal story of the sun-god who, after a struggle for existence and the development of his power in the early part of the year, at last rises in triumph into the midheaven of his glory, and bestows his life upon all creatures, ripening the corn and the grape, only to yield once more to the advance of winter.

The sun in the heavens, as the great life of the world, pursues this cycle of death and resurrection; and the smaller life in the seed follows a similar process—it sprouts and comes to fruit, which is garnered and sacrificed for the nourishment of man and other creatures; but just as Typhon did not utterly destroy Osiris, but left the fragments of His body through which His life was afterwards renewed, so does man not eat all the corn, but keeps some portion to be sown in the ground so that the processes of life may recur. Man in his turn grows through the same cycle of changes, through childhood, manhood and old age; and for him also there is no escape from the sacrifice that characterizes all life, but he is reborn again and again in his cycle of reincarnations.

The story of the seed is thus that of the ordinary man, but the story of the sun is that of the man who is becoming divine. In the Egyptian Mysteries they called him the Osirified, and the Christian mystics spoke of him as becoming one with Christ, as when S. Paul spoke to his followers as: "My little children, of whom I travail in birth again until Christ be formed in you."[25] It is the voluntary nature of the divine sacrifice that distinguishes it from the earthly sacrifices. Therefore the method of man's reaching divinity was always proclaimed to be unselfishness and self-sacrifice for the sake of others; and the entire

---

[24]Plutarch. *Moralia; De Iside et Osiride.*

[25]*Gal., iv, 19.*

story of Christ and of Osiris is but an epitome and example of how that sacrifice may be expressed on earth in human life, as it is in the heavens.

The researches of the initiate in the Mysteries of Osiris were still further extended to include man's true home, that higher section of the mental or heaven-world in which the ego functions in his causal body; and at the same time the great ceremony of raising was explained in many layers of interpretation as the descent of the Logos into matter, His mystic death and burial, and His rising again to a kingdom without end; and also as the personal descent of the soul into bodies, his resurrection from the death-in-life of the lower worlds of form, and his reincarnation upon earth once more.

The s. . .s of the Mysteries of Osiris were much the same as we have to-day, though the s. . .of g. . .and d. . .was that used in Scottish and American workings; but the words were different, being much more positive in character. The f. . .p. . .o. . .f. . .were identical with those we use now, and the g. . .or t. . .is likewise unchanged.

THE INNER MYSTERIES OF OSIRIS

Within this degree there was also an inner circle. The practical instruction was therein carried into the higher part of the mental plane, so that the fully trained initiate in the Mysteries of Osiris acquired full consciousness as an ego beyond the limitations of the one personal life which is all that most people know.

THE OFFICE OF MASTER

Beyond the Third Degree there opened out several lines of progress in the Mysteries. There was the work of holding office in the Lodges; that extended over many years, and gave splendid training to those who undertook it. Each officer in a Lodge has his own special work to do, his own aspect of the Deity to manifest, his own sacramental power to transmit to the Lodge of which he is a part; the course of training through successive offices was and is therefore of inestimable value in acquiring an all-round development of character. At the apex of the ancient Craft system, the degree of I.M. existed, which gave a far fuller power than had been conferred even in the Mysteries of Osiris, and enabled the Master to become a hierophant of the Mysteries in his turn, able to instruct and advance his Brn. in the secret wisdom of Egypt. In ordinary cases this splendid position was gained only late in life, and by the time the Master had ruled his Lodge he had had a most valuable training, that well might advance the course of his evolution more than several ordinary lives.

The same succession has been transmitted to us in Masonry to-day, and every I.M. is in possession of the power of the Egyptian priests of old; though it is certainly true that if he possessed also the knowledge of the Egyptian priests he could make far better use of the power.

THE HIGHER GRADES OF THE MYSTERIES

Beyond the teaching and training which were given in the Mysteries, classified in the three degrees which we have considered, the hierophants also made it their work to instruct and guide aspirants who had proved themselves fit for still further progress. We cannot say that there were in Egypt any organized degrees beyond the third, that of Osiris; but there was individual teaching, which led to the acquisition of still greater powers, and to the formation of links with beings at still higher levels.

The higher degrees of the Ancient and Accepted Scottish Rite of our modern days (which were established perhaps as late as the eighteenth century, when the Rite of Perfection or of Heredom was formed) reflect to some extent these more advanced lines of progress which existed in Egypt. We may therefore in the following brief account of them classify them as they are expressed in our Red, Black and White Freemasonry.

RED MASONRY IN THE MYSTERIES

For such M.M.s as were thought promising by the priests in charge (who were for the most part members of the three Grand Lodges), what we now call Red Masonry existed, as well as the teaching which is now included in our Royal Arch and kindred degrees, culminating in the splendid quest of the Knights of the Rose-Croix for the lost word, man's true divinity.

In the symbolic teaching corresponding to our degree of the Holy Royal Arch the aspirant was taught to clear away from the various levels of his consciousness all the veils which yet obstructed his vision of reality, and then in the power of that vision to recognize for himself the Hidden Light in every form, however deeply it might be buried and concealed from the eyes of the flesh. This was typified as a journey upwards, during which four veils were passed, and then by a search downwards for a hidden vault, deeply buried in the earth, in which the Name of God was concealed.

The central purpose of this stage was an actual realization in consciousness that the many are One. It was known to some extent among the uninitiated of the outer world that all the strange deities of Egypt were in reality only manifestations of One, but they did not in all probability realize the fact of unity with any degree of clearness. In what corresponded to the Royal Arch in Egypt we found for ourselves that God was immanent in all things and had descended into the very lowest that the lowest might come into being. The powers conferred at this stage enabled the candidate to realize this great truth to some extent; and a certain expansion of consciousness was given to him which quickened the growth of the intuitional principle within him, and so helped him to recognize the divinity in others.

There was a considerable interval between this stage and the next, during which the candidate was receiving instruction from the priests, and practising meditation upon what he had learnt. Gradually he came to realize that, although he had indeed found the divine Name, and had contacted for himself the Hidden Light of God, there was a further search still before him, in which he would penetrate deeper into the consciousness and being of the Deity. It was then that he began his second great quest, which led up through a number of stages, during which different attributes of the Deity were studied and to some extent realized, until it culminated in the magnificent illumination given in what we now call the Eighteenth Degree, that of the Sovereign Prince of the Rose-Croix of Heredom. The candidate then found the divine Love reigning in his own heart and in those of his Brn. He also learnt that God had descended and shared our lower nature with us in order that we might ascend to share His true nature with Him.

That link is still made for the Brn. of the Rose-Croix, and each should become a radiant centre of that love wherever he goes, forgetting himself utterly in the service of others. The splendid crimson Angels of the Rosy Cross, who now attend our Sovereign Chapters and pour out through them the fullness of their love for the helping of the world, were also known in ancient Egypt, and these were linked with the Sovereign Princes in their higher principles, so that their seraphic love also was at hand to be outpoured in blessing. To their guardianship the candidate was entrusted, and he had to realize his unity with the Angels as well as with his Brn.

At this stage the intuition or buddhi in the candidate, that hidden wisdom which is Horus or the Christ dwelling in man, was enormously quickened and aroused, so that the candidate became to some extent a manifestation of that eternal love who in later ages was called the Christ, and he was thereby enabled to work upon the emotional nature, which is a partial reflection of it in the matter of the astral world, so as to raise his power to love to greater heights than he could reach before. He now became a veritable priest, able to call down and pour forth the divine love for the helping of the world. A higher degree of this same most wonderful power enabled the Bro. to confer this expansion of consciousness and transmit these splendid links to others; and it is this power which is reserved in our modern Sovereign Chapters to the M. W. S. and those who have passed the Chair in the Rose-Croix degree.

Black Masonry in the Mysteries

Few indeed of our Egyptian Brn. appear to have passed beyond the Rose-Croix, for only the few needed anything further than the splendid revelation of the indwelling Love of God which they received in what we call the Eighteenth Degree. But for those few who felt that there was yet more to learn of the nature of God, and who eagerly wished to understand the meaning of evil and suffering and its relation to the divine plan, the prototype of our Black Masonry existed, the teaching and progress comprised in our degrees from the nineteenth to the thirtieth. This section of the Mysteries was especially concerned with the working out of karma in its different aspects, studied as a law of retribution, from one point of view dark and terrible. This is the inner kernel of truth lying behind the vengeance-elements in the degree of Knight K.H. The darker aspects of karma are largely connected with man's ignorance of the nature of God and confusion with regard to the many forms in which He reveals Himself, and thus the s . . . s of the 30° contain the heart of its philosophy. That degree would not be fully and validly conferred unless these s . . . s were duly communicated, since they express its inner meaning and purpose.

In the ancient instruction corresponding to this group of degrees it was taught that whatsoever a man sowed, that also must he reap, and that if he sowed evil the result would be suffering to himself. The karma of nations and races was also studied, and the inner working of the law upon the different planes was investigated by the inner sight, and shown to the student. The whole of what we now call Black Masonry led up to an explanation of karma as divine justice, this having been preserved for us in shadow in what is now the 31°, that of the Grand Inspector Inquisitor Commander, whose symbol is a pair of scales. In Egypt this pair of scales was taken as an emblem of the perfect balance of divine justice; the aspirant learnt that all the evil and horror associated with the working out of karma was indeed based on perfect justice, although it had appeared as evil to the lesser vision of the profane.

Thus the first stage of the higher instruction, that of the Rose-Croix or Red Masonry, was devoted to the knowledge of good, while the second stage, that of K.H. or Black Masonry, was devoted to the knowledge of evil. Next, in the first steps of what we call White Masonry, the crown of the whole glorious structure, the candidate learnt to see the underlying justice of that eternal God, Amen-Ra, who stands behind good and evil alike. In older days, before the *kali yuga,* in which evil predominates over good, the Knights K.H. wore regalia of yellow instead of black.

Our 30° links the Knight K.H. to the ruling rather than the teaching branch of the Great Hierarchy; he should become a radiant centre of perennial energy, which is intended to give him strength to overcome evil and to make him a real power on the side of good. The prevailing colour of the influence is an electric blue (that of the First Ray, quite different from the blue of the symbolic or Blue Lodges) edged with gold, including and yet not drowning the rose of the 18°. Associated with the degree there are also great blue Angels of the First Ray who lend their strength to the knight, somewhat as the crimson Angels assist the Excellent and Perfect Brn. of the Rose-Croix. A higher level of the same energy is transmitted in what to-day we should call the Chair of the Sovereign Commander, who has the ability to pass on the sacramental grace of the degree to others.

WHITE MASONRY IN THE MYSTERIES

The highest and last of the great sacramental powers of the Mysteries which have been transmitted to us is that which is now conferred in the 33°, that of the Sovereign Grand Inspector-General. In ancient Egypt, at the time when I knew it, there were only three who held the equivalent of that supreme degree, the Pharaoh and two others, who formed with him an inner triangle which was the heart of the whole system of the Mysteries, and the channel to them of the Hidden Light from the White Lodge behind. These three were all high Initiates of the Great White Brotherhood, and the Pharaoh possessed an even higher level of power than is usually given in the 33°, it being that of a Crowned and Anointed Sovereign.

The Brn. of this high Order may be said to have passed on from a conception of the divine justice to the certainty of knowledge and the fullness of the divine glory in the Hidden Light. The 33° links the Sovereign Grand Inspector-General with the Spiritual King of the World Himself—that Mighty Adept who stands at the head of the Great White Lodge, and in whose strong hands lie the destinies of earth— and awakens the powers of the triple spirit as far as these can as yet be awakened. The actual conferring of the degree was and is a very splendid experience when seen with the inner sight; for the Hierophant of the Mysteries (who in these modern days is the H.O.A.T.F.), stands above or beside the Initiator in that extension of His consciousness which is called the Angel of the Presence. If the recipient of the degree happens to be already an Initiate the Star (called in Egypt the Star of Horus) which marks the approval of the One Initiator once more flames out above him in all its glory; while in any case the two great white Angels of the rite flash down in splendour from the heavenly places, showing themselves as low as the etheric level that they may give their blessing to the candidate.

The Hierophant makes the actual links both with himself and with the reservoir of power set apart for the work of the Masonic Brotherhood, and through himself with that Mighty King whose representative He is, while the great white Angels of the Order remain as the guardians of the Bro. throughout life. He on the right hand has an aura of brilliant white light shot with gold, and represents Osiris, the sun and life, the positive aspect of the Deity; she on the left has an aura of similar light, veined with silver, and represents Isis, the moon and truth, the negative or feminine aspect of the divine glory. Their power is stern and splendid; and they give strength to act with decision, accuracy, courage and perseverance on the physical plane. They belong to the cosmic orders of Angels, those who are common to other solar systems besides our own, and their permanent centres of consciousness are on the intuitional plane, although their forms may always be seen hovering over the head of the initiate of this degree at the higher mental level. It is to be remembered that there is in reality no sex among these great Angels, yet one of them is preponderatingly masculine in appearance, and the other preponderatingly feminine.

When they think fit, they materialize themselves mentally and astrally—as at the greater ceremonies in Lodge—and they are always ready to give their blessing whenever it is invoked. They are inseparably one with the Sovereign Grand Inspector-General, linked to his higher self, never to desert him unless by unworthiness he first deserts them and casts them off. The symbols of the sun and moon are seen to-day on the gauntlets of the Sovereign Grand Inspector-General, and they are intended to refer to these great Angelic powers in the inner worlds.

The powers associated with the 33° appear to have been slightly modified since those ancient Egyptian times. The great white Angels seemed to be sterner and more rhadamanthine in ancient Egypt; to-day those who belong to the degree are in some ways gentler, though their power is no less splendid. This stage combined the wonderful love of Horus the Son with the ineffable life and strength of Osiris the divine Father, and Isis, the eternal Mother of the world; and this union of love with strength is still its most prominent characteristic.

It confers upon those who open themselves to its influence power similar to and only a little way below that of the first great Initiation, and those who enter the 33° should assuredly qualify themselves for that step before very long. Indeed, in the great days of the Mysteries this stage was accessible only to Initiates, and one feels that it ought only to be given to such now, just as it would seem appropriate that the marvellous gift of the episcopate should be conferred only upon members of the Great White Brotherhood. The power of the degree when in operation shows itself in an aura of dazzling white and gold, enfolding within it the rose and blue of Rose-Croix and K.H.; and in it also is manifested that peculiar shade of electric blue which is the especial sign of the presence of the King. The Sovereign Grand Inspector-General is the "Bishop" of Masonry, and if the life of the degree is really lived he should be an ever-radiating centre of power, a veritable sun of light and life and glory wherever he goes.

Such was the highest and holiest of the sacramental powers conferred in the Mysteries of ancient Egypt, such the highest degree known to us in Masonry to-day, bestowed in its fullness upon but very few. The opportunity to draw down its sublime glory is offered to all who receive the degree; how far it is taken and what use is made of the power is in the hands of the Bro. alone, for to use the power as it should be used needs high spiritual development and a life of constant humility, watchfulness and service. If he calls upon it for the service of others, it will flow through him mightily and sweetly for the helping of the world. If he neglects the power, it will remain dormant and the links unused—and Those behind will turn Their glance away from him to others more worthy. The power of the 33° is a veritable ocean of glory and strength and sweetness, for it is the power of the King Himself, the Lord who reigns on earth as Vice-Gerent of the Logos from eternity unto eternity.

THE STAGES OF THE OCCULT PATH

Behind the whole splendid scheme of the Egyptian Mysteries the Lodge of the Great White Brotherhood in that country ever stood in silence and secrecy, guarding them and using them as a channel of the Hidden Light—its very existence being unknown to all who remained outside the inner circles. The Brotherhood selected for initiation into its ranks only those who had fulfilled the ancient conditions imposed upon all candidates for that high degree, the qualifications for which were laid down in Part I of the manual of occult instruction now called *Light on the Path*, which represents the teaching of the Egyptian Lodge. Candidates were therefore generally chosen from among the Brn. who had received the higher instruction, and had prepared themselves by many years of meditation, study and service. Still, it sometimes happened that one might be chosen for Initiation who had not passed through the outer steps of the Mysteries, but in previous lives had prepared himself for it—for it is the ego who is initiated, not the mere personality of the lower planes.

There have always been five great Initiations, which in Christian teaching have been illustrated by stages in the life of the Christ as related in the Gospels, which contain elements derived from the teachings of the Egyptian Mysteries. The disciple Jesus was an initiate of the Egyptian Lodge, and therefore much of the Egyptian symbolism was adopted by His followers, and was later woven into the Gospel story. In *The Masters and the Path* I have given an account of certain of the ceremonies of Initiation used in the Great White Brotherhood at the present day. The Egyptian rituals were in some respects slightly different from these in form, although their essence was identically the same; for the Egyptian Lodge possessed the tradition handed down from the initiates of Atlantis, which was somewhat modified in later days, to suit the needs of the slowly-evolving humanity of the Aryan race.

THE FIRST THREE INITIATIONS

The first of the true inner Initiations was called the Birth of Horus, and corresponded in that great religion to the birth of Christ in Bethlehem in the Christian presentation. Horus was born of Isis, the Virgin-Mother; at his birth the Star shone forth, and the Angelic hosts sang their song of triumph; he was adored by shepherds and wise men, and saved from danger which threatened him from without. In *The Book of the Dead* it is said: "I know the power of the East, Horus of the Solar Mount, the Star of Dawn." The story of the Initiate is the story of the Sun-God, the universal Christ who is born into the heart of man, and His mystic birth is the purpose of the First Great Initiation.

If the candidate had not already passed through them, as most students in the Mysteries would have done, he had at this stage to undergo the trials by earth, water, air and fire, learning with absolute certainty that none of these elements could in any way harm him in the astral body. All this was preparatory to the taking up of service on the astral plane, for the Initiate had to fit himself to become a trained and useful servant of humanity both in this and in the other world.

The Second Great Initiation corresponds to that stage of the Christ-life which is typified by the Baptism, in which an expansion of the intellectual faculties takes place, just as a wonderful opening out of the emotional nature is the result of the First Initiation. It is at this stage that the inner trial typified by the temptation in the wilderness takes place in the life of the candidate. Then comes the splendour of the Transfiguration, when the Monad descends and transforms the ego into the likeness of His own glory.

THE FOURTH INITIATION

The Fourth Great Initiation corresponds to the Passion and Resurrection of the Christ; the candidate must pass through the valley of the shadow of death, enduring the utmost suffering and loneliness that he may rise forever to the fullness of immortality. This awful and wonderful experience is the reality which is reflected at an almost infinite distance in the degree of M. M.; through the portal of death he is raised to the everlasting glory of the Resurrection.

Certain portions of the ritual of this Fourth Initiation according to the Egyptian rite were curiously entangled with the Christian teachings, and became utterly materialized and distorted in somewhat the same way as the legend of Osiris became distorted in Egypt itself. The rubric of this part of the Initiation was as follows:

Then shall the candidate be bound upon the wooden cross, he shall die, he shall be buried, and shall descend into the underworld; after the third day he shall be brought back from the dead, and shall be carried up into heaven to be the right hand of Him from whom he came, having learnt to guide (or rule) the living and the dead.[26]

During the ceremony the candidate laid himself down upon a wooden cross, made hollow to receive and support his body. His arms were lightly bound with cords, the ends of which were left loose to typify the voluntary nature of the sacrifice. The candidate then passed into trance, left the physical body and passed in full consciousness on to the astral plane. His body was carried down into a vault below the temple and was placed in an immense sarcophagus, where it lay for three days and three nights in the heart of the earth.

During the mystical death of the body the candidate passed through many strange experiences in the astral world, and preached to 'the spirits in prison,' to those who had recently left the body in death and were still fettered by their passions and desires.

On the morning of the fourth day of his burial, the body of the candidate was raised from its sepulchre, and borne into the outer air at the eastern side of the great pyramid, so that the first rays of the rising sun might awaken him from his long sleep.

It was at this Initiation that the candidate was carried up into 'heaven,' to receive an expansion of consciousness on the spiritual plane, often called the atmic or nirvanic. That is the plane of absolute union, and that consciousness knows all from within, is one with all and in all. The Initiate thus was made "the right hand of Him from whom he came," being now pledged for ever to the service of God and man, and it was to be his work henceforward to guide the living and the dead towards the Hidden Light in which alone is peace.The great truth that all power which is gained is but held in trust, to be used as a means of helping others, has rarely been more clearly or more grandly set forth.

---

[26]*The Christian Creed*, by the Rt. Rev. C. W. Leadbeater, p. 98.

In *The Hidden Light in Freemasonry* I have drawn certain correspondences between the three degrees in Blue Masonry and the Great
Initiations, showing that the E.A. initiation reflects the great step of
entry on the probationary path, that the Passing may be compared to
the First Great Initiation, and that the Raising resembles the Fourth.[27]
We may now add the Mysteries of Egypt, and make the following table
of correspondences, always remembering, of course, that there are vast
differences of level between these Orders and the stages on the Path:

Masonic Degrees	Mysteries	The Path
E. A.	Isis	Probationer
F. C.	Serapis	Initiate
M. M.	Osiris	Arhat

The Fifth Initiation and Beyond

Only one more stage remains before human perfection is reached—
that which is typified by the Ascension into heaven. At this Fifth
Initiation the Adept ascends above all earthly life and becomes One
with that aspect of the Deity which in Christianity we call God the
Holy Ghost.[28]

And still there are higher stages, greater steps upon the Path, though
belonging no longer to human evolution but to the development of the
Superman. Even here our Masonic ceremonies reflect in symbol
something of those higher glories, giving the key to the whole vast
plan. Far above the grade of Adept, He who is the Christ stands as
the Lord of Love, the Teacher of Angels and men, and along this line
of interpretation His high stage of evolution is reflected in the 18°, which
is essentially a degree of Christhood. Equal with Him, but on the Ray
of Rule, stands the Manu, whose rank is mirrored at an almost in-

---

[27]*Op. cit.*, pp. 75 and 185.

[28]See *The Masters and the Path.*

finite distance in the 30°; and as the crown of the whole Hierarchy there reigns the One Initiator,[29] whose life and light and glory are adumbrated in the splendour of the 33°. Thus the whole wondrous plan of Masonic initiation is a shadow of things seen above "in the Mount"; and herein lies the greatness of our mighty brotherhood and its value to mankind.

Much lower down there are still correspondences. The 18° means glowing love and beauty, but that is mirrored in the position of the W. J. W.; the 30° gives a wonderful outpouring of strength, which is typified by the column of the W. S. W., while the wisdom and all-embracing sympathy of the 33° should be reflected in the attitude of the R. W. M. of the Lodge.

---

[29]*Ibid.*, Ch. xiv.

3

The Cretan Mysteries

THE UNITY OF THE MYSTERIES

THE group of beliefs and practices to which we give the name of the Mysteries has existed in many countries and in different forms, most of which have influenced Freemasonry to a greater or a lesser extent. Widely spread as they were, their unity of origin is to be seen in the fact that they had a certain framework which was always the same, although they showed divergences in minor matters. In those days, just as at the present time, a Bro. from a foreign Jurisdiction who wished to visit had to prove himself at the door of the Lodge; for whatever differences there may have been in the outer forms of the ritual, the s. . .s were always the same, for these are the keys to the sacramental powers lying behind all the systems of the Mysteries alike.

LIFE IN ANCIENT CRETE

One of the most striking instances of this unity is to be found in Crete, where the comparatively recent discoveries of Sir Arthur Evans have disclosed many Masonic symbols and forms, resembling very closely those of Egypt. Like Gaul in the days of Caesar, ancient Crete was divided into three parts or states—Knossos, Goulas and Polurheni. The King of Knossos was Overlord of the whole island, for the rulers of the other states acknowledged him as their leader, although they were perfectly free to manage their own internal affairs. There was also, in the south of the island, an independent city with a few miles of territory attached to it.

All these Kings were also *ex-officio* high priests, as in Egypt, and the King's palace was always the principal temple of his State. The people worshipped a dual deity—Father-Mother—and these two were regarded as one, though some men offered their devotion more to the Father-aspect, and some to the Mother. The Father, when spoken of separately, was called Brito, and the Mother Diktynna. No statues were made of these deities, but great reverence was paid to their symbol, which was a double-headed axe. (See Plate I, 1, following p. 50.) This was carved in stone and made in metal, and set up in the temples where one would naturally expect a statue, and a conventional drawing of it represented the deity in the writing of the period. This double axe was called *labrys,* and it was for it originally that the celebrated labyrinth was built, to symbolize to the people the difficulty of finding the Path to God.

Much of their religious service and worship was carried on out of doors. Various remarkable isolated peaks of rock were regarded as sacred to the Great Mother, and the King and his people went out to one or other of these on certain days in each month, and chanted prayers and praises. A fire was lit, and each person wove a sort of crown of leaves for himself, wore it for awhile, and then threw it into the fire as an offering to the Mother-God. Each of these peaks had also a special yearly festival, much like a Pardon in Brittany—a kind of semi-religious village fair, to which people came from all parts of the island to picnic in the open air for two or three days, and enjoyed themselves hugely. In one case a great old tree of enormous size and unusually perfect shape was regarded as sacred to Diktynna, and offerings were made under its branches. A vast amount of incense was burnt under it, and it was supposed that the leaves somehow absorbed and retained the scent, so when they fell in autumn they were carefully collected and distributed to the people, who regarded them as talismans which protected them from evil. That these dried leaves had a strong fragrance is undeniable, but how far it was due to the incense seems problematical.

The people were a fine-looking race, obviously Greek in type; their dress was simple, for the men in ordinary life usually wore nothing but a loincloth, except when they put on gorgeous official costumes for religious or other festivals. The women wore a cloth which covered the whole body, but was arranged something like an Indian dhoti in the lower part, giving rather the effect of a divided skirt.

The interior of the island was mountainous, not unlike Sicily, and there was much beautiful scenery. The architecture was massive, but the houses were curiously arranged. On entering, one came directly into a large hall like a church, in which the entire family and the servants lived all day, the cooking being done in one corner. At the back was a covered passage (as in the houses in Java at the present day) leading to what was in effect a separate building, in which were the sleeping rooms. These were quite small and dark—mere cubicles— but open all round for about two feet under the roof, so that there was ample ventilation. Round the wall of this hall under the roof usually ran a frieze of painted bas-relief—generally a procession, executed in the most spirited style.

The buildings were of granite, and there were many statues of granite, though also some made of a softer stone, and some of copper and wood. Iron was used by this race, but not much; the principal metal was copper. The pottery was distinctly peculiar; all the commonest articles were made of bright yellow earthenware, painted with all sorts of figures. These figures were generally on a broad white band round the middle of the pot, and the colours used were nearly always red, brown or yellow—very rarely blue or green. These were the common household pots; but for the table they had porcelain and glass—both very well made. Most of the glass was of a bluish-green tint, like some of the old Venetian glass—not colourless like ours. The richer people used many vessels of gold, wonderfully chased and sometimes set with jewels. These people were especially clever at jewellers' work of all sorts, and made elaborate ornaments. One sees among them no diamonds or rubies—chiefly amethysts, jasper and agate. But many ornaments were evidently imported, for they had statuettes and models in carved ivory.

These people had two kinds of writing, evidently corresponding to the hieroglyphic and the demotic in Egypt, but they were quite different from the Egyptian. A decimal system was used in calculating, and arithmetic generally seems to have been well understood. These Cretans were good sailors, and had a powerful fleet of galleys, some with as many as sixty oars. They used sails also—sails which were wonderfully painted; but apparently they employed them only when the wind was almost directly astern.

THE CRETAN RACE

These people were an arm or family of the fourth or Keltic sub-race of the fifth or Aryan race. In Chapter XIX of *Man: Whence, How and Whither* a brief history of that sub-race is given; it includes the following remarks on the subject of the origin of the Cretans:

The first section [of the fourth sub-race] to cross into Europe from Asia Minor were the ancient Greeks—not the Greeks of our 'Ancient History,' but their far-away ancestors, those who are sometimes called Pelasgians. It will be remembered that the Egyptian priests are mentioned in Plato's *Timaeus* and *Critias* as having spoken to a later Greek of the splendid race which had preceded his own people in his land; how they had turned back an invasion from the mighty nation from the West, the conquering nation that had subdued all before it, until it shivered itself against the heroic valour of these Greeks. In comparison with these, it was said, the modern Greeks—the Greeks of our history who seem to us so great—were as pigmies. From these sprang the Trojans who fought with the modern Greeks, and the city of Agade in Asia Minor was peopled by their descendants.

These, then, had held for a long time the sea-board of Asia Minor and the islands of Cyprus and Crete, and all the trade of that part of the world was carried in their vessels. A fine civilization was gradually built up in Crete, which endured for thousands of years. The name of Minos will ever be remembered as its founder or chief builder, and he was of these elder Greeks, even before 10,000. B.C.[1]

RECENT DISCOVERIES IN CRETE

It is only since the year 1900 that, largely owing to the work of Sir Arthur Evans, the modern world has come to know something about the Cretan civilization, and to realize that in age and splendour it compared even with the grandeur of ancient Egypt. But even now, though there is abundant appreciation of the archaeological value of the Cretan discoveries, not much attention has yet been given by Freemasons to the highly interesting fact that the Minoan civilization shows us the existence, five thousand years ago at least, of a Mystery-religion which in its symbols and general arrangements closely resembles our modern

---

[1]*Op. cit.*, pp. 309-10.

ritual. One feature of those Cretan Mysteries especially attractive to Co-Masons is that in them women were admitted as well as men. The admission of women was the practice of almost all the Mysteries of the ancient world, but clearer traces of the fact remain to-day in Crete than in any other country. These Mysteries do not lie in the direct line of Masonic descent; but the archaeological remains of initiatory rites are so plentiful and so strikingly similar to our present system as to be exceptionally interesting.

For those who are not conversant with the results of the excavations in Crete, it may be well to give a brief survey of the historical knowledge gained by their aid. Until recently most text-books of history taught that the Greek civilization began in the eighth century B.C. There were traditions of an older civilization, with a centre in Crete, where King Minos reigned in his palace in Knossos, and another on the mainland of Greece, where in the Mycenaean cities Agamemnon and his heroes had prepared for the expedition against Troy, but these accounts were taken to be of purely legendary character until the bold perseverance of Schliemann actually laid bare the walls of ancient Troy and discovered the tombs of the Mycenaean kings, and so compelled the historians to realize that in this case as in others legend had been truer than history.

The discoveries in Crete were even more striking. When Sir Arthur Evans began his excavations on the site of ancient Knossos he not only laid bare the palace of King Minos, but also a series of successive strata indicative of a continuous civilization of a very high character stretching over a period of several thousand years. It was shown that the old legends of the labyrinth of Crete and the terrible Minotaur, supposed to dwell in its innermost depths, were based on fact, not on fancy. It is now known also that at the time of the first dynasty in Egypt there flourished in the island of Crete a civilization as powerful as the Egyptian. With regard to it Sir Arthur Evans says:

The proto-Egyptian element in Early Minoan Crete is, in fact, so clearly defined and is so intensive in its nature as almost to suggest something more than such a connection as might have been brought about by primitive commerce. It may well, indeed, be asked whether, in the time of stress and change that marked the triumph of the dynastic element in the Nile Valley, some part of the older population then driven out may not have made an actual settlement on the soil of Crete.[2]

---

[2] *The Palace of Minos at Knossos,* vol. i, p. 17.

Though the civilizations of ancient Egypt and Crete have much in common, yet each had distinctly a genius of its own, and much of the similarity between them can be explained by the fact that for long ages not only the Delta, but Middle and Upper Egypt stood in continuous relation with Minoan Crete.

It is not our object to enter into a further description of this Minoan civilization, which in many respects was equal if not superior to that of our own times. We are here concerned chiefly with the religion and the ritual usages of the ancient Minoans, which in their details show such a remarkable likeness to modern Freemasonry. Since the Minoan script cannot yet be deciphered, we are but very partially informed about the thoughts and the beliefs of the Minoan race, but from the objects found and the monuments discovered some conclusions may be drawn which are sufficient for our present purpose.

WORSHIP IN CRETE

The main worship appears to have centred round the feminine aspect of the deity already mentioned who, like Isis amongst the Egyptians and Demeter amongst the later Greeks, symbolized the creative power and fostering care of mother-nature. Connected with her worship was the sacred tree, depicted in so many presentations of Minoan shrines, while the deity herself was associated with the dove, the lion, the fish and the snake, typifying her dominion over air, earth, water and the fire within the earth.

As I have written above, the most sacred symbol in Minoan worship was the double axe or labrys. This, mounted on a stone column, is found in the shrines of ancient Crete, and when depicted on any object or building invariably denotes its sacred character. (See Plate I, 1 and Plate IV, 1, following p. 50.)

It was always an emblem of the most High God, and is in reality the ancestor of the Master's gavel, which he bears because in his humble way he represents the All-Commander, ruling his Lodge in the name of the Spiritual King. In Crete we often find it associated with what is called the sacral knot (Plate I, 2, following p. 50). When thus combined it closely resembles the Egyptian *ankh,* the token of immortality. (Plate I, 3. following p. 50.)

The Mother-Goddess Dictynna denoted the productivity and creative power of nature; this double axe, especially when surmounted by the sacral knot, signified the eternal truth of death and resurrection, which was the central mystery of the religion of Crete as it was of that of

Egypt; and so it was often laid before her to typify the ever-recurring miracle of the rebirth of tree and grain from the death of winter. The very form of the labyrinth in the recesses of which this sacred emblem was concealed was in itself symbolical and full of meaning; it was based upon the cross, and the representations of it on seals and coins sometimes take the shape of the swastika (Plate I, 4, following p. 50).

Connected with this outer religious worship in ancient Crete there were Mysteries of initiation for the few, and it is in these that we find the main elements of similarity to Freemasonry. In the palace of Minos at Knossos, as also in the palace of Phaestos—another Cretan site— we find pillared crypts and chambers which were indubitably of a sacred and initiatory character. The most important of these rooms is the so-called throne-room in the palace of Minos, which derives its name from the magnificent sculptured throne which was found intact when excavated (see Plate II, 1, following p. 50).

THE THRONE ROOM

With regard to this room, Sir Arthur Evans says:

It is now clear that a large part of the West Wing of the Palace was little more than a conglomeration of small shrines, of pillared crypts designed for ritual use, and corresponding halls above. The best preserved existing chamber of this Quarter, the 'Room of the Throne,' teems with religious suggestion. With its elaborately carved cathedral seat in the centre and stone benches round, the sacral griffins guarding on one side the entrance to an inner shrine, on the other the throne itself, and, opposite, approached by steps, its mysterious basin, it might well evoke the idea of a kind of consistory or chapter-house. A singularly dramatic touch, from the moment of final catastrophe, was here, indeed, supplied by the alabastra standing on the floor, beside the overturned oil-jar for their filling, with a view, we may infer, to some ceremony of anointing. It is impossible to withhold the conclusion that the 'Room of the Throne' at Knossos was designed for religious functions.

The salient features in its arrangement (Plate II, 2, following p. 50), in fact, suggest an interesting comparison with a ritual chamber recently discovered in one of the kindred Anatolian sanctuaries. This is the 'Hall of Initiation' excavated by the British explorors in the sanctuary of Men Askaenos and a Mother Goddess, described as Demeter, near the Pisidian Antioch. The throne itself, the stone benches round, and the 'tank' on the opposite side to the throne, find all their close analogies, and are arranged in the same relative positions. In the Galatian Sanctuary we see, on a larger scale it is true, a chamber with a throne—in this case near, not actually against the back wall—to the right of the entrance, while opposite it on the left side on entering the chamber is an oblong tank. Here, too, along the back wall runs a rock-cut bench or divan, and the chamber was approached by an ante-room or *pronaos*.

Cult arrangements are often handed down almost unaltered through long periods of years, and the striking analogies here presented afford a real presumption for believing that the much earlier Room of the Throne at Knossos and its adjoining tank were devised for similar rites of initiation and purification. Like him who presided over these Anatolian rites, a Minoan priest-king may have sat upon the throne at Knossos, the adopted Son on earth of the Great Mother of its island mysteries. Such a personage, indeed, we may actually recognize in the Palace relief of a figure wearing a plumed lily crown and leading, we may believe, the sacral Griffin. It is probable, indeed, that in Crete the kingly aspect was more to the fore than in the religious centres of Asia Minor. But both the actual evidence from the palace site and the divine associations attributed to Minos lead to the conclusion that here, too, each successive dynast was 'a priest for ever after the order of Melchizedech' and 'made like unto the Son of God'.

There is little doubt that in the room thus described we find one of the Minoan temples of the Mysteries. Most probably, as Sir Arthur Evans suggests, the throne which is shown in the chamber was the seat of the Hierophant, and on the stone benches round the walls were ranged the Brn. who took part in the ritual. The candidates for initiation had to undergo a preliminary purification in the lustral basin before they could be admitted to the ceremonies.

THE THREE COLUMNS

A plan of this Minoan Temple is shown in Plate II, 2 (following p. 50). Facing the throne of the Hierophant were three columns, which are frequently found in the mystery religion of Crete and were closely connected with its rites. The evidence that the three columns bore a sacred meaning is to be found in one of the terra-cotta models belonging to a votive shrine, which often supply us with additional information about the Cretan Mysteries. (See Plate II, 3, following p. 50.) We will quote Sir Arthur Evans' description of the three columns surmounted by doves (which repeatedly occur in various models of Minoan shrines), and his explanation of their religious meaning:

But of all these remains, the highest religious interest attaches to a terra-cotta group belonging to some religious structure on a larger scale than the others. It consists of three columns on a common base, supporting in each case, above their square 'capital,' the round ends of a pair of beams on which a dove is perched (Plate II, 3, following p. 50). The square 'capital' itself and the beam ends above it must here be regarded as the equivalent, in an epitomized shape, of the roof beams and entablature of a building. In other words, they are the *Pillars of the House,* and the doves settled above them are the outward and visible sign of the divine presence and protection. A clay seal with a similar device of a dove perched above roof-beams resting on a column, itself set on an altar base as in the Lion's Gate scheme, has now come to light at Mycenae—a singular illustration of the Minoan source of its cult.

Of the columns themselves, each one may be regarded as a separate religious entity, since in place of a common entablature the superstructure is in each case separately rendered by a kind of architectural shorthand. This Trinity of baetylic pillars (which has many parallels in Semitic cult) itself recalls the triple arrangement seen in the case of the Temple Fresco at Knossos and of several late Minoan and Mycenaean shrines. The triple gold shrines of Mycenae are also coupled with seated doves.

The seated birds, as already observed, symbolize in this and other cases the descent of the divinity into the possessed object. At times, as in the above instances, it is the baetylic pillar or the cell that enshrines it. The celebrated scene on the sarcophagus of Hagia Triada shows raven-like birds brought down by ritual strains and libations on to the sacred Double Axes, which are thus 'charged' as it were with the divinity. The doves on the gold chalice from Mycenae and of 'Nestor's Cup' repeat the same idea.

But it was not only the cult object itself that could be thus sanctified by the descending emblem of spiritual indwelling. In the case of the gold plates from the Third Shaft Grave at Mycenae the doves are seen not only perched on the Shrine but on the head and fluttering from the shoulders of a nude female personage (Plate III, 2, following p. 50). So too the central clay image from the late 'Shrine of the Double Axes' at Knossos shows the dove settled on her head. In these cases we have either images of the Dove Goddess herself, reinforced by what may have been her older zoomorphic form, or of a priestess deified by the descent of the dove-spirit.

The extent to which primitive Minoan religious conceptions were familiar to the Semitic mind is here again illustrated by the striking parallel of the baptism in Jordan and the picture drawn by the evangelists of the Holy Spirit 'descending in bodily shape like a dove' and 'lighting on' Jesus. What has to be borne in mind in all these connexions is that it is not only the inanimate or aniconic object, such as the pillar or the sacred weapon, that may become, through due ritual, the temporary dwelling-place of the divinity, but that the spiritual Being may enter into the actual worshipper or votary in human form, who for the time becomes a God, just as the baptized Christian becomes *alter Christus.* This 'possession' is often marked by soothsaying and ecstatic dances, and an orgiastic dance on a Late Minoan signet, to be described below, finds its pictorial explanation in the descent of the goddess. Musical strains such as those of the lyre or the conch-shell or the sistrum of Egyptian cult were a means of invocation.

These highly interesting terra-cotta models illustrating the religious structures and ideas of the M.M. II Period are supplemented by an object—the scale of which answers to the same series as the group of columns—in the form of a portable seat (Plate II, 3, following p. 50). Within it are some remains of the lower part and attachments of a figure. It is evident that we have here a palanquin either for a divinity or for his earthly representative, the Priest-King, recalling the *sedia-gestatoria* still used by the Papa-Re at Rome.[3]

In its general arrangements the ritual chamber of the palace of Phaestos was similar to the Masonic temple in the palace of Minos, but it contained no throne—an omission which is explained by the portable seat found in the shrine. Evidently in some cases the initiator in the Mysteries was carried in procession and retained the seat in which he had been borne.

MODELS OF SHRINES

The accompanying figures (Plate III, 1; Plate IV, 1, 2, 3, following p. 50) show models of fresco paintings of Minoan shrines. In Plate III, 1, a gold plaque from Mycenae, we see again the three columns surmounted by the horns of consecration which, like the double axe, denote the sacred character of the object, and the ritual significance is further emphasized by the doves perched on the ends of the sacred horns. In looking at these illustrations of Minoan sanctuaries we must remember that the side walls of the chamber are flattened out in the picture and not drawn in perspective, so that we must in imagination fold the two side panels of the picture of the shrine forward so as to form three walls of a shrine room. Underneath the pillars in the different illustrations the floors are paved, as shown in Plate IV, 2 and 3 (following p. 50), in black and white squares similar to the mosaic pavement of the Masonic Lodge.

In the Minoan sanctuaries we have so far seen the seat of the Hierophant or Master on one side, the benches for the brethren round the walls, three sacred columns as the principal furniture of the temple and a mosaic pavement of alternating dark and light squares in the

---

[3]*Op. cit.*, pp. 222, 223, 224.

centre. In addition, in some of the model shrines we find on one side of the room two pillars side by side; this arrangement was also discovered with the two pillars standing in the excavation of the crypt in the Palace of Minos (see Plate V, 1, following p. 50). Of these crypts Sir Arthur Evans says:

There is clear evidence, as shown below, that such pillared crypts fulfilled a religious function and stood in relation to a columnar shrine above. There can be little doubt that we have here the remains of an important sanctuary facing the inner sea gate of the Palace.[4]

THE ALTAR OBJECTS

Still further evidence of the Masonic character of the Minoan rites is shown by the remarkable objects found in the temple repositories in which were kept the different altar-objects connected with the ritual worship in the chamber of initiation. Sir Arthur Evans has rearranged these objects on the altar ledge for which they were no doubt intended, and we show a reproduction of his arrangement in Plate V, 2 (following p. 50). Perhaps the most arresting feature is the marble cross in the centre of the altar. The cross with equal arms, or Greek cross, as well as the Latin cross and the swastika, are found repeatedly in connection with the Minoan cult, and since in all ages the cross has symbolized either the mystery of creation and the descent of the divine life into manifestation, or else the mystic death and resurrection of the soul, we have here striking evidence that these conceptions were also at the base of the Cretan Mysteries.

On either side of the cross on the altar ledge the figures wear aprons, which were clearly of a ritual character, for they are not to be met with in ordinary Cretan dress (see Plate V, 3, following p. 50). The apron was evidently double, extending both in front and at the back, and differed in details in the case of the goddess and her priestess. It is possible, and in some respects even probable, that both female figures found on the altar are worshippers of the cross and the triple snake, in which case the different character of the two aprons may well denote a difference in the rank or degree of the wearers. Evans expresses his opinion that the double aprons are of a ritual character.[5]

---

[4]*Op. cit.*, p. 404.

[5]*Op. cit.*, p. 503.

Various Symbols

There were also some lesser religious symbols and objects which are of such decidedly Masonic character that they are worth mentioning. In Plate VI, 1 (following p. 50), we see a relic of bone found in the temple repository which, as Evans says "is in the shape alternately of flowers and buds, suggested by those of a pomegranate". Further symbols familiar to Freemasons are the frequently recurring sun and moon, shown in our illustration (Plate VI, 2 and 3, following p. 50) on a bronze votive tablet from the Psychro cave, and a gold ring from Mycenae. With regard to the former Evans says:

The tree, dove and fish, which here appear as the vehicles of divine possession, aptly symbolize her dominion of earth, air and sea. The triple group of sacral horns further emphasize the threefold aspect of the cult, which also explains the triple basin of the Libation Table. So, too, we see the pillar shrines of the goddess, like that of the Knossian wall-painting, regularly divided into three compartments.

Both the votive tablet and the ring are full of religious meaning and Masonic symbolism, and well repay close study. They incidentally show how far the Minoan worship spread from Crete to the mainland. Similarly the introduction of the Masonic square as a decorative pattern on a vase found in Aphidna on the mainland of Greece is of interest as showing that with the spread of Minoan culture to the Mycenaean settlements the symbols of the Minoan mystery religion too were carried abroad. (See Plate VII, 1, following p. 50.)

The Statuettes

But these evidences of Masonic symbolism, decisive as they are, are surpassed by the testimony presented by a number of statuettes and votive figures found in Crete or in the outposts of Minoan civilization, which are represented in such indubitably Masonic attitudes (some of which now belong to the higher degrees) that even the most sceptical student must acknowledge that no chance can explain this similarity. (See Plates VII and VIII following p. 50.) It would not be in accordance with Masonic secrecy to mention the degrees to which the different attitudes belong, but all Masons will readily recognize them. Ridiculous as these statuettes are, if they were the only evidence found in Crete they would be sufficient to indicate the existence of Mysteries of a Masonic Character in that ancient civilization. But where that evidence is supported by the various proofs discussed above no doubt can remain that four thousand years ago and more there existed in Crete Mysteries in which Masonic signs and symbols were used, which admitted both men and women, and performed their rites in temples very similar to those of modern Freemasonry.

4

The Jewish Mysteries

The Jewish Line of Descent

ALTHOUGH our modern Freemasonic rites and symbols are derived
from Egypt, as has been shown in *The Hidden Life in Freemasonry*,
they have reached us for the most part through the Jews. The tradition
which has most influenced our modern Masonry is that of the Jewish
Mysteries, so the greater part of our ceremonies and s . . .s are now
cast in a Jewish form.

In *The Hidden Life in Freemasonry* it has been explained that many
of the traditions preserved in the Old Testament have a basis in fact,
although the actual events of Jewish history were magnified and
distorted through the lens of an almost fanatical patriotism by the later
compilers of the records. The Jewish scriptures as we have them to-
day were almost entirely rewritten after the return from the captivity;
and the priestly writers who did this work transfigured in a glow of
enthusiastic romance the poetic traditions of their nation.

The Jewish Migrations

The Jewish race is an offshoot of that Semitic people who formed
the fifth sub-race of the Atlantean root-race. Some four thousand years
before the great cataclysm of 75,025 B.C., which overwhelmed the first
Atlantean empire of Egypt, the Manu had led His especial followers

63

into the uplands of Arabia in order that they might be separated from the bulk of the Atlanteans, and that a new type might be evolved from them which would later be developed into the Aryan root-race. Strict injunctions were given by the Manu that there was to be no intermarriage with neighbouring races, so that the purity of the new stock might be maintained; and the idea of these men that they were a "chosen people" was fostered to that end. Shortly before the cataclysm some seven hundred of the best and most promising of these people were led into Central Asia by the Manu, and they grew there after many thousands of years into a great nation, the nucleus of the Aryan race that was later to rule the world.

About 40,000 B.C. the Manu led out the second sub-race of the new root-race to colonize Arabia once more, since the Semites who had been left behind were the closest of the Atlantean peoples to the new stock. Arabia became a great Aryan kingdom, excepting only a certain section of those inhabiting the southern part of the peninsula, who declined to recognize the Manu or to intermarry with His people, quoting His own regulation against Him in defence of their refusal. Later this tract of country was conquered by the Aryans, and a fanatical section of its inhabitants forsook their homes, and settled on the opposite coast of the Red Sea in what we now call Somaliland. Here they lived for several centuries, but in consequence of an attempt on the part of the majority to intermarry with the negroes of the interior, a fairly large minority of them withdrew from the community, and, after many wanderings, found themselves in Egyptian territory. The Pharaoh of the period, interested in their story, offered them an outlying district of his kingdom if they chose to settle there. Eventually some Pharaoh made a demand upon them for additional taxation and forced work which they considered an infringement of their privileges; and they once more undertook a wholesale migration under the leadership of him whom we now call Moses, and after further wanderings settled in Palestine, where they were known as the Jews, still strongly maintaining that they were a chosen people.[1]

During their sojourn in Egypt certain of them had been initiated into some of the degrees of the Egyptian Mysteries. Moses, as was said much later, "was learned in all the wisdom of the Egyptians",[2]

---

[1] See *Man: Whence, How and Whither*, Ch. xiv and xvi, *passim*.

[2] Acts, vii, 22.

and he seems to have been the real founder of the Jewish Mysteries, much as tradition suggests, introducing into them the succession of I.M.s which he had received from the Egyptian priests. Our investigations have not confirmed the events related in the early chapters of the book of Exodus with regard to the ten plagues and the smiting of the Egyptians; the Jews departed without much opposition, and after many years of wandering in the wilderness conquered various tribes and took possession of Palestine. Indeed their migration seems to have been inspired to some extent by the Manu. During their wanderings they used a tent for the celebration of their Mysteries, preserved in Hebrew tradition as the tabernacle; in this they worked in essence the Egyptian rituals, though the whole celebration was under such conditions on a much smaller and less splendid scale. These are the facts lying behind the Masonic tradition of the First or Holy Lodge.

THE PROPHETS

It appears that Moses was also acquainted with the great ritual of Amen as worked in the Mysteries of Egypt, and some portion at least of this tradition was transmitted to his successors. There arose in later times a school in connection with the Mysteries, the members of which had the idea of personifying the children of Israel as one Being who might shed blessing over all nations; and they attempted to arouse among them the sense of unity necessary for this purpose partly by means of ritual. There were also the schools of the prophets, who were trained in the Mysteries and studied the deeper teaching enshrined in the ancient rites. One such school is mentioned in the Old Testament as existing at Naioth under the direction of the prophet Samuel,[3] and there were others later at Bethel and Jericho.[4]

These schools were not so much concerned with prophecy in our modern sense of foretelling the future, as with endeavouring to instruct the people by preaching; they seem to have resembled in many ways the preaching friars sent out by the Roman Church during the middle ages, the Franciscans and other Orders. These preachers were chosen from among the Levites, and were sent forth to proclaim the deeper teaching in a popular form. It is probable that many of the greater Jewish prophets belonged to a later development of these schools—

[3] I Sam., xix, 20.

[4] II Kings, ii, 2, 5.

Isaiah, Jeremiah, Ezekiel and others—but they were always somewhat pessimistic in their outlook, even though several of them unquestionably touched high levels of consciousness in their visions. Their method was apparently to throw themselves into a state of tremendous exaltation, and then to look up into a higher plane through a kind of shaft which they had opened. It was in this way that Ezekiel saw the vision of the four Kings of the elements. These Great Ones can be seen clearly only with the sight of the spiritual or nirvanic plane; it does not appear that Ezekiel had touched that exalted level directly, but he became aware of it in his ecstasy as though looking up to it from below.

THE BUILDERS OF K. S. T.

Something both of the inner powers and of the Egyptian rituals had been faithfully handed down from generation to generation from the days of Moses until King Solomon came to the throne of his father David. There is some truth in the tradition preserved in the Bible, although there are exaggerations and mistakes in the accounts which have come down to us, and much of the inner meaning of the symbols had been forgotten. King Solomon seems to have been a man of considerable force of character and some occult knowledge, and the great ambition of his life was to weld his people into a strong and respected kingdom, able to take an influential place among the nations around. To that end he built the temple in Jerusalem to be the centre of the religious worship of his people and a symbol of their national unity; it was perhaps not quite so magnificent as tradition relates, but the King was nevertheless extremely proud of it and considered it to be one of the great achievements of the age.

In this work he was assisted by his ally, Hiram King of Tyre, who supplied a quantity of material for the building, and lent many clever craftsmen to aid in the work; for the Phoenicians were more skilled in building than the Jews, who were chiefly a pastoral people. Also about fifty years before some of the wandering bands of Masons who called themselves the Dionysian Artificers had settled in Phoenicia, so King Hiram was able to supply many expert workmen. This alliance is a matter of secular history, for Josephus tells us that even in his day copies of the letters which passed between the two Kings existed in the Tyrian archives and might be consulted by students.[5] Hiram Abiff

---

[5]Josephus. *Ant.*, viii.

was also a real personage, though he did not meet his death in the manner recorded in Masonic tradition. He was a decorator rather than the actual Architect of the Temple, as the biblical records clearly tell us. "He was filled with wisdom and understanding, and cunning to work all works in brass."[6] He was "skilful to work in gold, and in silver, in brass, in iron, in stone, and in timber, in purple, in blue, and in fine linen, and in crimson; also to grave any manner of graving, and to find out every device which shall be put to him".[7]

Josephus confirms the tradition that he was an artist and a craftsman rather than an architect: "This man was skilful in all sorts of work, but his chief skill lay in working in gold and silver and brass, and he did all the curious work about the temple as the King wished."[8] He was the son of a widow of Naphtali, and his father was a man of Tyre, a worker in brass before him. Since so much responsibility rested in his hands, and he was so skilful an artist, he appears to have been in the close confidence of King Solomon, and a member of his council. He was evidently treated as an equal by the two Kings, and that is one of the reasons which influenced Bro. Ward to translate Hiram Abiff as "Hiram his father," and to represent the King of Tyre as sending his abdicated father to superintend the decoration of the temple.

THE RECASTING OF THE RITUALS

But King Solomon's plans for the consolidation of his people were not yet complete; by the building of his temple he had formed an outer centre of national worship, and he now desired that the Mysteries, the heart of his people's religion and the centre of their spiritual consciousness, should also be purely Jewish in their form. The ceremonial handed down from the days of Moses was still Egyptian, and the initiates of the mysteries were yet symbolically engaged in building the great pyramid, the House of Light, and in celebrating the death and resurrection of Osiris. Even though it had no corresponding halls of initiation, King Solomon desired that for the future his temple should take the place of the House of Light, and become the spiritual centre of the Jewish Mysteries. King Hiram of Tyre warmly supported this

---

[6] I Kings, vii, 14.

[7] II Chron., ii, 14.

[8] Josephus, *Ant.*, viii.

idea; he himself had inherited initiatory rites which had been derived from the Mysteries of Chaldaea, a very ancient line of tradition running parallel with the Mysteries of Egypt from Atlantean days, and having its own chief halls of initiation in Babylon. He, too, felt that a centre nearer home and in friendly hands was eminently desirable, and he therefore co-operated in the plan of Judaizing the ancient rites and focusing them upon the temple in Jerusalem.

At first, it appears, the two Kings sent an embassy to Egypt to consult the Pharaoh in the matter, telling him of the temple which they had built, and asking for some recognition of the Jewish branch of the Mysteries. The Pharaoh did not accept their proposals with any degree of enthusiasm, but rather implied that no foreigner could possibly understand the Mysteries of Egypt. The Egyptians of the period seem to have regarded their Jewish brethren with something of the same feeling that the Grand Lodge of England might have towards the Grand Orient of Hayti if it should propose alterations in the ritual, and their interest in the new venture was decidedly cold. We find no confirmation of the story of the marriage of King Solomon to Pharaoh's daughter, as is related in the Bible; indeed, this union is now generally rejected by the critics as impossible, for according to the Tell el-Amarna tablets, an Egyptian princess might not marry a foreigner.[9]

THE MINGLING OF TRADITIONS

On the return of their embassy from Egypt King Solomon and King Hiram called together the council at Jerusalem, and it was decided that they should proceed immediately with the work of recasting the rituals into the Jewish form. It is an interesting fact that three distinct lines of tradition were represented in the persons of the three chief members of the council, and of each of these we can find traces in our modern workings. King Solomon himself had inherited the Egyptian line of succession derived from Moses; King Hiram of Tyre preserved the Chaldaean descent; while Hiram Abiff brought with him another line of tradition, not derived from either of these sources.

This last line was strange and terrible—a line probably perpetuated through savage and primitive tribes who had bloodthirsty customs of mutilation and human sacrifice. I think it must be to this line that Bro. Ward refers in his remarkable work *Who was Hiram Abiff?* in which

---

[9]Peake's *Commentary on the Bible*, p. 296.

he adduces a vast amount of evidence to show that our traditional history is based upon the myth of the death and resurrection of Tammuz, and is in reality an account of the ritual murder of one of the Priest-Kings of that religion. He points out that most primitive races enact a drama in which some one, usually a priest or king, represents a god who is slain and comes to life again; that in earlier times at any rate such a representative was really killed and offered up as a sacrifice to ensure fertility; that we first hear of this myth of Tammuz in connection with Babylon, and that the tribes in the neighbourhood of Judaea were all addicted to the worship of that deity. In fact, among the Jews themselves we find the prophets blaming the Hebrew ladies for taking part in the ritual mourning for him.[10]

Solomon himself was by no means definitely monotheistic, and his people betrayed a distinct tendency to run after strange gods. There seems much evidence to prove that the love-song attributed to him in the Bible is really a ritual hymn to Astarte, for whom he built a temple quite near to that of Jehovah. There is considerable uncertainty as to whether Balkis, Queen of Sheba, was a real person, or only a personification of Astarte. Bro. Ward explains that the festivals of the two patron saints of Freemasonry, S. John the Baptist in summer and S. John the Evangelist in winter, are only a perpetuation of the feasts of the old fertility cult at the summer and winter solstices; that similar cultural rites are found in other lands, Teutonic, Celtic and Greek, that they also survived among the Essenes, and that the Knights Templars brought back from Syria a story very similar to that of the 3°. The tale of Jonah, he remarks, has always been understood as a myth of death and resurrection, and he also was sacrificed to appease a deity, and obtain salvation for others, just as was the Priest-King of old. He quotes many instances of foundation and consecration sacrifices; and, holding as he does that Hiram Abiff was the father of that other Hiram who was King of Tyre, he writes:

The Phoenician and Jewish followers of the old Tammuz cult no doubt felt that the Great Goddess had been cheated of her just dues when Hiram Abiff was not slain, according to ancient custom, on the accession of his son, and were confident that if he were not sacrificed when the temple was completed its future and stability would be endangered.... So I consider that the Phoeni-

---

[10]Ezekiel, viii, 14.

cian workmen, with or without the consent of Solomon, killed the old King of Tyre, Abibaal or Hiram Abiff, as a Consecration Sacrifice.[11]

While we can hardly accept the suggestion that the ancestry of our modern rite is wholly Syrian, we cannot doubt that the influence of the third line of tradition especially contributed by Hiram Abiff was very considerable. We note also that it seems to have been especially concerned with the working of metals.

All that is found in our modern rituals about Lamech and his sons, about Jubal, the founder of the art of music, and Tubal Cain, the first artificer in metals, appears to belong to the line of tradition which Hiram Abiff introduced.

This council was the originator of the greater part of our modern Masonic working; the main outline of the Egyptian ritual was carefully preserved (although King Solomon on more than one occasion referred to his brother of Tyre on points of detail) together with the s. . .s, and although the w. . .s were given in Hebrew, for the most part their meaning remained the same. King Solomon himself seems to have been largely responsible for our ceremony of raising; he it was who, at the instance of Hiram Abiff, changed the legend of Osiris into that of the master builder who attempted to escape by the S., N., and E. g. . .s and was s. . .n because he would not divulge the s. . .s of a M.M. The name of the original master builder was not of course given as now, for he himself assisted in the construction of the legend; neither was there any fatality connected with the actual building of the holy temple. The insertion of the present name was the work of Rehoboam, when he succeeded to the throne of Solomon his father, as I have said in *The Hidden Life in Freemasonry;* so the story came to be applied to the person of Hiram, the widow's son.

A very curious tradition still exists in the 3° of the rite of Mizraim. In that rite the central figure of the legend is not H.A., who is said to have returned to his family after the completion of the temple; but the story is carried back to the days of Lamech, whose son Jubal, under the name of Harrio-Jubal-Abi, is reported to have been slain by three traitors, Hagava, Hakina, and Heremda. (Mackey's *Encyclopaedia,* art. *Mizraim.)* The rite of Mizraim, as we shall see later, is extremely old, and may well have incorporated another tradition than that handed down in Europe; for it appears to have been introduced from the East

---

[11]*Who was Hiram Abiff?* by J.S.M. Ward, p. 191.

towards the end of the eighteenth century. It may be that we have here another echo of that line of tradition which Hiram Abiff represented on the council of King Solomon.

Such was the important work undertaken by the second or Sacred Lodge. The succession of I.M.s was handed down into the new dispensation, and thenceforward Masters of Lodges deriving their succession from the Mysteries of the Hebrews have always sat in the Chair of King Solomon, while the two Wardens occupy those of Hiram King of Tyre and Hiram Abiff. Thus there is a very real truth behind our Masonic tradition.

The original traditional history as adapted by King Solomon contained much more of the legend of Osiris, and was altogether more coherent and reasonable than it is to-day; for there was a resurrection of the master-builder as well as a death, and the search of Isis for the body of Osiris was reflected in the search of certain craftsmen for the body of the Master. But this was rather in the nature of a verbal charge than a piece of ritual working, and it was therefore more likely to become distorted in the course of ages. This is exactly what took place. The ceremonies were handed down from age to age with very few changes, but they were at several epochs clothed in a new set of words, which reflected the spirit of the times; while the legend associated with the ritual of the 3° became sadly marred in its passage throughout the centuries, until in its present form it is a mere shadow of the glorious teaching of the Mysteries of Egypt from which it was derived.

THE TRANSMISSION OF THE NEW RITES

The Mysteries were transmitted from generation to generation for the next three hundred and fifty years, during the survival of the kingdom of Judah. In 586 B.C. the city of Jerusalem was destroyed by Nebuchadnezzar, and the people were led captive into Babylon. During the captivity the Mysteries were interrupted, and it does not seem probable that they were seriously worked during the fifty years of exile. Nevertheless, the succession of I.M.s remained unbroken, and when the people returned from Babylon to rebuild the temple, they also tried to reconstruct their rites of initiation.

Herein we find the facts underlying the tradition of the third or Grand and Royal Lodge; for Zerubbabel, the prince of Judah, and Jeshua, the high priest, were largely instrumental in this work of restoration and renewal. The same difficulty recurred again, for it was never allowed to write down the rituals; once more it was necessary to rely upon memory for the major part of the tradition, and only a very few could have recollected the actual workings in the days before the captivity. Nevertheless they succeeded in reconstructing the rites with tolerable accuracy, although once more the traditional history suffered distortion through being imperfectly remembered. Such is the story of that line of succession which eventually found its way into the Roman Collegia, in the first place by direct descent from the teaching of King Numa, then by the migration of the rites of Attis and Cybele to Rome about 200 B.C., and again through the medium of the returning soldiers of the armies of Vespasian and Titus. From these Collegia it has been handed down with singularly little change in essentials to our modern Lodges.

Besides the three Craft degrees which formed the main structure of the Jewish Mysteries, there were also other Masonic traditions handed down from Egypt. That which is now the Holy Royal Arch had its place in the working, while the ideas contained in what we now call the Mark degree were associated with the 2° as the Arch was with the 3°. Although in English working the period of the Arch is represented to be that of Zerubbabel and the Second Temple, the Irish Chapters refer the whole legend to the days of King Josiah, while the Royal Arch of Enoch, which differs considerably in detail, though the symbology has the same significance and purpose, is described as belonging to the time of King Solomon himself. The absence of a fixed period is noteworthy as indicating that the historical setting is only of secondary importance, and that the main purpose of the degree is to convey symbolical instruction.

THE ESSENES AND THE CHRIST

The tradition of the Mysteries was transmitted from century to century, until we find it among the Essenes, who also appear to have inherited Chaldaean rites. It was in this school that the disciple Jesus lived in preparation for His ministry, after receiving a high initiation into the true Mysteries of Egypt. The Essenes had among other Chaldaean rites inherited what was afterwards known as the Mithraic eucharist, the ceremony of bread and wine and salt, which, as we shall see later, was transmitted through the ages until it was incorporated in the modern degree of the Rose-Croix of Heredom. The consecration of those elements was and is wonderful, though there is not so full a descent of the Divine Presence as in the corresponding ritual of Amen used in ancient Egypt. It seems probable, however, that the Lord Christ took the Mithraic supper as the basis of His holy eucharist, and while preserving the ancient symbolism of the elements changed them into His own special vehicle, symbolized as His Body and Blood—the very closest and most intimate of all the sacraments known to man.

The Mithraic eucharist brought the worshipper into close touch with the divine Life; the mystic supper of the Rose-Croix lifts the Sovereign Prince into a wonderful union with Christ, the Lord of love; in the ritual of Amen the Brn. bowed to each who had partaken of the sacrament saying, "Thou art Osiris." The holy eucharist of the Christian Church is the last and most wonderful of all, for in it we receive Him, the Lord of Love, and the sacred Host is just as fully and perfectly His vehicle as was the body of Jesus in Palestine two thousand years ago. It seems probable that He took the existing sacrament which was regularly celebrated in the Essene community, and transfigured it into another and holier eucharist, which has become the glory of His Church from generation to generation.

KABBALISM

With the tremendous impetus given by the coming of the Lord the mysteries received a greater inspiration than had been theirs since the days of Moses. Part of the mystic teaching belonging to them later passed into writing, and in the Kabbala we find fragments of the symbolic knowledge which was once the exclusive property of the initiates. So close are the analogies between certain of the doctrines of the Kabbala and those of the earlier degrees of Masonry that it has been supposed that Kabbalistic students were responsible for the introduction of speculative Masonry into our modern Craft. The student of occultism does not hold this view, for he knows that our speculative rituals belong in substance to a far older past than the eighteenth century, and that they perpetuate the tradition of the Jews, who derived it from the Mysteries of Egypt. He sees in the literature of the Kabbala a written and exoteric portion of certain teachings belonging to the Jews, though handed down along an independent line, which may nevertheless have crossed that of our own Craft and influenced it to

some extent in later days. There is much in the Kabbala which throws
light upon our ceremonies and symbols, and a study of Kabbalistic
Theosophy may be of both profit and interest to the Mason.

The briefest summary is all that we can attempt here.[12] The literature
of the Kabbala represents a growth of many centuries under the influence of many types of thought—Jewish, Gnostic, Neo-Platonic, Greek,
Arabic and even Persian—and it has never been fully translated into
any European language. It consists of certain great texts written in
Hebrew and Aramaic, and a mass of commentaries upon them compiled by Jews of many lands and many ages. The most important texts
are the *Sepher Yetzirah,* which explains the mystic meanings underlying
the Hebrew alphabet, and erects a vast system of mystical and occult
speculation upon the combinations and permutations of the various
letters; and the *Sepher ha Zohar,* or *Book of Splendour,* which is a
medley of history and legend, of fable and of fact, of mysticism and
fantastic speculation which, like all such literature, contains priceless
gems of occult wisdom hidden in a mass of rubbish. Both these texts
claim to date from the second century A.D., but in reality they were
not written down until a later period, the former being completed about
the tenth century, and the latter before the thirteenth. They became
known to the educated people of Europe about the time when
speculative Masonry was beginning to emerge into the light of day
(that is during the seventeenth century) through various Latin works,
the chief of which are Baron Knorr von Rosenroth's *Kabbala
Denudata,* the *OEdipus AEgyptiacus* of Athanasius Kircher, the *De
Arte Cabalistica* of Reuchlin and a Latin translation of the *Yetzirah.*
As Bro. A. E. Waite, our chief authority in this field, has pointed out:

The written Jewish tradition presupposes throughout a tradition which did
not pass into writing. The *Zohar,* for example, which is its chief memorial,
refers everywhere to a great body of doctrine as something perfectly well-
known by the circle of initiation for which the work was alone intended.[13]

The skeleton of this body of doctrine has reached us in the symbolism of Masonry, although along so different a line; and in the

---

[12]See *The Secret Tradition in Israel, The Secret Tradition in Freemasonry,
A New Encyclopaedia,* all by Bro. A.E. Waite.

[13]*Secret Tradition in Freemasonry,* I, 64.

Kabbala we may find a clue to much that is obscure in our modern rituals.

THE SPIRITUALIZATION OF THE TEMPLE

Two mystical concepts found in the *Zohar* relate directly to our subject—the spiritualization of the temple of King Solomon, and the doctrine of the lost word, both of which have their roots in the Egyptian Mysteries, as we have already seen. King Solomon's temple formed the physical basis for a vast structure of mystical speculation and inquiry; for its measurements and proportions were held to have a relation to those of the universe, and all the sacred objects which it contained had their macrocosmic and microcosmic interpretations. The Shekinah or divine glory which irradiated the innermost sanctuary, the Holy of Holies, was interpreted not only as the divine Presence which hallowed the visible temple, but as God immanent in His universe and indwelling in the heart of man.

Furthermore, the idea of the Jews that some day the temple should be rebuilt is itself spiritualized and transformed, and it was taken as an allegory of the attainment of divine perfection both in man and the universe. The Jews, whose rich Oriental minds delighted in exuberant and complex allegory, conceived a veritable city of temples, of which King Solomon's was but the symbol—temples and palaces each relating to a different aspect or plane of nature and forming an intricate system of reflections and correspondences. The prototype of all this wealth of symbolism is found in the Mysteries of Egypt, wherein the measurements of the great pyramid were studied as emblematical of the proportions of the universe, and contained vast stores of occult and astronomical lore. The Jews applied what they knew of the Egyptian system to the temple of King Solomon, reflecting the wisdom of Egypt through the lens of their own fiery and poetical temperament, whence some portion of it gradually passed on the one hand into written and exoteric literature, and on the other was handed down in the secret Lodges of Masonry.

THE LOSS OF THE DIVINE NAME

The second great doctrine of Kabbalism which concerns us here is the loss of the divine Name, or rather of the correct method of pronouncing that Name. The Jews thought of this Name as a word of four

letters, J. H. V. H., which we generally read as Jehovah. The tradition relates that the Omnific Word which, being the Name of God,
commanded all the creative forces of Nature, was pronounced by the
high priest once a year on the day of atonement, but that after the
exile the true pronunciation was lost. The consonants remained, but
the vowel points essential to correct articulation had been forgotten.
(The present Masoretic system of vowel points was introduced only
in the tenth century A.D.) This was woven into a beautiful allegory
of the descent into matter and of the fall of man; for immersed in matter
as we are at our present stage of evolution, we cannot utter the word
or know the divine Nature in its fullness, but can perceive only the
outer shell of things, represented by the remaining consonants. And
even this we do not understand, and therefore for even that much of
the Divine Name a substituted secret is necessary. And so in the tradition whenever the word Yahweh occurred in the reading of the Law,
the name Adonai (meaning "my Lord") was substituted for it. (The
modern word Jehovah is made by using the consonants Jhvh, and
intercalating the vowels from the word Adonai.) The tradition looks
forward to a future when time or circumstances shall have restored
the genuine method of pronunciation, and man will return to the God
from whom he came forth, able to utter the word in all its mighty
power, to command the forces latent in his own divinity.

All this was interwoven with the doctrine of the Logos, the Word
of God, expounded so admirably by Philo, and known to all Christians
from the opening words of the Gospel of S. John; for the whole tradition of the divine Word is derived from the Mysteries of Egypt. The
true Tetragrammaton was not the Name of God in Hebrew, but another
and far more ancient word, which has ever been known to initiates
of high degree. A Christian development of this symbolism forms the
device of a jewel worn by a certain high official in the Scottish Rite.
Under the old covenant the word was lost, and even when restored
through the discovery of a certain secret vault, its true pronunciation
was unknown; the end of the quest was not yet reached, though it was
in sight. The new covenant added in the centre yet one letter more,
the mystic *Shin,* emblematical of fire and of the Spirit; and so the Word
Jehovah became Jeheshua, the Name of the Christ. Which things are
an allegory, for it is only by the finding of the Christ in the heart that
the lost word can be rediscovered, and that very finding brings the

knowledge of the true Tetragrammaton—that secret of man's eternal being, which from the beginning has been written upon the cross of sacrifice and always kept hidden in the heart of the world among the secret things of God.

Such is a brief outline of those Jewish Mysteries, the tradition of which was carried to Rome, and thence passed down through the Collegia into the mediaeval guilds, finally emerging in the eighteenth century in the speculative rituals of the Craft degrees, in the Holy Royal Arch and the degree of Mark Master Mason, and in those other emblems and ceremonies which have been incorporated into certain of the subsidiary grades belonging in their symbolic time to the old covenant. The Jewish Mysteries are the source of our present tradition, for the three Craft degrees are, and always have been, the basis of the whole system of Masonic initiation, since they enshrine the relics of the Lesser and Greater Mysteries of Egypt, which alone can be termed degrees in their original form. But before we pass on to our next link in the Masonic chain of descent—that of Rome and its Colleges—it may be well to touch upon certain of the other great Mystery-systems which were famous in the ancient world.

5

The Greek Mysteries

THE ELEUSINIAN MYSTERIES

WE come now to the Mysteries of Greece, of which the best-known and most important in classical times were the Eleusinian. There seems to be a widely-spread delusion, the origin of which we can trace to the writings of the Christian Fathers, that the Mysteries of antiquity were kept secret because they contained much that was improper, and that would not bear the light of day. That is not so in the least, and I am in a position to bear direct testimony, having been myself an initiate of the Mysteries, that there was nothing whatever in them of an objectionable character. The teachings were all of the highest and purest nature, and they could not but benefit very greatly all who had the privilege of being initiated into them. In classical and post-classical times many of the greatest men have borne witness to their worth. A few quotations—samples of many—will be sufficient to show this.

Sophocles, the great tragic poet, says of them:

Thrice-happy are those mortals who after the contemplation of the Mysteries go down into the realms of Hades; for there they alone will possess true life: for the rest there is naught but suffering.[1]

Plato says through the mouth of Socrates in that wonderful death-scene in the *Phaedo:*

---

[1]Sophocles fr. 348, quoted Foucart: *Les Mysteres d'Eleusis*, p. 362.

I fancy that those men who established the Mysteries were not unenlightened, but in reality had a hidden meaning when they said long ago that whoever goes uninitiated and unsanctified to the other world will lie in the mire, but he who arrives there initiated and purified will dwell with the Gods.[2]

Cicero was initiated into them and held them in the highest reverence,[3] while Proclus tells us in the last days of the pagan faith:

The most holy Rites of Eleusis vouchsafe to the Initiates enjoyment of the good offices of Kore when they shall be delivered from their bodies.[4]

It is true that in the time of the decadence of Rome there were degenerate ceremonies connected with the Mysteries of Bacchus, which involved orgies of a very unpleasant character, but they were in no way connected with the original Eleusinian Mysteries, which by that time had faded almost entirely into the background.

The modern world knows little of the truth about the Greek Mysteries, for their activities and doctrines were really kept secret. Apart from the strong pressure of public opinion, which treated the slightest violation of secrecy as an act of terrible impiety, we hear of the death-penalty being inflicted in a case of the accidental intrusion of two non-initiates into the sacred enclosure at Eleusis during the celebration of the Mysteries.[5] Very little, therefore of direct fact has reached us from pagan sources; the greater part of our information comes from the Christian writers, Hippolytus, Clement of Alexandria, Origen, Arnobius and others, who were engaged upon destroying as much as possible of the pagan religion, and therefore always spoke of the Mysteries in the worst possible light. Something is known of a few of the exterior tests that were applied to candidates, and of the teaching that was given through the various myths. When people outside pressed for information, and would not be put off, the officials permitted so much to be revealed.

THE ORIGIN OF THE GREEK MYSTERIES

The original founder of the Greek Mysteries was Orpheus, who was an incarnation of the same great World-Teacher who had come to Egypt

---

[2]Plato. *Phaedo.* Loeb. Edition, p. 241.

[3]Cic. *De. Leg.*, II, 14.

[4]Proclus. *Comment. in Plat. rem pub.* quoted Foucart, loc. cit., p. 364.

[5]Livy. xxxi, 14.

in 40,000 B.C. as Thoth or Hermes, to preach the doctrine of the Hidden Light. But now the method of His message was different; for it was spoken to a different race.

About 7000 B.C, He came, living chiefly in the forests, where He gathered His disciples around Him. There was no king to bid him welcome, no gorgeous court to acclaim Him. He came as a singer, wandering through the land, loving the life of Nature, her sunlit spaces and her shadowed forest retreats, averse to cities and to the crowded haunts of men. A band of disciples grew around Him, and He taught them in the glades of woodland, silent save for the singing of the birds and the sweet sounds of forest life, that seemed not to break the stillness.

He taught by song, by music, music of voice and instrument, carrying a five-stringed musical instrument, probably the origin of Apollo's lyre, and He used a pentatonic scale. To this He sang, and wondrous was His music, the Angels drawing nigh to listen to the subtle tones; by sound He worked upon the astral and mental bodies of His disciples, purifying and expanding them; by sound He drew the subtle bodies away from the physical, and set them free in the higher worlds. His music was quite different from the sequences, repeated over and over again, by which the same result was brought about in the Root-stock of the Race, which it carried with it into India. Here He worked by melody, not by repetition of similar sounds; and the rousing of each etheric centre had its own melody, stirring it into activity. He showed His disciples living pictures, created by music, and in the Greek Mysteries this was wrought in the same way, the tradition coming down from Him. And He taught that Sound was in all things, and that if man would harmonize himself, then would the Divine Harmony manifest through him, and make all Nature glad. Thus He went through Hellas singing, and choosing here and there one who would follow Him, and singing also for the people in other ways, weaving over Greece a network of music, which should make her children beautiful and feed the artistic genius of her land.[6]

This wonderful tradition of the Mysteries of Orpheus was handed down for thousands of years until in classical times we find, on the one hand the Orphic Schools, of which that of Pythagoras was a splendid offshoot, and on the other the greatest of all the Greek Mysteries, those of Eleusis, which preserved much of the ancient teaching in a ceremonial form. A relic of the tradition of Orpheus is found in the fact that the hierophant of the Eleusinian Mysteries was always chosen from the sacred family of the Eumolpidae, the descen-

---

[6]*Man: Whence, How and Whither*, p. 316ff.

dants of the fabled Eumolpus, whose name meant the sweet singer; and one of the most important qualifications for the office was the possession of a beautiful and resonant voice, with which the sacred chants might be correctly intoned.[7]

THE GODS OF GREECE

The Greek idea of worship was very different from our modern conceptions. It must not be supposed that any of the educated Greeks believed in the mythology of their religion as literal fact. Men sometimes wonder how it was possible for great nations like Rome or Greece to remain satisfied with what we commonly call their religion—a chaos of unseemly myths, many of them not even decent, describing gods and goddesses who were distinctly human in their actions and passions, and were constantly quarrelling amongst themselves. The truth is that nobody *was* satisfied with it, and it never was at all what we mean by a religion, though it was no doubt taken literally by some ignorant people. All cultured and thinking men took up the study of one or other of the systems of philosophy, and in many cases they were also initiates of the school of the Mysteries; it was this higher teaching that really moulded their lives, and took for them the place of what we call religion—unless, indeed, they were frankly agnostic, as are so many cultured men now. Some of these weird myths, however, were explained in the Mysteries and were seen to enshrine a hidden teaching relating to the life of the soul.

Nevertheless many of the gods of Greece were real personages, who played their parts in the lives of the people, and were channels to them of the divine blessing. The chief aspect of the outer religion of Greece was the cult of the beautiful. It was known in Greece that every true work of art radiated an atmosphere of joy and beauty; therefore the Greeks surrounded themselves and their worship with every kind of lovely thing. They knew that the gods manifested themselves through beauty, were aspects of and channels for the One Beauty; and thus they gathered streams of the divine influence around them and so outpoured blessing upon the world. The gods of Greece were not the same as those reverenced in Egypt; they represented somewhat different aspects of the one eternal God in forms suited to the development of

---

[7]*Les Mysteres d'Eleusis.* Paul Foucart. Paris, 1914, p. 170.

the Celtic subrace, which was essentially an artistic, as the Egyptians had been a scientific, people. As students of the occult side of religion are aware, each subrace has its own especial presentation of truth, its own divine forms through whom worship is offered to the Supreme; and the type of religion is formulated by the World-Teacher Himself in accordance with the development and culture which are to be the distinguishing characteristic of that race and its contribution to the world-plan of evolution. In Greece, as in Egypt, there was a multiplicity of these divine forms, some of them represented and ensouled by great Angels, who may be compared to some extent to those adored in Christian lands—S. Michael, S. Gabriel, S. Raphael and others. The gods of Greece were no less real than these great ones, although they belonged to an entirely different type, resembling rather the presiding Angels of the various countries than the Rulers of the nine orders of the Angelic hosts.

Pallas Athene, the grey-eyed goddess of wisdom, was a magnificent and splendid Being, who practically governed Athens in the old days through her devotees. Her influence was enormously stimulating, but she was not so much an embodiment of compassion or of love, as is the Blessed Virgin Mary, but rather of efficiency and of that perfect accuracy of form that is the essence of all true art. Much of the wonderful art of Greece was inspired directly by her; and to satisfy her it had to be the very highest and truest and most accurate. She could not tolerate a single line misplaced, even in the smallest thing. There was something of polished steel about Athene; she was cold and keen like a rapier, tremendously powerful, keeping the people up to the highest, the noblest, the purest, the most beautiful; and yet less for the sake of an abstract love of beauty than because it would have been a disgrace to be otherwise than beautiful. There was practically no emotion connected with Pallas Athene; we had an intellectual appreciation of her greatness, an intense devotion along mental lines, a splendid enthusiasm in following her; but we should not have ventured upon anything like personal affection. She kept Athens in perfect order, directing it, governing it, brooding over its people with her wonderful inspiration; and she watched the development of her city with the closest interest, determined that it should be ahead of Sparta and Corinth and the other cities of Greece.

Hera was a real personage likewise, but very different from Pallas Athene. She was one of the many incarnations or forms of the feminine aspect of the First Ray, and was thought of as the Queen of Heaven; she corresponds most closely to the Indian goddess Parvati, the *shakti* or power of Shiva, imaged as His consort, as Hera was the consort of Zeus.

Dionysus was the Logos Himself, just as Osiris had been in Egypt, though in a somewhat different aspect; and the legend of His death and resurrection corresponded closely with that of Osiris, and was taught with the same signification in the Mysteries of Greece. Phoebus Apollo, the God of the Sun and of music, whose symbol was the lyre, seems originally to have been Orpheus; so that in venerating him the Greeks in reality offered their love to the great World-Teacher. Demeter and her daughter Persephone or Kore were especially reverenced at Eleusis. These two deities were personifications of the great forces of nature, the first of the brooding motherhood of the earth, and the second of that creative life which makes the earth to flourish and blossom with corn and flowers and fruit, and then withdraws once more at the onset of winter into a kind of hibernation—a hidden life within, only to burst out again as though in a new incarnation under the influence of spring. Demeter appears to correspond with Uma, the Great Mother, still venerated in India.

Aphrodite, the goddess of Love—"immortal Aphrodite of the broidered throne," as Sappho calls her—represented the feminine aspect of the Deity as the divine compassion; she was called the "foam-born" because she was mystically supposed to have risen from the waters of the ocean. Swinburne describes her in magnificent lines:

> Her deep hair heavily laden with the odour and colour of
> flowers,
> White rose of the rose-white water, a silver splendour, a
> flame...

who, at her mystic birth,

> Came flushed from the full-flushed wave, and imperial, her
> foot on the sea.
> And the wonderful waters knew her, the winds and the
> viewless ways,
> And the roses grew rosier, and bluer the sea-blue stream of
> the bays.

This beautiful symbolism of her name refers to the form side of the Deity, the root of matter—called the "deep sea," or the "virgin sea"—

which is impregnated with the divine life and beauty, and so gives birth to the loveliest of forms. The title "foam-born" is particularly appropriate when we consider that all forms are built up of aggregations of bubbles blown in the "deep sea," the aether of space. All this was explained to the initiates of the Mysteries. The same mystical idea lies in the title of Our Lady Mary, "Star of the Sea"; although she embodies in herself a fuller manifestation of the divine love in the perfection of eternal motherhood, and indeed unites in her person many Aspects of the Deity that were divided in Greece. There were, however, two sides of the cult of Aphrodite. The higher side was embodied in *Aphrodite Ouranios,* the heavenly Aphrodite, who was indeed "the Mother of fair love"; but there was a lower aspect of her worship as *Aphrodite Pandemos,* the earthly, common love, which leads to much evil and base desire, unworthy of the name love; and this aspect was the most prominent in the days when the old religion had become outworn and corrupt. Aphrodite corresponds to some extent with Lakshmi in India.

The gods were connected with the Mysteries, and worked with and through their faithful followers; but even in the Mysteries there was less of devotion and more of intellectual appreciation than in our religion to-day. In studying different branches of the Mysteries as worked in different lands we can but give certain analogies—we cannot hope to make exact comparisons; and the difficulty is still greater when we try to compare the ancient with the modern faiths—their whole outlook was so different from ours.

THE OFFICIALS

The control of the Eleusinian Mysteries in classical times lay in the hands of two families: the Eumolpidae and the *Keryces* or heralds, who were also connected with the worship of the Pythian Apollo at Delphi. Most of the officers were chosen from these two families, although there were also important civil representatives of the Athenian State who were responsible for the public ceremonial of the Mysteries as well as for the control of finance.

The chief officer was the hierophant, chosen for life by lot from the Eumolpidae. He alone had the guardianship of the Hallows (Hiera), those sacred treasures which were so carefully preserved at Eleusis and played so great a part in the ceremonial magic of the Mysteries. He was invariably a man of advanced age and distinguished position, and in his hands lay the supreme control over the secret ceremonial.

Next to him in rank stood the Dadouchos, the bearer of the double torch, chosen for life from the family of the Keryces. Both these officials had houses in the sacred enclosure at Eleusis, into which only initiates might enter; but while the hierophant remained in almost entire seclusion, the Dadouchos often took a prominent part in public affairs. A third official was the Hieroceryx, or sacred herald, who also was chosen for life from the family of Keryces; one of his duties was to make the solemn proclamation to the *Mystae* before their initiation into the Greater Mysteries, to preserve silence upon sacred matters. A fourth official was the Priest of the Altar, chosen also from the Keryces, who in later times was responsible for the sacrifices. In the great days of the Mysteries animal sacrifices were never offered, but, as in all religious systems, a time came when the tradition had become formalized and much of the inner knowledge had been withdrawn. It was then that certain teachings upon the meaning of sacrifice and its place in the spiritual life were distorted and materialized into the cruel superstition that it was necessary to sacrifice animals to the Diety.

There were also two women hierophants, dedicated to the two goddesses who presided over the Mysteries, Demeter and Kore; and in addition to them there was a priestess of Demeter, who appears to have been closely connected with certain other rites of the goddesses open only to women (Thesmophoria, Haloa), as well as with the Mysteries of Eleusis. A number of minor officials also took part in the ceremonial. As in Egypt, women were admitted to the Mysteries on equal terms with men, and no distinction was made between the sexes save in the matter of office. The instruction of the candidates was placed in the hands of the Mystagogues, who taught under the supervision of the hierophant and prepared the initiates for the celebration of the Mysteries, communicating to them certain formulae which would be required in the course of the ceremonial. An enclosed order of priestesses lived in retreat at Eleusis, vowed to celibacy and dedicated to the higher life. It seems probable that these are the ''bees'' of whom Porphyry and various grammarians speak.[8]

THE LESSER MYSTERIES

The Eleusinian Mysteries were divided into two degrees, the Lesser and the Greater. We see no trace of the tri-gradal system suggested by some scholars, although there were special ceremonies for the

---

[8]*Les Mysteres d'Eleusis*. Foucart, Ch. VI and VIII, *passim*.

installation of the principal officers. The Lesser Mysteries were celebrated in the Temple of Demeter and Kore at Agrae, near Athens, in the month of March. In them teaching was given upon the life after death in the intermediate or astral world, just as in the Lesser Mysteries of Egypt, and in this sense it is possible to compare the Lesser Mysteries with our Masonic 1°, although the details of the ceremonial do not exactly correspond. The ceremony was conducted by the hierophant of Eleusis, assisted by his various officers; and the initiates of this degree were called mystae.

The ceremonies opened with a preliminary purification or baptism in the waters of the Ilissus, during which certain ritual formulae were recited; they were continued in the secrecy of the temple, in which representations of the astral world were shown to the candidate, and instruction given upon the results of certain courses of action in the life after death. In earlier days when the hierophant directing the studies described the effect of some particular vice or crime, he used his occult power to materialize some good example of the fate which his words portrayed, in some cases, it is stated, enabling the sufferer to speak and explain the condition in which he found himself as the outcome of his neglect while on earth of the eternal laws under which the worlds are governed. Sometimes, instead of this, a vivid image of the state of some victim of his own folly would be materialized for the instruction of the neophytes.

In the days of the decadence, just as in Egypt, there remained no hierophant who possessed the power to produce these occult illustrations, and consequently their place was taken by actors dressed to represent the sufferers, and in some cases by ghostly images projected by means of concave mirrors—or even by cleverly executed statuary or mechanical figures. Of course it was perfectly understood by all concerned that these were only representations, and no one was ever led to suppose that they were original cases. Certain of our ecclesiastical writers, however, failed to realize this, and some of them spent much time and ingenuity in "exposing" deceptions which never deceived anyone, least of all those who were specially concerned with them. Besides this teaching upon the exact results in astral life of physical thought and action, much instruction was given in cosmogony, and the evolution of man on this earth was fully explained, again with the aid of illustrative scenes and figures, produced at first by materialization, but later imitated in various ways.

The initiates of the Mysteries had a number of proverbs and aphorisms peculiar to themselves. "Death is life, and life is death" was a saying which will need no interpretation for the student of the inner side of life, who comprehends; at least to some extent, how infinitely more real and vivid is life on any other plane than this imprisonment in the flesh. "Whosoever pursues realities during this life will pursue them after death; whosoever pursues unrealities during this life will pursue them also after death," was another statement entirely in line with the facts of post-mortem existence, and it empha-sizes the great truth upon which we so often find it necessary to insist, that death in no way changes the real man, but that his disposition and his mode of thought remain exactly what they were before.

The myths of the exoteric religion of the country were taken up and studied in the Eleusinian Mysteries, as in the Mysteries of Egypt. Among those relating to the life after death was that of Tantalus, who was condemned to suffer perpetual thirst in Hades: water surrounded him on all sides, but receded from him whenever he attempted to drink; over his head hung branches of fruit which receded in like manner when he stretched out his hand to touch them. This was interpreted to mean that everyone who dies full of sensual desire of any kind finds himself after death still full of desire, but unable to gratify it.

Another story was that of Sisyphus, who was condemned always to roll uphill a huge block of marble, which as soon as it reached the top rolled down again. That represents the condition after death of a man full of personal ambition, who has spent his life in making plans for selfish ends. In the other world he goes on making plans and work-ing them out, but always finds at the point of completion that they are nothing but a dream. The liver of Tityus was ceaselessly devoured by vultures. This was symbolical of the raging desire that tears at a man until it is burnt out by suffering. In many such ways desire is purified and the man is able to pass onwards to the life of the heaven-world, which was the subject of instruction in the Greater Mysteries.

Within the Lesser Mysteries, just as in the Mysteries of Egypt, there existed an inner school for the training of specially selected candidates. These were taught to awaken the senses of the astral plane, so that the teaching given in the Mysteries could be verified by them at first hand. As in Egypt, the severe tests of courage were applied only to the small proportion of those who entered the Mysteries who intended to take up positive occult training, and become active workers on the astral and higher planes. Tens of thousands of people were initiated without them. One classical author mentions a gathering of thirty thousand initiates. All serious-minded people gravitated towards these Mysteries, much as the better class of young men and women of our day go to the great Universities, and in addition many were interested in one or other of the systems of philosophy.

This inner school was kept secret, so that none even of the initiates knew of its existence until actually received into it. The dress of the mystae was the dappled fawn-skin (Nebris),[9] a fitting emblem of the uncontrolled astral body, which in this 1° had to be trained and brought into subjection by the will. This dress corresponded with the leopard-skin worn by the Egyptian priests, and the tiger or antelope skin so often used by the Eastern Yogis.

THE GREATER MYSTERIES

The Greater Mysteries were held at Eleusis in the month of September (Boedromion), and in connection with their celebration all Greece went into holiday, and splendid public processions took place, in which the whole populace, both initiates and non-initiates, joined. These public processions have been described in detail by contemporary writers; but beyond these exoteric descriptions nothing of the Greater Mysteries is known to the outer world save through a few obscure hints. On the 13th Boedromion the young men gathered at Eleusis to form the escort of the solemn procession to Athens, which was distant from Eleusis some twelve miles. On the 14th the Hallows (Hiera) were solemnly escorted to the great city, accompanied by the hierophant and his officers, the members of the priestly families, the college of priestesses and the retinue of the Eleusinian temple. The Hallows were treated with the deepest reverence; they were conveyed in great wicker baskets secured with bands of purple wool, and placed upon a ceremonial car. Only the hierophant and his ministers were allowed to handle them, and none but initiates might even see them, under pain of death. During the rest of the year they remained in a shrine or chapel (Anactoron) in the temple at Eleusis, and were guarded with the utmost care and awe, as being of divine origin.

When the procession reached the outskirts of the city of Athens, the Hallows were met by the magistrates and people, and were escorted

---

[9]*Recherches sur les Mysteres du Paganisme.* Par M. le Baron de Sainte-Croix. Ed., Paris, 1817. Tome I, p. 347.

with all magnificence and pomp to the Eleusinion at the foot of the Acropolis. Like the mother temple at Eleusis, this was surrounded by high walls, and no one but the initiates was ever allowed to enter. On the 15th day of the month, the day of the full moon, the mystae who were to be advanced to the Greater Mysteries assembled, and the solemn proclamation was made, enumerating those to whom access to the Mysteries was forbidden....''Whoso hath unclean hands...whoso hath an unintelligible voice''.[10] This latter qualification has been taken to mean that only Greek-speaking people could be admitted to the Mysteries; but M. Foucart suggests the more probable explanation that the voice must be free from impediment in order that the sacred formulae might be pronounced correctly; and he compares this qualification to the Egyptian title *Maat-heru,* which meant not only ''true of voice'' but one who is able to wield the occult powers of sound without mistake.[11] When we remember the tradition of Orpheus and realize how great a part sound played in the Greek Mysteries, we may understand that this conjecture is not without foundation.

On the 16th. day of the month the mystae took a ceremonial bath of purification in the sea; on the 17th and 18th various public processions took place in Athens; while the mystae remained secluded in the temple, receiving instruction and preparing themselves by meditation for their initiation into the Greater Mysteries. On the 19th. the great procession of the initiates to Eleusis was formed, the Hallows were carried back to their ancient resting-place with the fullest possible pomp and splendour, and the candidates and Brn. marched in triumph to the temple of initiation accompanied by vast crowds of people.

First came the car of Iacchos, bearing the statue of ''the fair young God'', who was one of the forms of Dionysus, the ''Blazing Star of nocturnal Initiation'' as Aristophanes calls him;[12] next marched the young men, myrtle-crowned, with shields and lances glittering in the sunlight, whose duty and privilege it was to escort the sacred Hallows, borne aloft upon the ceremonial car in the great wicker baskets, still bound with purple wool; after them came the hierophant and his

---

[10]Libanius, quoted Foucart. *op. cit.,* p. 311.

[11]*Ibid.,* p. 149.

[12]Aristophanes. *Frogs,* 346.

officers, dressed in their purple robes and wearing myrtle crowns, followed by the mystae in charge of the mystagogues. After them marched the vast company of initiates and people, arranged according to their tribes and demes, and preceded by the civil magistrates and the council of the five hundred; and the whole splendid throng was followed by a train of baggage-animals carrying bedding and provisions for the few days' sojourn at Eleusis.

The procession arrived at the sacred village after nightfall, and glowed like a river of fire in the blazing light of the torches carried by all the people; and after a tremendous ovation the Hallows were carried into the sacred enclosure by the hierophant, who placed them once more in the secret shrine within the hall of initiation (Telesterion). The next two days, during which the actual ceremonial instruction took place, were spent by the initiates within the enclosing walls of the temple, and the whole glorious celebration concluded with a festal assembly held outside the temple walls, in which all the citizens took part, afterwards returning quietly to their homes.[13]

In the Greater Mysteries the teaching upon the life after death was extended to the heaven-world; they thus corresponded to some extent to out 2°. The initiates were named epoptae, and their ceremonial garment was no longer a fawn-skin, but a golden fleece—whence, naturally, the whole myth of Jason and his companions. This symbolized the mental body, and the power definitely to function in it. Those who have seen the splendid radiance of all which pertains to that mental plane, who have noticed the innumerable vortices produced by the ceaseless emission and impact of thought-forms, who remember that a brilliant yellow is especially the colour which manifests intellectual activity, will acknowledge that this was no inapt representation.

In this class, as in the lower one, there were two types—those who could be taught to use the mental body, and to form round it the strong temporary vehicle of astral matter which has sometimes been called the mayavi rupa—and the far greater majority who were not yet prepared for this development, but could nevertheless be instructed with regard to the mental plane and the powers and faculties appropriate to it. As in the Lesser Mysteries men learned the exact result in the intermediate world after death of certain actions and modes of life on the physical plane, so in the Greater Mysteries they learnt how causes

---

[13]*Les Mysteres d'Eleusis.* Ch. XI and XII *passim.*

generated in this lower existence worked out in the heaven-world. In the Lesser the necessity and the method of the control of desires, passions and emotions was made clear; in the Greater the same teaching was given with regard to the control of mind.

Further teaching upon cosmogenesis and anthropogenesis was also continued. In the Greater Mysteries instead of being instructed only as to the broad outlines of evolution by reincarnation (which does not appear to have been clearly taught in the outer religion), and the previous races of mankind, the initiates now received a description of the whole scheme as we have it to-day, including the seven great chains of worlds and their positions in the solar system as a whole. Their terms were different from ours, but the instruction was in essence the same; where we speak of successive life-waves and outpourings, they spoke of aeons and emanations, but there is no doubt that they were fully in touch with the facts, and that they represented them to their pupils in wonderful visions of cosmic processes and their terrestrial analogies.

Just as in the case of the after-death states, these representations were at first produced by occult methods; and later, when these failed them, by mechanical and pictorial means, the results of which were greatly inferior. Illustrations of the development of the human embryo, shown by picture or model in the same way as we might show some of them by means of a microscope, were employed to teach by the law of correspondences the truth of cosmic evolution. We may remember how Madame Blavatsky adopted in *The Secret Doctrine* a similar method of illustrating the same evolutionary processes.[14] It is probable that a misunderstanding of the representation of some of these processes of reproduction was distorted into an idea of indecency, and so the seed was sown from which sprang later the false and foolish accusations of the ignorant and bigoted Christians.

The culmination of the ceremonial of the Greater Mysteries was the exposition of an ear of corn. Of this Hippolytus speaks:

The Athenians, while initiating people into the Eleusinian Rites, likewise display to those who are being admitted to the highest grade at these Mysteries, the mighty, marvellous, and most perfect secret suitable for one initiated into the highest mystic truths: I allude to an ear of corn in silence reaped. This ear of corn is also considered among the Athenians to constitute the perfect

---

[14]*Op. cit.*, Vol. iii, p. 441.

and enormous illumination that has descended from the unportrayable One, just as the hierophant himself declares.[15]

This symbol referred to the divine life of God, ever-changing, ever-renewed, buried in the earth of the lower planes, only to rise in other forms to a fuller and more abundant life, passing from manifestation to manifestation without end. This was explained by the hierophant to the initiates, and the simplicity of the symbol and the beauty and profundity of the meaning underlying it formed a fitting climax to a wonderful ceremony.

THE MYTHS OF THE GREATER MYSTERIES

The meaning of various myths was explained in detail in the instruction given to the initiates. The legend of Persephone or Proserpine (Kore) is clearly an occult parable of the descent of the soul into matter. If we remember how the story tells us that Proserpine was carried away while she was plucking the flower of the narcissus, at once we have a suggestion of connection with that other myth of the soul's life. Narcissus is represented to have been a young man of extraordinary beauty who fell in love with his own reflection in a pool of water, and was so much attracted by it that he fell into the pool and was drowned, and was afterwards changed by the gods into a beautiful flower. It was taught that the soul was not originally immersed in matter, and need not have been so, but for the fact that she was attracted by the image of herself in the lower conditions of matter, symbolized by water. Beguiled by this reflection, she identifies herself with the lower personality, and is for the time sunk altogether in matter; yet nevertheless the divine seed remains, and presently she springs up again as a flower. It was while Proserpine was stooping to Narcissus that she was seized and carried off by Desire, who is the king of the lower world; and although she was rescued from complete captivity by the effort of her mother, yet after that she had to spend her life half in the lower world, and half in that above, that is to say, partly in incarnation and partly out of it.

The Minotaur, which was slain by Theseus, was the personality in man, "half animal and half man". Theseus typifies the higher self, who has been gradually developing and gathering strength until at last he can wield the sword of his divine father, the Spirit. Guided through

---

[15]Hippolytus. *Refutation of All Heresies,* Bk. V, iii (Ante-Nicene Library Ed.).

the labyrinth of illusion which constitutes these lower planes by the thread of occult knowledge given him by Ariadne (who represents intuition), the higher self is enabled to slay the lower and escape safely from the web of illusion; yet there still remains for him the danger that, developing intellectual pride, he may neglect intuition, even as Theseus neglected Ariadne, and so failed for the time to reach his highest possibilities. The legend of the slaying of Bacchus by the Titans, the tearing of his body into fragments and his resurrection from the dead, was also taught, with the same interpretation as that given to the legend of Osiris in the Mysteries of Egypt—the descent of the One to become the many, and the reunion of the many in the One through suffering and sacrifice.

THE MAGIC OF THE GREATER MYSTERIES

In the Eleusinian Mysteries the initiates were brought into close communion with the Deity through specially consecrated food and drink. Cups of highly-magnetized water were given to them, and consecrated cakes were eaten during the ceremonies of initiation. S. Clement of Alexandria gives us the formula or pass-word of the Eleusinian Mysteries, which some have taken to refer to this sacrament: "I fasted; I drank the draught; I took from the chest; having tasted, I placed in the basket, and from the basket into the chest".[16] In many religions we find a similar method of conveying the divine blessing to the people.

The Hallows (Hiera) already mentioned were physical objects extremely highly magnetized, through which much of the magical side of the Mysteries was performed. They were the personal property of the priestly family of the Eumolpidae, being handed down from generation to generation; and their solemn exposition and the explanation of the symbolical teaching connected with them was one of the features of the Eleusinian ritual.[17]

One of these was the caduceus, the rod of power, surrounded by the twisting serpents and surmounted by the pine-cone. It was the same as the thyrsus; and was said to be hollow and to be filled with fire. In India it is a stick of bamboo with seven knots in it, which represents

---

[16]Clem. Alex. *Exhortation to the Greeks.* Loeb. Ed., p. 43 (Lobeck.)

[17]Foucart. *Op. cit.*, p. 150.

the spinal column with its seven centres or chakras. When a candidate had been initiated, he was often described as one who had been touched with the thyrsus, showing that it was not a mere emblem, but had also a practical use. It also indicated the spinal cord, ending in the medulla, while the serpents were symbolical of the two channels called in Eastern terminology *Ida* and *Pingala;* and the fire enclosed within it was the serpent-fire which in Sanskrit is called *kundalini*. It was laid by the hierophant against the back of the candidate, and thus used as a strong magnetic instrument in order to awaken the forces latent within him, and to free the astral body from the physical, so that the candidate might pass in full consciousness to the higher planes. To help him in the efforts that lay before him the priest in this way gave the aspirant some of his own magnetism. This rod of power was of the greatest importance, and we can understand why it was regarded with so much awe when we realize something of its occult potency.

There was also the *krater* or cup, always associated with Dionysus, and emblematical of the causal body of man, which has ever been symbolized by a cup filled with the wine of the divine life and love. The tradition of this passed down through the ages and became mingled with that of the Holy Grail, which played so great a part in early mediaeval romance and legend.

Among the holy symbols there were also highly-magnetized and richly jewelled statues, which had been handed down from a remote past, and were the physical basis of certain great forces invoked in the Mysteries; and a lyre, reputed to be the lyre of Orpheus, on which certain melodies were played and to which the sacred chants were sung. There were also the toys of Bacchus, with which he was playing when he was seized by the Titans and torn to pieces—very remarkable toys, full of significance. The dice with which he plays are the five Platonic solids, the only regular polygons possible in geometry. They are given in a fixed series, and this series agrees with the different planes of the solar system. Each of them indicates, not the form of the atoms of the different planes, but the lines along which the power works which surrounds those atoms. Those polygons are the tetrahedron, the cube, the octahedron, the dodecahedron and the icosahedron. If we put the point at one end and the sphere at the other we have a set of seven figures, corresponding to the number of planes in our solar system.

In some of the older schools of philosophy it was said: "No one can enter who does not know mathematics." That meant not what we now call mathematics, but that science which embraces the knowledge of the higher planes, of their mutual relations, and the way in which the whole is built by the will of God. When Plato said: "God geometrizes," he stated a profound truth which throws much light upon the methods and mysteries of evolution. Those forms are not conceptions of the human brain; they are truths of the higher planes. We have formed the habit of studying the books of Euclid, but we study them now for themselves, and not as a guide to something higher. The old philosophers pondered upon them because they led to the understanding of the true science of life.

Another toy with which Bacchus played was a top, the symbol of the whirling atom pictured in *Occult Chemistry*. Yet another was a ball which represented the earth, that particular part of the planetary chain to which the thought of the Logos is specially directed at the moment. Also he played with a mirror. The mirror has always been a symbol of the astral light, in which the archetypal ideas are reflected and then materialized. Thus each of those toys indicates an essential part in the evolution of a solar system.

The Hidden Mysteries

The two divisions of the lesser and greater mysteries above-mentioned were generally known, but it was not known that there was always, behind and above those, the greater mystery of the Path of Holiness, the steps of which are the five great Initiations already mentioned. The very existence of the possibility of that future advancement was not certainly known even by the initiates of the Greater Mysteries until they were actually fit to receive the mystic summons from within. If one thinks of the conditions of that time one can readily understand the reason for that secrecy. The Roman Emperors, for example, knew of the existence of the Lesser and the Greater Mysteries, and insisted upon being initiated into them. We know from history that many of the Emperors were hardly of a character to be allowed to play a leading role in a religious body, but it would have been very difficult for the hierophants of the Mysteries to refuse entrance to an Emperor of Rome. As was once said: "One cannot argue with the master of thirty legions." Many of the Emperors would certainly have killed anyone who stood in the way of anything they wished; so the existence of the true Mysteries was not made public; and no one knew of them until he was deemed, by those who could judge, worthy to be admitted into them. The teaching of these higher degrees is still open to the worthy, and to the worthy alone; but certain conditions must be fulfilled, as I have explained in *The Masters and the Path*.

Thus the Mysteries of Eleusis corresponded closely with those of Egypt, though they differed in detail; and both these systems led their initiates, when properly prepared, to that Wisdom of God which was "before the beginning of the world". We in Masonry do not inherit the Eleusinian succession directly, although something of its inspiration and influence was transmitted to certain of the mystic schools of the Middle Ages. Nevertheless our rites have the same purpose, symbolize the same invisible worlds, and are intended to prepare candidates for the same august reality that lies behind all true systems of the Mysteries alike.

THE SCHOOL OF PYTHAGORAS

The great philosopher Pythagoras was born in Samos about 582 B.C., and was the founder of the school that bore his name and studied his teachings in Greece, Italy, Egypt and Asia Minor. Mr. G. R. S. Mead says of the Pythagorean school:

The finest characters among women with which ancient Greece presents us were formed in the School of Pythagoras, and the same is true of the men. The authors of antiquity are agreed that this discipline had succeeded in producing the highest examples not only of the purest chastity and sentiment; but also a simplicity of manners, a delicacy and a taste for serious pursuits which was unparalleled.[18]

Pythagoras travelled through many of the countries of the Mediterranean basin, studying for some years in Egypt, where he was initiated at Sais. He was also initiated into the Eleusinian, Kabeiric and Chaldaean Mysteries, and thus was thoroughly versed in all the hidden knowledge of the ancient world. In addition to his travels round the shores of the Mediterranean, Pythagoras journeyed to India, where he met the Lord Buddha and became one of His disciples. He spent some years in India, and it is reported that he had the high honour of an interview with the next World-Teacher, the holy Child Shri Krishna, who blessed him and sent him back to Europe to found his system of philosophy and of esoteric instruction. Thus in the

---

[18]*Orpheus:* G.R.S. Mead, p. 265, 266.

Pythagorean school many lines of tradition met together, and were blended into a comprehensive teaching upon the hidden side of life.

There is a curious old writing called the Leyland-Locke MS., which was at one time in the Bodleian Library, but recent investigators have been unable to trace it. Its genuineness has been disputed by some authorities, "but," says Bro. Ward, "in my opinion on quite inadequate grounds."[19] Its reputed date is 1436, and it is written in the quaint old English of the period, and in the form of question and answer. In the part referring to Freemasonry it asks where it began, and the answer is that it began with the first men of the East, who were before the first men of the West. Then it asks who brought it to the West and the answer is: "The Venetians, etc."

It then continues:

How comede ytt (Freemasonry) yn Engelonde?

Peter Gower, a Grecian, journeyed for kunnynge yn Egypte and yn Syria, and yn everyche londe whereat the Venetians hadde plauntedde Maconrye, and wynnynge entraunce yn al Lodges of Maconnes, he learned muche, and retournedde and worked yn Grecia Magna wachsynge and becommynge a myghtye wysacre and gratelyche renowned, and here he framed a grate Lodge at Groton, and maked many Maconnes, some whereoffe dyd journeye yn Fraunce, and maked manye Maconnes wherefromme, yn process of tyme, the arte passed yn Engelonde.

This is said to have much puzzled John Locke until he realized that Peter Gower was Pitagore—the French pronunciation of Pythagoras, that Groton was Crotona, and the Venetians the Phoenicians.

No wonder that Mackey says "It is not singular that the old Masons should have called Pythagoras their 'ancient friend and brother'."

About 529 B.C. Pythagoras settled in Crotona in the south of Italy, remaining there until he was forced by political troubles to remove to Metapontum. At Crotona he became the centre of a widespread and influential organization, a religious brotherhood which extended over all the Greek-speaking world. "Number is great and perfect and omnipotent, and the principle and guide of divine and human life," said Philolaus, and the sentence expresses the keynote of the Pythagorean system. Number is order and limitation, and alone makes a cosmos possible. By numbers nature moves, and to understand

---

[19]*An Outline History of Freemasonry,* by J.S.M. Ward, p. 24.

numbers is to be the master of nature. Hence the Pythagorean sought to understand the nature of numbers, and to trace their working in the universe, whether in the vast ordered movements in the heavens, or in the arrangements of the earth. Hence also his devotion to mathematics, a science which (as far as Europe is concerned) may almost be said to have been created by Pythagoras, so much did he add to it and systematize it; he found it but a number of scattered and unrelated facts, and left it a science. Metempsychosis or reincarnation was an essential part of the Pythagorean teaching; the purification of the soul being thus accomplished by repeated descents into matter and withdrawals into the invisible worlds, in order to transmute experience into faculty.

THE THREE DEGREES

The Pythagorean schools worked in close association with the teaching of the Mysteries, but without the ceremonies; they gave a philosophical exposition of the same great facts of the inner worlds. In those schools the pupils were divided into three degrees which corresponded almost exactly with those of the early Christians, who called them the stages of purification, illumination and perfection respectively —the last one including what S. Clement of Alexandria calls the "scientific knowledge of God". In the Pythagorean scheme the first degree was that of the *akoustikoi* or hearers, who took no part in the discussions or addresses, but kept absolute silence in the meetings for two years, and devoted themselves to listening and learning.

At the end of that time, if otherwise satisfactory, the students were eligible for the second degree, that of the *mathematikoi*. The mathematics which they learnt were not, however, confined to what we now mean by that term. We study this science as an end in itself, but for them it was only a preparation for something much wider, higher and more practical. Geometry, as we now know it, was taught in the outer world in ordinary life as a preparation; but inside these great schools the subject was carried much farther, to the study and comprehension of the fourth dimension, and the laws and properties of higher space. It can be fully understood only if we take it thus as a whole, not in mere fragments, and as an introduction to higher development. It leads a man upwards towards the understanding of all the octaves of vibrations, as to vast areas of which science knows nothing as yet, towards the intricate occult relations of numbers, colours and sounds, the various three-dimensional sections of the mighty cone of space, and the true shape of the universe. There is a vast amount to be gained from the study of mathematics by those who know how to take it up in the right way; it helps us to see how the worlds are made.

The *mathematikoi* brought geometry, mathematics and music into relation with one another, and worked out the correspondences between them, which are very remarkable. Everyone who knows anything about music is aware that there is a fixed proportion between the lengths of the strings which produce certain tones. A piano can be tuned according to a certain system of fifths, and the relation of the different tones to one another can be expressed by the number of vibrations of each tone; so a harmonious chord can be stated mathematically. This was first discovered simply by experiment; later the mathematicians found out what the proportions should be, and again by experiment they were found to be exact. But the peculiarity is that the numbers which produce a harmonious chord have the same relation to one another as that which exists between certain parts of the Platonic solids. Our scale, so different from the old Greek scale, which consisted of five tones, can still be deduced from the proportions of those five Platonic figures, which were studied over two thousand years ago in Greece. One might think that there cannot be much relation between mathematics and music, but we see by this that they are both parts of one great whole.

The third degree of the Pythagoreans was that of the *physikoi*—not physicists in our modern sense of the word, but students of the true inner life, who learnt how to distinguish the divine life under all its disguises, and so were able to comprehend the course of its evolution. The life exacted from all these pupils was of the most exalted purity. Mackey gives the following account of the school at Crotona:

The disciples of this school wore the simplest kind of clothing, and, having on their entrance surrendered all their possessions to the common fund, they submitted for three[20] years to voluntary poverty, during which time they were also compelled to a rigorous silence. The scholars were divided into Exoterics and Esoterics. This distinction was borrowed by Pythagoras from the Egyptian priests, who practised a similar mode of instruction. The exoteric scholars were those who attended the public assemblies, where general ethical instructions were delivered by the sage. But only the esoterics constituted the true

---

[20]This should be two only.

school, and these alone Pythagoras called, says Iamblichus, his companions and friends. Before admission to the privileges of the school, the previous life and character of the candidate were rigidly scrutinized, and in the preparatory initiation secrecy was enjoined by an oath, and the severest trials of his fortitude and self-command were imposed. The brethren, about six hundred in number, with their wives and children, resided in one large building. Every morning the business and duties of the day were arranged, and at night an account was rendered of the day's transactions. They arose before day to pay their devotions to the sun, and recited verses from Homer, Hesiod, or some other poet. Several hours were spent in study, after which there was an interval before dinner, which was occupied in walking and in gymnastic exercises. The meals consisted principally of bread and honey.

Although we do not find any direct connection between the School of Pythagoras and the degrees of modern Masonry, yet the influence of Pythagoras upon our Mysteries was profound, as Masons have always recognized. The tradition of the Pythagoreans passed into the Neo-Platonic schools; and from thence much of the inner teaching came into Christian hands, and formed the basis of many of those schools of mystic instruction which enshrined in mediaeval times certain of the secrets now preserved in the higher degrees of Masonry. There is a succession of ideas as well as of sacramental power; and the school of Pythagoras may certainly be said to be one of the links in the chain of Masonic philosophy, even though to-day the greater part of that philosophy has faded from our rites. To Pythagoras is attributed the discovery of the 47th proposition of Euclid, which now forms the jewel of the I. P. M. in English Masonry, and is the basis not only of a great portion of exoteric geometry but, in a mystical sense, of the whole system of the Mysteries, and indeed of the universe itself. It is impossible exactly to estimate the influence of any given line of tradition. We cannot say more than that some of the Pythagorean teachings, probably transmitted along several mutually-interacting lines of descent, became mingled with the Masonry of the Middle Ages and formed part of the inner instruction that was associated with the ceremonies handed down among the operative builders from Jewish sources. These were preserved under binding pledges of secrecy, and emerged in speculative Masonry after the Reformation, thus forming part of our present Masonic system.

OTHER GREEK MYSTERIES

Another line of tradition is that of the Mysteries of Dionysus (or as the Romans called him, Bacchus), which approached more closely to the Egyptian scheme of initiation than the Eleusinian rites. They were celebrated throughout Greece and Asia Minor, but principally at Athens; they were carried to Rome, and afterwards formed a link in the chain of Masonic descent. Their central legend deals with the slaying of Dionysus by the Titans and his subsequent resurrection.

The mysteries commenced with the consecration of an egg, symbolizing the mundane egg from which all things came. The candidate was crowned with myrtle, clothed in the sacred robes, exhorted to have courage, and then led through dark caverns amid the howling of wild beasts and other fearful noises, while flashes of lightning revealed monstrous apparitions to his sight. After three days and nights of this kind of experience, he was laid on a couch in a solitary cell; there was a sudden crash of waters, typifying the deluge, and the murder of Dionysus was enacted, his limbs being scattered on the waters. Then, amid lamentations, commenced the search of Rhea for the remains of Dionysus, and the apartments were filled with shrieks and groans, accompanied by the frantic dances of the Corybantes. Suddenly the body was found, the scene changed to one of joy, and the aspirant was released from his confinement. After that he descended into the infernal regions, where he saw the sufferings of the wicked and the rewards of the good, and afterwards became an epopt or seer—one who could look upon the world from above, see it as a whole, and therefore understand it. Among the followers of this Bacchic form of the Mysteries were the celebrated Dionysian Artificers, a secret society, bound by the most rigid pledges never to reveal their s... and p... w..., and employing emblems adopted from the building trade. These wandering bands of workmen built temples all over Syria and Asia Minor, just as the bands of Freemasons afterwards built churches in Europe. Bro. Ward writes of them:

They appear to have reached Asia Minor from the south-east, and, according to Strabo, could be traced through Syria and Phoenicia, via Persia and India. Apparently they reached Phoenicia about fifty years before the building of K.S.'s temple, and it is their presence which alone explains how that temple came to be built. Indeed, the Bible itself makes it abundantly clear that the temple was not built by Jews, who at that time were an agricultural race, quite incapable of undertaking the task of building such an elaborate edifice.

From the same source we learn that the chief architects and men came from Phoenicia, and Phoenician letters have been found on what are believed to be the foundations of the first temple... From Phoenicia they spread first into Asia Minor, and thence into Greece, from which country Greek colonists no doubt in the course of time carried members of the guild to Magna Grecia, which was the early name for South Italy.[21]

It is said that this cult of Dionysus survived up to 1908 in Thrace, in a slightly modified form at Viza, and may still exist.[22]

In the same land of Phoenicia, the mysteries of Adonis or Tammuz were celebrated at Byblos or Gebal, where lived the Gibelim or Stone-squarers, deriving their name from that of the town. The legend of these mysteries is an interesting combination of those of Egypt and Eleusis, the death and resurrection of Adonis being interwoven with a theme upon his exile and return for six months of the year, which reminds us of the fate of Persephone.

This cult appears in many forms, some of them savage and sanguinary, evidently derived from the dark and debased delusions of prehistoric and even cannibal tribes. Some hint of these may be seen in the account given on p. 000.

The mysteries of Attis and Cybele in Phrygia had many points in common with the last-named, the death and resurrection of Attis being the central myth. Other mystery-cults existed also, all teaching similar ideas. That of the Kabeiroi in Samothrace, which was held in great honour in the ancient world, is thought by some scholars to be the oldest of them all—a theory which is supported by the barbarous names of the deities involved. But even these are myths of death and resurrection, the god being in this case called Kasmillos.

It seems probable that when Virgil, in the sixth book of the *Aeneid*, depicted the descent of Aeneas into hell, he intended to give a representation of what happened in some of these Mysteries.

---

[21]*An Outline History of Freemasonry*, by Ward, p. 22.

[22]R. M. Dawkins, *Journal of Hellenic Studies*, xxvi (1906), pp. 191-206.

6

The Mithraic Mysteries

ZARATHUSTRA AND MITHRAISM

THE Mysteries of Mithra were in many ways similar to those of Greece, but they always had certain characteristics which were especially their own, and the line of succession which they transmitted was distinct from that of the three degrees of Blue Masonry; some of the more important features of its ritual seem to have passed over into the 18°. There was a strong military flavour about them, and they demanded from their devotees a purity of life which was almost ascetic.

Just as the Mysteries of Egypt and Greece arose respectively from the incarnations of the World-Teacher as Thoth and Orpheus, so did the Mithraic scheme arise from His incarnation as the first Zarathustra about 29,700 B.C. in Persia. It taught of Mithra, Captain of the hosts of the God of Light and Saviour of mankind.

MITHRAISM AMONG THE ROMANS

It is said that Mithraism was first transmitted to the Roman world during the first century B.C. by the Cilician pirates captured by Pompey; but, as we have already seen, it was before that time in the possession of the Essene communities in Palestine. For nearly two centuries it attained no great importance in Rome, and it was not until the end of the first century A.D. that it began to attract serious attention. Towards the close of the second century, the cult had spread rapidly through the army, the mercantile class and the slaves, all of which classes were largely composed of Asiatics. It throve especially at the military posts, and in the track of trade, where its monuments have been discovered in greatest abundance. Some twenty of the Mithraic temples still remain, and they show certain points of resemblance to our Masonic Lodges. The temple was rectangular, with a raised platform at the east end, often apsidal in form; continuous benches ran along its walls on the longer sides for the accommodation of the Brn., and the ceiling was made to symbolize the firmament.

Jerome (*Epist.* cvii) tells us that the system consisted of seven degrees: *Corax,* the Raven, so-called not only because the raven was the servant of the sun in Mithraic mythology, but because the raven can only imitate speech and not originate ideas for himself;[1] *Cryphius,* the Occult, a degree in the taking of which the mystic was perhaps hidden from others in the sanctuary by a veil, the removal of which was a solemn ceremonial; *Miles,* the Soldier, signifying the holy warfare against evil in the service of the God; *Leo,* the Lion, symbolic of the element of fire, which played so great a part in the Persian faith; *Perses,* the Persian, clad in Asiatic costume, a reminiscence of the ancient origin of the religion; *Heliodromus,* the Courier of the Sun, with whom Mithra was identified; and *Pater,* the Father, a degree bringing the mystic among those who had the general direction of the cult for the rest of their lives.

It is not easy to trace exact correspondences between these seven stages and our own degrees, because of the difference between the systems. The Corax is fairly parallel with the E. A., and the Cryphius and Miles with the F. C., the latter being distinguished from the former by additional knowledge which may not inaptly be compared with that of the Mark degree. These three classes together were regarded to some extent as servitors; the next stage, Leo, was the first whose members were called ''participants'' and admitted to the Mithraic sacrament. We may consider the three stages of Leo, Perses and Heliodromus as divisions of the M. M. degree; the first gave access to the full fellowship of the Mithraic brotherhood, the second passed him who received it through a most impressive ceremony in the course of which he was symbolically slain and raised to life in honour of

---

[1]Cf. the *Akoustikoi* of the Pythagoreans, and the fact that the due-guard of the 1° shows that the E. A. must confine himself to what is taught in the V. S. L.

Mithra, and the third put him in possession of additional knowledge equivalent to that which is supposed to be given to us in the Holy Royal Arch; for only when he had that knowledge of the name and qualities of the deity was he fitted to go forth as a messenger of the Sun to bear his strength and life through the world. The Pater corresponded to our I. M., who alone can confer the various degrees and pass on the succession to posterity.

THE MITHRAIC RITES

The Mithraic cult was essentially a religion of soldiers, a veritable brotherhood of arms. Women were never admitted to their rites of initiation, although it seems probable that in earlier times there were separate degrees for them. The power flowing through the rites gave especially courage and purity, and the demands upon the candidates in both these respects were exceedingly high. There was an intensity of brotherly feeling between the initiates of Mithra which is rarely realized in our Lodges to-day; they were pledged to fight for the right, and they stood shoulder to shoulder against all foes.

The Mithraic sacrament consisted of bread and wine and salt, and was consecrated at a solemn ceremony in the Mysteries, being linked to that aspect of the Deity which was represented by Mithra, and intensely charged with force along the characteristic lines of purity, courage and brotherhood, helping to bind the brethren together into a body corporate as soldiers of Light and Truth. This same Eucharist has been transmitted to us to-day through the Culdee line of tradition, in the ceremonial of the Rose-Croix of Heredom; but the forces flowing through it have been modified to some extent, so that instead of a Brotherhood of Arms we have now a Brotherhood of Love. The power of love takes the place of the military influence of courage, although the method of consecration in the higher worlds is the same. This is due to a blending with the Egyptian line of tradition.

The analogies between Mithraism and Christianity are very close; they are well summarized thus in the *Encyclopedia Britannica:*

The fraternal and democratic spirit of the first communities, and their humble origin; the identification of the object of adoration with light and the Sun; the legends of the shepherds with their gifts and adoration, the flood, and the ark; the representation in art of the fiery chariot, the drawing of water from the rock; the use of bell and candle, holy water and the communion; the sanctification of Sunday and of the 25th of December; the insistence on moral conduct, the emphasis placed upon abstinence and self-control; the doctrine of heaven and hell, of primitive revelation, of the mediation of the Logos emanating from the divine, the atoning sacrifice, the constant warfare between good and evil and the final triumph of the former, the immortality of the soul, the last judgment, the resurrection of the flesh and the fiery destruction of the universe—these are some of the resemblances. . . . At their root lay a common Eastern origin rather than any borrowing.[2]

The Great Powers behind evolution appear at one time to have thought seriously of making Mithraism the religion of the fifth subrace instead of the maimed Christianity which had rejected its own gnosis and put aside its Mysteries. But the ideal of Mithraic purity was so high that it would probably have been impossible for men to follow it during the Dark Ages; and another very serious objection to the system was that it absolutely excluded women. Mithraism was allowed therefore to sink into the background and finally to pass out of sight of the outer world. Nevertheless the ancient succession is still guarded and the rites are preserved in the custody of the H. O. A. T. F.; so Mithraism may yet have its part to play in the religious life of the future.

In addition to the Mysteries of Mithra, there was an Atlantean tradition of the Mysteries—that to which we have already referred as the Chaldaean line of succession. In the days of its splendour the Chaldaean rituals put the initiate into relation with the great Star-Angels who were adored in that mighty faith; and a relic of this tradition is still found in the hidden side of certain of the degrees of the rites of Memphis and of Mizraim. The Chaldaean method of seating the Principal Officers of a Lodge is still preserved in Continental Masonry, and has passed also into certain of the higher degrees.

THE ROMAN COLLEGIA

We may now return to the main line of Masonic descent, that of the three Craft degrees. We have already seen how the Jewish Mysteries handed down the essentials of our Masonic rites; it remains for us to trace their transmission to our modern Lodges. The next link in the chain is the Roman Collegia, in which the transition from speculative to operative Masonry took place.

We have seen that the science of architecture was always closely connected with the Mysteries, and that our Masonic Craft ritual when properly worked is designed to build a superphysical temple of the

---

[2]*Ency. Brit.* (11th Edn.), Art. *Mithras.*

Ionic order of architecture, which was chosen because it is the vehicle of the special type of force which flows through Craft Masonry.[3]

Other forms are built by the higher degrees, belonging to different kinds of architecture, according to the influences which are to be radiated through them; so we see that we are in the presence of a science of spiritual building, of which material architecture is but the reflection in the dense matter of the physical plane. Each order of architecture expresses an idea and is the channel of certain types of influence associated with that idea, attracting the attention of certain kinds of Angels who work along the lines of that idea in the invisible worlds. Each sub-race has its own characteristic type of architecture as well as its own type of music, and these are often utilized by the Great Ones behind in order to impress upon the people certain characteristics which are necessary for their evolution.

The principles of this inner science of building were taught in the ancient Mysteries, and the temples of the different faiths were planned by the priests with full knowledge of the hidden side of what they were doing; it was for this reason that builders were always associated with temples and temple-worship, and the secrets of building were carefully guarded as part of the teaching of the Mysteries. Thus the confusion between speculative and operative, which was purposely effected at the breaking-up of the Roman Empire, presented no difficulties to the Powers behind, since those two aspects had always worked in close association, and it was merely a question of emphasizing the one, and of temporarily withdrawing the other into yet further silence and secrecy. No essential change was required.

THE WORK OF KING NUMA

Plutarch tells us that the Roman Collegia were originally founded by Numa, the second king of Rome, who lived during the seventh century B.C.[4] Numa is a half-legendary figure to our modern historians; but he was a very real personage, and the true founder of the Roman Mysteries as well as of the trade guilds. Plutarch says of his character:

He was endued with a soul rarely tempered by nature and disposed to virtue, which he had yet more subdued by discipline, a severe life, and the study

---

[3]See *The Hidden Life in Freemasonry,* p. 120.

[4]Plutarch's *Life of Numa,* A. H. Clough, Vol. i, p. 152.

of philosophy. . . . He banished all luxury and softness from his own home, and, while citizens alike and strangers found in him an incorruptible judge and counsellor, in private he devoted himself not to amusement or lucre, but to the worship of the immortal Gods, and the rational contemplation of their divine power and nature.[5]

Numa was "deeply versed, so far as anyone could be in that age, in all law, divine and human,"[6] says Livy; while Dio Cassius tells us that he shaped the political and peaceable institutions of Rome, as Romulus had determined its military career.[7] In addition to all his external ability, he was far advanced on the Path of Holiness, and was a high Initiate of the White Lodge. His especial work was laying down, at the very beginning of the Roman State, the inner foundation of Rome's future greatness; he moulded both her outer religion and her inner Mysteries, which in later days were to be the channel of that spiritual force which would make Rome mighty among the nations, one of the greatest empires that the world has ever known.

Numa sent messengers to Egypt, to Greece, to Chaldaea, to Palestine and other lands, to study all existing systems of the Mysteries, so that he might adopt in Rome those most suited to the development of his people. His high occult rank opened all doors; and like Pythagoras, an even greater Initiate, who came later, he was enabled to synthesize many lines of tradition into one comprehensive whole. The system which appears to have been adopted in Rome was that of the Mysteries of Dionysus or Bacchus, which, as we have already seen, closely corresponded to the Egyptian system; and here we have the first of the links with the Dionysian Artificers of whom Masonic tradition so persistently speaks.

Numa introduced the Egyptian line of succession, and thus the hierophants of his Mysteries were I. Ms. after the manner of the priests of Egypt and the Masons of to-day. This succession appears to have been handed down in secret among the Colleges of Architects until the time when Christianity began to dominate the Roman world at the beginning of the third century A.D. The fortunes of the Colleges or guilds which were thus formed were very varied; gradually they rose

---

[5]*Ibid.*, pp. 130, 131.

[6]Livy., Bk. I, xviii (Loeb Ed.)

[7]Dio's *Roman History,* Loeb. Ed., p. 29.

to great political power, were abolished by the senate about 80 B.C., and restored again twenty years later. The Emperors issued edicts against them from time to time, but those which could prove their antiquity or religious character were permitted to remain in existence. They were finally abolished in A.D. 378.

THE COLLEGES AND THE LEGIONS

Of these Colleges of Architects one was attached to every Roman Legion, building for it fortifications in time of war and in time of peace temples and houses. It was thus that the Roman Mysteries were brought to Northern Europe. Wherever the Romans settled, the Collegia worked their rites, and in process of time native soldiers were initiated into their ranks, until the system became deeply-rooted in each Roman colony. Closely connected with these rites were those of Mithra which, as we have seen, were also spread by the Roman armies, although the two systems were always kept separate and distinct.

The organization of the Colleges, as extant records show, corresponded in many ways with that of our modern Lodges. "Tres faciunt Collegium" — "Three make a College" was one of their principles; and the rule was so indispensable that it became a maxim of civil law. The College was ruled by a *Magister* or Master, and two *Decuriones* or Wardens; and among other officers were a treasurer, sub-treasurer, secretary and archivist.[8] There was also a *Sacerdos* or Chaplain, who was in charge of the religious side of the work. The members of the College consisted of three grades corresponding closely to Apprentices, Fellows and Masters; and records point to the fact that they possessed semi-religious rites which were kept rigidly secret, and also that they attached symbolic interpretations to their tools, such as the square and compasses, the plumb-rule and level. They took pagan gods as their patrons in much the same way as the guilds which succeeded them adopted Christian patron saints. The Four Crowned Martyrs, the patron saints of Masonry, were Christian members of a College who were tortured to death by the Emperor Diocletian for refusing to make a statue of Aesculapius.[9] They were later confused with the tradition of the Four Brothers of Horus.

---

[8] R. F. Gould: *History of Freemasonry,* Vol. I, p. 42.

[9] J. S. M. Ward: *Freemasonry and the Ancient Gods,* pp. 144, 145.

Bro. J. S. M. Ward describes a building of the Collegia unearthed at Pompeii in 1878, which had been buried in A.D. 79, during the great eruption of Mount Vesuvius. It contains striking Masonic correspondences. There are two columns, and on the walls are interlaced triangles. Upon a pedestal in the centre was found an inlaid marble slab with a skull, level and plumb-rule and other Masonic designs in mosaic work. A fresco in another building close by shows a figure in the act of making the F. C. H. S.[10] The Roman Colleges of Architects were brought to Britain by the Roman army. One legion under Julius Caesar established a colony at Eboracum or York, later to be so prominent in Masonic legend and tradition; and another centre was at Verulam, afterwards known as S. Albans.

THE INTRODUCTION OF THE JEWISH FORM

The introduction of the Jewish form of the Masonic ceremonies was intentionally arranged by the Powers who stand behind Freemasonry about the time when Christianity was gaining ascendancy in the Roman Empire. It would have been almost impossible to continue the Mysteries of Bacchus or those of Mithra in their original form, while there was so much opposition between the Christian faith and the old Pagan religion. No such opposition was in Roman days felt towards the Jews, among whom the Christian faith arose and had its early nurture; and the Jewish form of the Mysteries was therefore adopted by the White Lodge as the best means of transmitting the ancient rites through the Dark Ages, when the Church rigorously persecuted all who were not in agreement with her doctrines. The chief agent in the work of transition was He who was then known as S. Alban, but whom to-day we revere as the Master the Comte de S. Germain, the Head of all true Freemasons throughout the world. I have given some account of Him and His Roman incarnation in *The Hidden Life in Freemasonry.*[11]

THE TRANSITION TO THE OPERATIVES

The Mysteries of Bacchus quite naturally and gradually gave place to the Jewish form of the same tradition as Christianity grew more

---

[10]J. S. M. Ward: *Freemasonry and the Ancient Gods*, pp. 115, 116.

[11]*Op. cit.*, pp. 12-16.

and more powerful; for this was not incompatible with the Christian faith as the Greek and Egyptian traditions would have been; and the speculative secrets were more and more confused with operative terminology until the transition was complete. When the Roman Empire of the West was destroyed, political power came more and more into the hands of the Church, which grew very suspicious of secret societies, and suppressed them with great vigour. She did not, however, persecute the operative Masons, whom she regarded as a body of men wisely guarding the secrets of their trade, which she supposed to be concerned with the measurements of columns and arches, quantities for the mixing of mortar, and other such things.

The Masters of the White Lodge, therefore, intentionally confused the symbolical with the operative working and thus preserved Blue Masonry, but permitted the higher wisdom to sink for the time out of sight. Thus they provided for such of the egos born in Europe as could not develop under the cruder teaching which was mis-called Christianity.

This effort to preserve the Mysteries in the Dark Ages was successful because the speculative Masons adopted as much as they could of the operative Masons' terminology, and entrusted them with some of the secrets. The latter then faithfully carried on the forms without comprehending more than half of what they meant.

Then those who held philosophical ideas of which the Church would not approve allied themselves with the operative masons, became members of the fraternity, and attended their meetings; they did not come into the guilds as operative masons, and therefore were not bound as apprentices, but were *free* masons *accepted* into the operative body, but not belonging to it by right of physical-plane work. The tradition of the Collegia passed into the Lodges of the guilds, as we shall see in the next chapter, and the ancient succession of I.M.s, which we in Britain trace through S. Alban, was handed down unbroken from century to century. In consequence of this persecution, and the partial restoration of Masonry in different forms in different countries, its outward history had been obscured and confused in the greatest possible degree. It is a matter that might no doubt be elucidated by long and painstaking research, but it would be a task involving far too great an expenditure of energy and time.

7

Craft Masonry in Medieval Times

EVOLUTIONARY METHODS

THE theory of human evolution ordinarily put before us is that of a
slow upward progress of man from extremely primitive and almost
animal conditions through the Stone Age, the Bronze Age, the Iron
Age, until he has arrived at his present level, which is by this hypothesis
the highest which he has yet attained. This view is only partially true;
it is only on the one hand in a very broad and general sense covering
a development lasting many millions of years, and on the other in a
purely local sense affecting one or two subraces, that it can be said
to be true at all, for it leaves entirely out of account some of the most
important factors in the case.

Let no one ever doubt that evolution is a fact—that God has a plan
for man, and that that plan is one of eternal advancement and unfoldment, carrying him on to heights of glory and splendour of which
at present we have no conception.

Yet we doubt not through the ages one eternal purpose runs.
And the thoughts of men are widened with the process of the suns.[1]

But if we wish to understand anything of this wondrous scheme we
must begin by trying to grasp its general principles. First, it is no mere

---

[1] *Locksley Hall,* by Lord Tennyson.

haphazard growth; it is being definitely directed from behind by a body of perfected men which we call the Great White Brotherhood—a body which exists to carry out the will of the Logos of the solar system. It works through machinery so vast and complicated that from the physical plane we can never see more than a tiny corner of its operation, and so we constantly misconceive and underrate it.

Secondly, its method of working is cyclical. The soul of man grows by occupying a succession of bodies, each of which is born, grows slowly to maturity, lives its life, learns (or fails to learn) its lesson, and then dies. Just so humanity grows by incarnating in a succession of races, each of which passes through its stage of youth, adolescence, full manhood and decay. Often the period of decay seems sad, both with the man and with the race; often the student of history cannot but regret the passing of a once mighty and splendid civilization to make way for a savagery possibly more virile, but certainly in its youth coarser and cruder.

A flagrant example of that was the destruction of the gentle and beautiful civilization of Peru by the incredibly cruel and atrocious methods of the invading Spaniards; another very similar case was the utterly unjustifiable attack upon the civilization of Rome by the ferocious hordes of Goths and Vandals from the north. So coarse, so brutal were they that their very names have become a proverb, and we use them to-day to indicate the extremes of clumsiness and wanton destruction. Yet they also were an instrument in the hand of the divine power, and their crass ignorance contained within itself the seed of certain qualities which were in danger of dying out and being forgotten among the decaying races which they were destined to leaven and partially to replace.

The Withdrawal of the Mysteries

Even before the destruction of the Roman Empire the withdrawal of the Mysteries as public institutions had taken place; and this fact was mainly due to the excessive intolerance displayed by the Christians. Their amazing theory that none but they could be "saved" from the hell which they themselves had invented naturally led them to try all means, even the most cruel and diabolical persecutions, to force people of other faiths to accept their particular shibboleth. As the Mysteries were the heart and stronghold of a more rational belief, they of course opposed them bitterly, quite forgetful that in the earlier days of their religion they had claimed to possess as much of the inner knowledge as any other system.

THE CHRISTIAN MYSTERIES

Even to-day it is quite commonly thought that Christianity had no mysteries, and some of its followers boast that in it nothing is hidden. That mistaken idea has been so sedulously impressed upon the world that it leads many people to feel a certain distaste for the wiser faiths which met all needs, and to think of them as unnecessarily hiding part of the truth or grudging it to the world. In the old days there was no such thought as this; it was recognized that only those who came up to a certain standard of life were fit to receive the higher instruction, and those who wished for it set to work to qualify themselves for it. Knowledge is power, and people must prove their fitness before they will be entrusted with power; for the object of the whole scheme is human evolution, and the interests of evolution would not be served by promiscuous publication of occult truth.

Those who maintain the above-mentioned opinion about Christianity are unacquainted with the history of the Church. Though many of the early Christian writers are bitterly hostile to the Mysteries, they indignantly deny the suggestion that in their Church they have nothing worthy of that name, and claim that their Mysteries are in every way as good and deep and far-reaching as those of their 'pagan' opponents. S. Clement says: "He who has been purified in baptism and then initiated into the little Mysteries (has acquired, that is to say, the habits of self-control and reflection), becomes ripe for the greater Mysteries, for Epopteia or Gnosis, the scientific knowledge of God."[2] The same writer also said: "It is not lawful to reveal to profane persons the Mysteries of the Logos."

Origen, the most brilliant and learned of all the ecclesiastical Fathers, also asserts the existence of the secret teaching of the Church, and speaks plainly of the difference between the ignorant faith of the undeveloped multitude, and the higher and reasonable faith which is founded upon definite knowledge. He draws a distinction between "the popular irrational faith" which leads to what he calls "somatic Christianity" (the merely physical form of the religion) and the "spiritual Christianity" offered by the Gnosis or wisdom. He makes it perfectly

---

[2]Quoted in *Some Glimpses of Occultism*, Ch. ii.

clear that by "somatic Christianity" he means that faith which is based on the gospel history. He says of it: "What better method could be devised to assist the masses?" In Dean Inge's *Christian Mysticism* he is quoted as teaching that:

The Gnostic or sage no longer needs the crucified Christ. The eternal or spiritual gospel which is his possession shows clearly all things concerning the Son of God Himself, both the Mysteries shown by his words and the things of which his acts were the symbols. . .Origen regards the life, death and resurrection of Christ as only one manifestation of a universal law, which was really enacted not in this fleeting world of shadows, but in the eternal counsels of the Most High. He considers that those who are thoroughly convinced of the universal truths revealed by the incarnation and the atonement need trouble themselves no more about their particular manifestations in time.[3]

Here we see distinct and repeated references to the hidden teaching, greater far than anything known to the Church of the present day, and carrying those who study it to a much higher level than is ever now attained by the disciples of orthodoxy. What has become of this magnificent heritage of Christianity? It is true that everything the Church knows is now given out, but that is only because she has forgotten the mysteries which she used to keep hidden. This is one of the principal reasons why she has lost control of her more intellectual sons, and has therefore failed in her duty to educate and instruct the people in the most important things of life, and has left our age the most unpractical one ever known.

We have come into this world to live our lives, not to make money, and on the way in which we live depends the condition of our future births. One would think, therefore, that people would be taught all about these things in school. It is certain that every one must die, but nobody tells us anything that is worth knowing about that important matter. On the contrary, exoteric Christianity in the days of its power positively forbade those who knew to say anything on the subject, and enforced with the most terrible weapons its incredibly foolish commandment: "Thou shalt not think."

Happily all this wonderful wisdom is not lost, for much of it is preserved to us in the teachings of Freemasonry. There were many thousands of people at the time when Christianity began to dominate the world who still clung to the ancient tradition, who preferred to

---

[3]*Op. cit.*, p. 89.

state their views in the older forms. As Christianity grew narrower and more aggressive, and less tolerant of fact, those who knew something of the truth, and wished to preserve its enshrinement in those older forms, had more and more to keep their meetings secret; for the Church was exceedingly intolerant towards anyone who dared to differ from her, even in minor matters.

THE REPRESSION OF THE MYSTERIES

In A.D. 399 the Emperor Theodosius issued his celebrated edict, which was a heavy blow to the outer manifestation of the ancient pagan faith:

Whatever privileges were conceded by the ancient laws to the priests, ministers, prefects, hierophants of sacred things, or by whatsoever name they may be designated, are to be abolished henceforth, and let them not think that they are protected by a granted privilege when their religious confession is known to have been condemned by the law.

By A.D. 423 the penalties against those who clung to the old beliefs had become severe, for in a later edict of the same Emperor we find:

Although the pagans that remain ought to be subjected to capital punishment if at any time they are detected in the abominable sacrifices of demons, let exile and confiscation of goods be their punishment.[4]

Wherever possible the temples of the gods were destroyed, the ancient libraries were burnt, the statues and other relics were broken in pieces by the brutal hands of the savage Christians—and what destruction remained to be accomplished in the Western Empire was completed by the no less barbarian invaders. So perished the outer worship of the gods of Greece and Rome; the Mysteries were withdrawn into inviolable secrecy, which remained unbroken until after the Reformation, when the Church had lost her power to burn and torture all who did not at least pretend to be in agreement with her doctrines.

THE CROSSING OF TRADITIONS

This retirement took place in several countries simultaneously, so several traditions arose which, like the mystery-systems from which

---

[4]*Codex Theodosianus* XVI, 10, 14, 23, quoted in *A Source Book for Ancient Church History.* Ayer, p. 371.

they were derived, differed considerably in their details, though they were always based upon a common plan. These traditions have crossed and recrossed one another constantly throughout the centuries, have influenced each other in all sorts of secret ways, have been carried from country to country by many messengers; so that the Masonry which emerged in the eighteenth century bears the signature of many lines of descent, of many interacting schools of mystical philosophy.

Behind all these different movements, utterly unknown except by the few disciples charged with the work of keeping alight the sacred fire during the Dark Ages, stood the White Lodge itself, encouraging all that was good in them, guiding and inspiring all who were willing to open themselves to such influence.

By efflux of time the true philosophy has gradually faded out of them again and again, and from time to time the adepts have taken advantage of some favourable opportunity to restore a little of it— sometimes by founding a new rite or school, sometimes by instigating the establishment of additional degrees in an existing rite. We see, therefore, a number of parallel and equally valid streams of tradition running down in secret throughout the Middle Ages, and emerging here and there in movements which are to some extent known in the outer world. The real continuum of Masonry may thus be compared to the roots of a plant creeping along under the ground, and giving forth apparently separate plants at intervals. There are, however, more or less broken lines of outward descent that may be traced up to a certain point on the physical plane; it is with these that we shall especially concern ourselves in the following chapters.

THE TWO LINES OF DESCENT

We have already indicated that the only portion of the Masonic tradition which was anciently divided into definite degrees is that which we now call Craft or symbolic Masonry—the direct descendant of the Lesser and the Greater Mysteries of Egypt and Judaea, and closely akin to the Mysteries of Greece. Greater sacramental powers were conferred and deeper spiritual instruction was given to the few who were endeavouring to prepare themselves for the true Mysteries of the White Lodge; but these cannot be called degrees after the manner of Craft Masonry, for even in ancient Egypt they were not organized as such. Both these lines of sucession passed down through the Middle

Ages; the Craft degrees were deliberately confused with operative building, and were thus transmitted, although in secrecy, in the outer world, but the higher instruction still belonged only to the few, and was handed down in far deeper secrecy still, being introduced from time to time into the heart of various mystical schools, which were much more exclusive in their choice of members than the operative builders.

With the Craft degrees were associated the kernel of those ceremonies which we now attach to the Honourable Degree of Mark Master Mason, connected, as always, with the 2°, and the Supreme Order of the Holy Royal Arch of Jerusalem, worked in conjunction with the 3°. Our present rituals for these are not therefore necessarily ancient, for all have been subjected to much modern recasting and editing. A body of legend and tradition explanatory of the ceremonial appears also to have been handed down; and the relics of this have in comparatively recent times been manufactured into separate ceremonial degrees—such, for example, as certain of the earlier stages of the Ancient and Accepted Scottish Rite, and their kindred among the side or additional degrees worked in England and America.

The Culdees

A noteworthy line of tradition, connected with Craft Masonry to some extent, but even more with the Royal Order of Scotland and the 18°, is found among the Culdees of Ireland, Scotland and York. Few trustworthy sources of information exist concerning them, though they have been the centre of many beautiful dreams; but they are thought by scholars to have been either an ancient monastic order with settlements in Ireland and Scotland,[5] or in a wider sense to have represented the monks and clerics of the Celtic Church without limitation, as well as those understood to be their successors in later times.[6]

We hear of them in Ireland from the ninth to the seventeenth centuries; from the ninth to the fourteenth centuries in Scotland, where they had several influential monastic communities, including one upon the holy island of Iona, which had been one of the greatest spiritual

---

[5]*Enc. Brit.*, Art. *Culdees* (Eleventh Ed.).

[6]*Hist. Freemasonry*, R. F. Gould, Vol. I, p. 47.

centres of Celtic Christianity long before the word Culdee is mentioned in the historical records concerning it. In Wales in the twelfth century there was a strict community of Culdees living in the island of Bardsey, the holy island of Wales; while in England we find them as officiating clergy in the Cathedral Church of S. Peter at York during the reign of King Athelstan, who was so closely linked with English Masonic tradition.[7] It is said that after requesting the prayers of the Culdees for victory over the Scots, when he was successful he granted them a perpetual endowment of corn, to enable them to continue their works of charity.

Their name has been derived from the Celtic *Cele-De,* meaning Companion or Servant of God, and from the Latin *Colidei,* worshippers of God; others have thought that it came from the Celtic *cuill dich,* meaning men of seclusion; but the etymology of the word is not certainly known. Godfrey Higgins claimed that the word Culdee was the same as Chaldee, and ascribed to them an Oriental origin, although he adduces no authentic evidence for his views.[8]

CELTIC CHRISTIANITY IN BRITAIN

Students of English Church History know that Christianity was introduced into Great Britain long before the missions of S. Patrick and S. Augustine; and there has been a persistent feeling that this Christianity was not that of Rome, but had affinities rather with the Eastern rites.[9] Many traditions, none of them substantiated by authentic records, bear witness to this belief, and point the way to a truth in the background. There is the beautiful legend of Joseph of Arimathaea and the Holy Thorn of Glastonbury; there is the story told by Theodoret and Fortunatus that S. Paul visited Britain, which appears to receive some confirmation from S. Clement of Rome; while Eusebius, the great ecclesiastical historian, mentions that some of the twelve apostles

---

[7]*Hist. Freemasonry,* R. F. Gould, Vol. I, p. 50 ff.

[8]Quoted by Bro. A. E. Waite: *A New Encyclopaedia of Freemasonry,* Art. *Culdees.*

[9]Neander, *General History of the Christian Religion and Church,* Vol. i. p. 117. Quoted Gould, *loc. cit.*

visited the British Isles.[10] Indeed it was not until the twelfth century
that Celtic Christianity was finally brought into line with the usages
of Roman Catholicism.[11]

The holy island of Iona, once the heart of the old Celtic Church,
lies off the west coast of Scotland among the Inner Hebrides. It was
called Hy or Icolmkill (the island of Columba of the Church), and
by the Highlanders Innis nan Druidhneah (the isle of the Druids),
implying that before the coming of S. Columba in A.D. 563 it had
been a hallowed centre of the ancient worship of the Celts.[12] The monks
of Iona spread their learning over Sootland and Northern England,
and the early Celtic Bishops owned the abbot of Iona as their spiritual
head. In 717 the monks of Iona were expelled from Scotland by the
Pictish King Nechtan; but their place was largely filled by the Culdees
of Ireland,[13] who appear to have been followers of the same tradition.
No mention is made of the Culdees in Scotland after A.D. 1382.[14]

We find that the early British Church, of which the Culdees were
the later survivors, possessed a beautiful and mystical form of Christianity derived from Eastern sources and closely connected with the
traditions of the Essenes, who were the immediate followers of Our
Lord. It had the apostolic succession of the Christian Church, but its
teachings were less defined and rigid, more mystical and poetic than
the Roman scholasticism which in later days so completely absorbed
it. In addition to the Christian sacraments, certain secret rites were
brought to Britain by the original missionaries, rites belonging to the
Mithraic line of succession, which, as we have already seen, were
practised among the Essenes; and there may also in all likelihood have
existed among them a succession of Jewish Masonry unconnected with
the Roman Collegia.

THE DRUIDIC MYSTERIES

These various lines of tradition were assimilated to some extent with
the indigenous Mysteries of the Druids, which, however, had lost much

---

[10]*Foundation Stones.* Austin Clare, p. 16.

[11]*Enc. Brit., loc. cit.*

[12]*Enc. Brit.,* Art. *Iona.*

[13]*Enc. Brit.,* Art. *Culdees.*

[14]Gould, *loc. cit.*

of the splendour of former times; and even the outer Christian rites became touched with that peculiar beauty which is the heritage of the Celt. We find confirmation of the ancient legend that the splendid Celtic race called the Tuatha De Danaan, which flourished in ancient Ireland, came originally from Greece through Scandinavia; and the same is true of other offshoots of the Celtic stock which settled in Wales, Cornwall and Brittany. They all formed a branch of that Fourth Subrace from which the later Greeks and Romans were also descended; and the origin of the Mysteries of the Druids may be traced to the great World-Teacher, in His incarnation as Orpheus, the singer of Hellas, though they were also influenced somewhat by the still older Mysteries of Ireland which date from Atlantean times. The lyre of Apollo became the harp of Angus; and the old worship of God as the divine beauty manifesting through music thus passed down into Britain.

The Druidical Mysteries had a certain influence on the imported Roman or Norman rites. They are compared by Strabo and Artemidorus to the rites of Samothrace, and by Dionysius to those of Bacchus, while Mnaseas refers to their Kabiric correspondences. We learn from Diogenes Laertius and from Caesar that the Druidic method of instruction was by symbols, enigmas and allegories, and that they taught orally, deeming it unlawful to commit their knowledge to writing. It is said that their ceremonies of initiation required much physical purification and mental preparation. In the first degree the aspirant's symbolical death was represented, and in the third his regeneration from the womb of the giant goddess Ceridwin and the committal of the newly-born to the waves in a small boat, symbolical of the ark. Their doctrines were similar to those of Pythagoras—including reincarnation and the existence of one Supreme Being. Apart from a few stray references in classical authors, we know of them today chiefly through the Bardic songs attributed to the Welsh poet Taliesin, of the sixth century A.D., who claimed Druidic initiation. Culdees of York blended Christian mysticism with these pre-Christian rites, and so linked them with modern Masonry.

There have been many other mysteries, such as those of Ireland, closely connected with the Druids, and of Scandinavia, wherein the death and resurrection of Balder was the chief theme, and no doubt all these were connected with the source of our present Masonry, being branches of the same tree, even though external traces of their relationship in the past have disappeared.

The Holy Grail

As part of this indirect heritage from the Greek Mysteries came the well-known symbol of the *Krater* or Cup, which in the intermingling with early British Christianity was identified with the Sangreal, the Chalice used by our Lord at the Last Supper for the founding of the Holy Eucharist. King Arthur, who has often been supposed to be an imaginary hero, was a very real and most lovable and sagacious ruler, of whom England may well be proud; his Round Table also is fact and not fiction, and among its Knights there was a rite of the Christian Mysteries centring round the beautiful story of the quest for the Holy Grail. Some there were who took the legend literally and undertook endless physical-plane pilgrimages in search of an earthly cup; others knew that the mystical meaning of the finding of the Holy Grail is the union between the higher and the lower self, which is one of the qualifications for initiation into the true Mysteries of the White Lodge; for the Chalice symbolically represents the causal body into which the "blood" of the Mystery is poured. "I am the cup, His love the wine." The Mysteries of the Holy Grail were simultaneously celebrated in various centres, both in Great Britain and on the Continent, where they doubtless became mingled with other lines of tradition; and in them we find clear traces of one of those secret schools in which the flame of the hidden wisdom burnt bright during the early Middle Ages. The tradition of the Grail and its spiritual Knighthood passed into literature through the hands of Chretien de Troyes, Wolfram von Eschenbach and other writers, whence on the one hand we derive the *Morte d'Arthur* of Sir Thomas Malory, from which Tennyson drew the materials for his *Idylls of the King,* and on the other the glorious music of *Parsifal,* in which Wagner reconstructed so magnificently the German tradition of the Grail Brotherhood.

Heredom

In Scotland these secret Mysteries of the East and West were handed down from generation to generation in various centres, one of the chief of these being the sacred island of Iona. Among the initiates of the Culdee rites Iona was called Heredom. Heredom is said in Masonic tradition to be a mystical mountain, and as such it is indeed the mount of Initiation beyond the veils of space and time; but it was also the secret name of the physical centre of the Mysteries—and this centre was Iona. Another such secret centre in mediaeval days was the Abbey of Kilwinning; and thus, the rites which derive in part from Culdee sources have always styled themselves as of Kilwinning and of Heredom.

The Saxon invasion of Britain drove the Celtic inhabitants of the plains to the mountains of the west and north; and thus there was a further mingling of the Jewish Mysteries of the Collegia with the Culdee rites. The Culdees of York were among the guardians of the Masonic tradition in the tenth century, and the Old Charges tell us that an assembly of Masons was held at York during the reign of King Athelstan, when a reorganization of the Craft took place. For many centuries York was a powerful centre of Masonry; and we have a curious piece of testimony given in 1835, by Godfrey Higgins, who claimed to be in possession of a Masonic document by which he could prove that "no very long time ago" the Culdees or Chaldaeans of York were Freemasons, that they constituted the Grand Lodge of England, and that they held their meetings in the crypt under the great cathedral of that city.[15] As we shall presently see, it was at York that certain important Masonic degrees emerged in the eighteenth century.

The monks of the Celtic Church were largely responsible for the introduction of Christianity into Germany. "Wherever they came they raised Churches and dwellings for their priests, cleared the forests, tilled the virgin soil, and instructed the heathen in the first principles of civilization."[16] Some German authorities have held that the monks directing these operations owed much of their success to the remnants of the Roman Colleges of Gaul and Britain, and ultimately laid the foundations of the craft guild system in Germany. Gould rejects this view on the ground that at the time of the Celtic influence there were no craft guilds in Germany;[17] but nevertheless some of the secret rites and traditions of the Celtic monks passed into the German monasteries and formed one of the lines of descent of those stonemasons who built the great German cathedrals in the Middle Ages.

In Scotland the Celtic Mystery-tradition passed down independently

---

[15]Quoted in Waite's *New Encyclopaedia*, Art. *Culdees*.

[16]Gould. *Hist. Freem.*, Vol. I, p. 107.

[17]Gould. *Hist. Freem.*, Vol. I, p. 109.

of the later operative Lodges, for there is no trace whatsoever of any high degrees in the extant Minutes of Mother Kilwinning, No. 0 upon the roll of the Grand Lodge of Scotland, which date from 1642.[18] There is truth in the legend of the coming of certain of the French Knights Templars to Scotland after their proscription in 1307, and there was an intermingling of their doctrines also with the Scottish rites. One line of descent crossed from Scotland to France, where it was blended in the eighteenth century with the Egyptian tradition to form the rite of Heredom or of Perfection under the Council of the Emperors of the East and West, as will be further explained in Chapter XI. Another line was handed down in Scotland and England, becoming blended with Jewish Tradition, and Emerged in the Degrees of HRDM-RSYCS in what we now call the Royal Order of Scotland. The curious rhymed ritual of the Royal Order bears internal evidences of age, and although its Christianity has been ruthlessly edited in protestant interests there are yet traces of the old mystical ideas of the Celtic Church.

[18]*History of the Lodge of Edinburgh* (Mary's Chapel, No. I) D. Murray Lyon, pp. 340, 434.

8

Operative Masonry
in the Middle Ages

THE TEMPORARY CUSTODIANS

IN a complete study of mediaeval operative Masonry it would be necessary to include a treatise upon the various schools of mediaeval architecture and the tendencies, national and economic, which influenced their creation and development. In this book we are concerned with the operative builders only in so far as they were the temporary custodians of the speculative science of the Mysteries; but the study of architecture is of considerable value to the Mason; for it is the physical-plane reflection of mighty ideas in the inner worlds, and by the study of architecture certain of the laws of spiritual building may by analogy be reached and understood.

As Masons, our speculative ancestry is noble and magnificent, for we are in that respect the lineal descendants of the kings and prophets and priests of old who have been the bearers of the Hidden Light to men through countless generations; but of our operative forefathers who so faithfully guarded the tradition in the days of darkness we may also be proud, for their art at its zenith was unsurpassed in richness and splendour by the achievements of any other age in Europe; the great cathedrals and monasteries which they built to the glory of God and in the service of His Church are touched with the finger of divine inspiration, so that the cold marble is transfigured into almost unbelievable grace and delicacy; they are veritable dreams of beauty materialized into stone. The operative Masons, too, have handed down to us many of their customs and usages; and it is well that we should understand these in addition to what we have derived from other sources.

When Europe was overrun by the Germanic tribes and the Empire of the West was destroyed, the Roman Collegia for the most part disappeared with the other fruits of civilization. The Mysteries enshrined in them survived in a more or less repressed form in Italy, France and England, although they were kept extremely secret for fear of the barbarian invaders. It was from these survivals that the Lodges of the guild Masons of the Middle Ages were derived.

DECLINE OF THE COLLEGIA

Mackey shows how the Collegia declined after the fall of Rome, and how new guilds were started and old ones revived under the patronage of the Christian clergy, and asserts that after the tenth century the whole of Europe was perambulated by bands of wanderers called Travelling Freemasons, who erected churches and monastaries in the Gothic style. Authorities differ seriously in opinion as to whether the fraternities who built the great cathedrals were joined together by any central organization. There is much in the similarity of style of building in the different countries, and in the Masonic signs upon the buildings, to indicate their connection, but the central organization must have allowed its branches great latitude, since the differences in style are also great. The cathedrals that the Travelling Freemasons built with such great skill and artistic inspiration were laid out upon a symbolic plan, usually based upon the cross and the *vesica piscis*, and there is some evidence that they moralized upon their tools. Undoubtedly these were men of the loftiest intellect and spirituality, and we modern speculative Masons have no reason to be ashamed of our associations with such operative craftsmen.

THE COMACINI

The first signs of a revival in the art of building, the first stirrings of that creative spirit which was to blossom in later years in the full glory of the Gothic, are to be found in Lombardy, where originated the style called Romanesque, which eventually spread all over Europe. According to tradition, the College of Architects from Rome removed during the last days of the Empire to the safe refuge offered by the little republic of Comum, once the home of Pliny, and made its retreat upon the lovely island still known as Isola Comacina in Lake Como in Northern Italy.[1] In A.D. 568 the surrounding country fell into the hands of the Lombards or Longobards, so-called from their long beards and uncouth appearance, whose original home had been in the lower basin of the Elbe; and although at first they were detested by the Italians, with surprising rapidity they developed enthusiasm for the arts and refinement of the land they had conquered.[2]

The first mention in contemporary records of the celebrated Comacine Masters, who were descended from that Roman College, occurs in the code of the Lombard King Rothares (643), in which they figure as Master Masons with power to make contracts for building works and to employ workmen and labourers.[3] They are mentioned also in the *Memoratorio* of King Luitprand in 713,[4] when they received the privileges of freemen in the Lombard State. To their creative genius Romanesque architecture is due; and in all probability they adapted the traditional Roman methods to the requirements of their Lombard masters. It is clear from the Edict that they were highly-skilled architects. From a letter from Theodoric the Great to an architect whom he had appointed, we learn that the profession was highly developed, and an architect had to be able to construct a building from foundation to roof, and also decorate it with sculpture and painting, mosaic and bronzework. This inclusiveness prevailed in all the mediaeval schools up to 1335, when the Siennese painters seceded; and subsequently other branches also separated themselves into distinct guilds.

The first dawn of the new style (c. 600) was followed by a long period of obscuration, not unlike that Dark Age which in the evolution of Greek art followed the Dorian conquest. Then, with a strange suddenness, sprang forth (c. 1000) in wonderful perfection the new style, and rapidly extended itself over much of western and northern Christendom—the rapidity of this extension being easily explainable by the fact that master-builders and workmen were

---

[1] *The Cathedral Builders,* Leader Scott, pp. 11, 140.

[2] *History of Art,* H. B. Cotterill, Vol. I, p. 232.

[3] *The Cathedral Builders,* p. 5.

[4] *Ibid.,* p. 24.

often summoned to great distances from well-known centres of architecture. In the same way as Venice and Ravenna sent to Constantinople for Byzantine builders, Charles the Great and many other princes, as well as cities, procured from Italy skilful Romanesque architects, such as the Comacine Masters, and the characteristics of this Lombard Romanesque are found not only in Germany and France but even in England.[5]

Italian chroniclers relate that architects and builders were sent by Pope Gregory the Great to England with S. Augustine, and we learn from the Venerable Bede that S. Benedict Biscop set out for Gaul to search for masons to build the monastic church at Monk Wearmouth "according to the Roman style he had always loved".[6] S. Boniface visited Italy before undertaking his great mission to Germany in A.D. 715; Pope Gregory II gave him instructions and credentials, and sent with him a large following of monks versed in the art of building, and of lay brethren who were also architects to assist him.[7] Leader Scott contends that these builders were Comacine Masters, and bases her arguments upon the evidence of building methods and the similarity of the styles employed, In like manner she traces the Comacini into France and Normandy, Southern Italy and Sicily, and even to Ireland— in fact wherever the Romanesque style of building has penetrated.

The Comacine Lodges

The Comacine Guild not only inherited the building traditions of the Collegia, but also their secret Mysteries; and it was largely owing to the impulse given by them that a general revival of the existing Lodges of Europe took place. A very considerable interchange of influence occurs at this time; new Lodges were founded and old Lodges were restored, for, although the primary inspiration came from Italy, the builders in the different countries soon learnt to modify the new style in accordance with national requirements and taste. Many of the higher brethren, the Magistri of the Guild, were men of wide culture and refinement, who knew much of the inner meaning of the rites and ceremonies handed down amongst them; and it may well be that some among them possessed the knowledge now belonging to the higher degrees, for high degree signs are occasionally found upon their work.

---

[5]*History of Art,* Vol. I, p. 230.

[6]*The Cathedral Builders,* pp. 143, 154.

[7]*Ibid.,* p. 133.

The majority of the craftsmen, however, probably knew little more than that there was a symbolical meaning to their ceremonies and tools, and tried to order their lives accordingly.

As Bro. J. S. M. Ward has pointed out very clearly, the Comacini show marked analogies with our modern Masonic system. They were organized into Masters and Disciples under the rule of a Gastaldo or Grand Master. Their working-places were called Lodges. They had Masters and Wardens, signs, tokens, grips, pass-words and oaths of secrecy and fidelity. The Four Crowned Martyrs were their Patron Saints; they wore white aprons and gloves, and among the symbols associated with them we find the Lion of Judah, King Solomon's knot, the square and compasses, the level and plumb-rule, and the rose and compasses.

On a pulpit at Ravello, in one of their buildings of the thirteenth century, Jonah is seen coming out of the whale's mouth, making the F. C. H. S.[8] At Coire Cathedral in Switzerland, which is Romanesque in style and contains abundant evidence of Comacine work, several figures on the capitals of the pillars in the choir and sanctuary are depicted making Masonic s . . .s, notably the F. C. H. S., the G. and R. S., and several s . . .s now associated with the Rose-Croix, Knights Templars, and other high degrees in Freemasonry.[9] In the town-hall at Basle there is a fresco by Hans Dyg, painted in 1519, in which we may see the same s . . .s, and also one of the Mark degree. King Solomon's knot is the traditional name among the Italians of to-day for the elaborate interlaced stonework executed by the Comacine Masters up to the eleventh century. It consists always of a single strand woven and interwoven in the most complex and beautiful designs. Leader Scott calls it "that intricate and endless variety of the single unbroken line of unity—emblem of the manifold ways of the power of the one God who has neither beginning nor end".[10]

OTHER SURVIVALS OF THE COLLEGIA

Before passing on to the rise of Gothic architecture, which marks the climax of operative achievement in the Middle Ages, it will be

---

[8]*Freemasonry and the Ancient Gods,* J. S. M. Ward, Ch. xviii, *passim.*

[9]*An Outline History of Freemasonry,* J. S. M. Ward, p. 34.

[10]*The Cathedral Builders,* p. 72.

well if we indicate certain other survivals of the Collegia and their Mysteries; for although the great impulse to restore the art of building came through the Comacine Masters, other Lodges had existed in Europe from Roman days which, under the influeuce of Italian inspiration, regained their power and vitality. In France especially it is clear that the organization of the Collegia was never fully destroyed and that the craft-guilds (Corps d'Etat) of the Middle Ages were derived from them in unbroken continuity.

The true origin of the corporation is found in the social life of the Romans, and amongst the vanquished Gauls, who always formed the principal population in the cities, and faithfully preserved under their new masters the remembrance and traces of their ancient organization.[11]

Roman civil architecture, industry, art—in one word, the whole Roman tradition—was perpetuated in France till the tenth century. Even the German conquerors, while preserving their own national laws, customs, and usages, accepted the Gallic industry much as they found it.[12]

Not only was the trade organization preserved without break; the inner Mysteries of the Colleges of Architects were transmitted to the mediaeval building guilds of France, though they were no doubt strongly influenced by the Italian Masters who practised the same Mysteries and the same glorious Craft.

THE COMPAGNONNAGE

An interesting survival of the mediaeval craft-guilds of France is seen in an association of French journeymen for mutual support and assistance during their travels. Practically nothing was known about the practices of the Compagnonnage before the nineteenth century, although a partial revelation of one of the sections composing it (Enfants de Maitre Jacques) had been extracted by the Doctors of the Sorbonne in 1651, who not unnaturally stigmatized their proceedings as impiety and sacrilege. In 1841 the *Livre du Compagnonnage* was published by Agricol Perdiguier, a French workman of some culture, who undertook the task of revealing as much of the history and tradi-

---

[11]Levasseur, *Histoire des Classes Ouvrieres en France*, Vol. i, p. 104, quoted Gould i, p. 182.

[12]Monteil, *Histoire de l'Industrie Francaise*, Preface by C. Louandre, p. 76, quoted *ibid.*, p. 183.

tions of the Compagnonnage as his oath would permit, in order to put an end to the strife which ceaselessly occurred between its different sections.

The Compagnonnage consisted of three organizations perpetually at war with one another, each of which had an interesting traditional history and claimed a traditional chief. The oldest division was that of the Sons of Solomon, originally consisting of stonemasons only, although joiners and locksmiths were admitted later; the second was that of the Sons of Maitre Jacques, who likewise admitted members of these three trades and later of many others, notably saddlers, shoemakers, tailors, cutlers, and hatters; while the third section followed Maitre Soubise, and was originally composed only of carpenters, although at a later date plasterers and tilers were also admitted. It is generally conceded that the Sons of Solomon were the oldest of all; and another remarkable fact is that the masons (to be carefully distinguished from the Stonemasons) were never admitted at all. Houses of call belonging to these three associations existed in the more important towns of France; and travelling journeymen had the right to lodging and assistance in finding work in the houses belonging to their fraternity.

The three sections of the Compagnonnage preserved legends concerning King Solomon and his temple. Little is known of the form of the legend current among the Sons of Solomon, but there are curious indications that the story of the death of Hiram (which is not contained in the Bible) was known to them. Perdiguier tells us little, but he gives certain hints:

An ancient fable has obtained currency amongst them (the Sons of Solomon) relating, according to some, to Hiram, according to others, to Adonhiram; wherein are represented crimes and punishments. Again he tells us "that the joiners of Maitre Jacques wear white gloves, because, as they say, they did not steep their hands in the blood of Hiram".

Furthermore with regard to the use of the word *chien* bestowed upon all the Compagnons du Devoir, he says:

It is believed by some to be derived from the fact that it was a dog which discovered the place where the body of Hiram, architect of the Temple, lay under the rubbish, after which all the companions who separated from the murderers of Hiram were called *chiens* or dogs.

Some have thought, and among them Perdiguier himself, that these are indications of a legend which may have been borrowed from the Freemasons; but they clearly point to an independent line of tradition handed down among the stonemasons of France. Maitre Jacques and Maitre Soubise have also their traditional histories, likewise going back to the days of Solomon's Temple; and in that of the former an elaborate account of the death of Maitre Jacques is given, which may likewise be an echo of the death of another and greater Master—for it is clearly intended to be symbolical. There is also a suggestion that it was taken to refer to the death of Jacques de Molay, the last Grand Master of the Knights Templars. Much yet remains to be discovered about the Compagnonnage, for no full investigation into its records has yet taken place; and it may well be that future research will show clearly that the speculative Masons of England and the operative journeymen of France derive their traditions from a common ancestry in the ancient Mysteries. This at least was the opinion of R. F. Gould, the greatest of our Masonic historians.[13]

THE STONEMASONS OF GERMANY

Another line of survival of the ancient tradition is found among the Stonemasons of Germany. We have already traced the influence of two streams of tradition into Germany, one emanating from Britain through the Celtic monks, and another coming from Italy through S. Boniface. The craft guilds of Germany developed independently of monastic influence, but according to Gould it is probable that in the twelfth century the skilled masons of the monasteries amalgamated with the craft builders in the towns, and together formed the society afterwards known throughout Germany as the Steinmetzen.[14]

We know from the Torgau Ordinances of 1462 that the Stonemasons venerated the Four Crowned Martyrs as their patron saints, and the Strasburg Constitutions of 1459 contain a devout invocation of the names of the "Father, Son, and Holy Ghost; of our gracious Mother Mary; and of her blessed servants, the Holy Four Crowned Martyrs of everlasting memory".[15] From the *Brother-Book* of 1563 we learn

---

[13]See Gould. *Hist. Freem.*, Vol. I, ch. iv and v, for a complete account of what is known of the French Craft Guilds and the Compagnonnage.

[14]*Concise History of Freemasonry*, R. F. Gould, p. 17.

[15]Gould, *Concise History*, p. 19.

that they had a greeting and a grip which might not be described in writing;[16] and a curious piece of testimony came to light at the beginning of the nineteenth century, when a certain architect, who had joined a survival of the Stonemasons and was subsequently admitted into Masonry, recognized the E. A. grip as identical with that of the Steinmetzen of Strasburg.[17] A ceremony of admission was in use among them; but what it was is not known.[18]

At Daberan in Mecklenburg there is a carving of the Last Supper, wherein the apostles are depicted in well-known Masonic attitudes,[19] while according to the *Bulletin* of the Supreme Council of the Ancient and Accepted Scottish Rite (Southern Jurisdiction, U.S.A.) the legend of Hiram Abiff is carved in stone at Strasburg.[20] In the cathedral at Wurzburg two pillars, inscribed Jachin and Boaz, originally stood at the porchway or entrance, but they have now been moved within the building. Stieglitz in his *Early German Architecture* says that they were intended to bear a symbolic reference to the fraternity.[21] A bas-relief in a convent near Schaffhausen depicts a figure making one of the s. . .s of an I. M.[22] In the year 1459 the Stonemasons of Germany united to form a Grand Guild, governed by four Head Lodges, of which Strasburg was the chief. So close are the parallels between its organization and that of modern speculative Masonry that many German writers have held that the Steinmetzen were the originators of the speculative system. As a matter of fact there appears to have been no interchange in modern times between the two corporations, and modern German Craft Masonry is clearly derived from England.[23]

The English Guilds

Three distinct lines of tradition contribute to the Masonry of the English guilds. One line was preserved among the Celts, as we have

---

[16]Gould: *Hist. of Freem.*, Vol. i, p. 128.

[17]*Ibid.*, p. 146.

[18]*Concise History*, Gould, p. 22.

[19]*An Outline History of Freemasonry*, J. S. M. Ward, p. 35.

[20]*Op. cit.*, vii, 200.

[21]Gould: *Concise Hist.*, p. 24.

[22]*An Outline History of Freemasonry*, J. S. M. Ward, p. 11.

[23]Gould: *Concise History*, pp. 18, 24.

already seen, and became mingled in later times with streams from other sources. Secondly, the Roman Collegia survived to some extent in England after the departure of the Romans; the Saxons found them there and did not interfere with them.[24] Thirdly, there was the influx of Continental builders, beginning in the time of S. Augustine, but greatly augmented after the Norman Conquest under the patronage of Archbishop Lanfranc, the first Norman Archbishop of Canterbury, a Lombard by birth and a celebrated patron of building even before he came to England.[25] All these streams of tradition were represented in the mediaeval guilds, and were handed down in various centres. The French craft-guilds preserve accounts similar to those found in our English Old Charges regarding the assistance given to Masons by Charles Martel.[26]

The secret Mysteries of the Craft, common, save for certain unimportant local modifications, to all these lines of descent, Celtic, Saxon and Continental, were handed down in the Lodges of the mediaeval Masons, which were the units of organization and labour within the guilds; they were never written down, but were transmitted orally from generation to generation, the succession passing down from Master to Master as in the present day. The primary work of the Lodges was of course operative, and the speculative ritual which was handed down so faithfully in essentials was regarded as an ancient heritage to be scrupulously transmitted to posterity; but it is unlikely that any but the few recognized its true purpose, or thought of it as containing more than a merely moral code of life. It is due to the rigid observance of the O. "never to write those secrets" (an O. which would have been enforced by certain pains and penalties not unknown to Masons today), that no trace of the ritual can be found in any document prior to 1717; and it is because of this lack of all records that many Masonic scholars believe that it was compiled only at the beginning of the eighteenth century. Even in the fourteenth and fifteenth centuries, when the Old Charges were written down, no mention is made of the Legend of Hiram; for this formed part of the secret ritual and therefore might not be divulged. A figure representing God the Son in the porch of

---

[24]Coote—cited in *The Cathedral Builders*, Leader Scott, p. 140.

[25]J. S. M. Ward: *Freemasonry and the Ancient Gods*, p. 147.

[26]Gould: *Concise History*, p. 30.

Peterborough Cathedral is depicted as making the F. C. H. S.[27] showing that this s... at least was known to our old operative brethren.

THE RISE OF GOTHIC ARCHITECTURE

The climax of mediaeval operative building was reached in the twelfth and thirteenth centuries in the rise and development of Gothic architecture, which was inspired directly by the Head of all true Freemasons throughout the world, as part of the plan for the development of the fifth or Teutonic sub-race. Many theories have been advanced to account for the rapid development of the new style.

Whether the wonderful change of style that in a few years spread over a great part of Western Christendom was due primarily to the discovery of the possibilities of the pointed arch or those of the so-called ogival vaulting is much disputed. Probably it was due to both, and also of course to certain movements, social and political, which were bound to favour immensely any such new enthusiasm; for a new national consciousness was rapidly gaining strength, especially in France, and cities and communes were beginning to vie in erecting vast buildings—first cathedrals and later civic edifices—the architects being now mostly laymen, the founders and donors often municipal bodies and rich citizens, and the workmen not seldom volunteers from the people. The old monastic era of Romanesque suddenly gave way to that of a new, popular, and civic architecture, and in a surprisingly short time much the same had happened as that which we noted after the passing of the fateful year A.D. 1000, when, according to old Raoul Glaber, Christendom cast aside its outworn attire and put on a fresh white robe of new-built Churches.[28]

We, however, do not need to speculate or theorize as to the causes of the rapid development of the new style, for we have the advantage of knowing that the movement was all the time being definitely steered from behind by the H. O. A. T. F. and a corps of able assistants under his direction.

As I have already said, architecture has a powerful effect upon the consciousness of the people, for it is one of the means chosen by the White Lodge to influence the development of the various nations according to the plan of the Great Architect of the Universe. To understand the significance of the Gothic style, we must consider for a moment an important fact of occult history, that which is technically

[27]J. S. M. Ward, *Op. cit.*, p. 116.

[28]Cotterill, *History of Art*, Vol. I, p. 278.

known to students as the cyclic change of Ray. The seven rays, or types of the divine consciousness and activity, to one or other of which all living things belong, influence the world in turn, and this cyclic change produces the modifications of outlook which are to be noted as century succeeds century.

Each race and sub-race has its own especial qualities to develop. The fifth root-race, to which we ourselves belong, is engaged as a whole in the unfolding of intellect; but each of its sub-races has likewise a quality to cultivate. The fourth or Celtic sub-race was concerned with the evolution of intellect through the emotions, and so produced the beauty-loving peoples whom we see in Greece and Ireland; while the fifth or Teutonic sub-race, to which the Anglo-Saxons and Scandinavians belong, is striving to awaken the intellect working in the concrete mind, and so is producing the scientific and industrial nations which lead the world to-day.

This cyclic change of Ray, which is also part of the great plan, produces other, but no less definite modifications in the corporate consciousness. In Greece we saw something of the fifth ray, the ray of knowledge, working upon the fourth sub-race with its love of beauty, resulting in that intellectual type of art so characteristic of the classical age; the Middle Ages show forth the qualities of the sixth ray, the ray of devotion, working upon the fifth or Teutonic sub-race, and producing as its characteristic intellectual fruit scholastic philosophy with its hair-splitting intellectuality based upon an almost fanatical devotion.

Devotion, indeed, was the great characteristic of the Middle Ages. The twelfth and thirteenth centuries, so rich in the annals of Christian mysticism, were adorned by men and women whose power of devotion reached heights rarely touched in any other age. The great S. Bernard (who among many other noted works gave their Rule to the Order of Knights Templars), Richard of S. Victor, S. Hildegarde, S. Francis of Assisi and S. Antony of Padua, and a little later S. Bonaventura and S. Thomas Aquinas—all these have shone forth as a light unto many generations. Profound changes took place in the Catholic Church during these significant years, and Europe rose from the dark ages into the full glory of an era of culture and art. Gothic architecture was intended to lift the devotion of the masses to greater heights than had been induced by the contemplation of the flatter Romanesque style;

by its soaring lines and ever-ascending curves, by the richness of its ornamentation and the splendid complexity of its design, by its amazing grace and delicacy, it had power to raise the hearts of men on the wings of its silent music to the very throne of God Himself, to mould and enrich their devotion in unseen subtle ways, to pour out upon them spiritual influences which would aid in the great work of transformation which had to be accomplished.

The change from Romanesque to Gothic, then, was brought about deliberately. The inspiration was given to certain master-builders in the different countries by the H.O.A.T.F., and the erection of the splendid cathedrals of the period was carried out by travelling bands of Masons passing from centre to centre, and doubtless employing the local builders upon the actual work of construction. This, as we have said, was an age of devotion, and every stone was carved with the utmost care to the glory of God, and thereby charged with the adoration of the skilful craftsmen who worked so unselfishly. The powerful spiritual influences generated by all this loving care have contributed in no small degree to the extraordinary beauty of the Gothic cathedrals, and to the power which they possess even in the present day of evoking devotion and reverence from all who approach them.

The particular expressions of Gothic vary in the different countries, and even in different parts of the same country; that is always the case in every style of building. But behind the whole order of Gothic architecture there is one great idea, that of soaring, passionate devotion ever rising to the feet of God; and that is found with national modifications in England, France, Germany, Italy and Spain. This was the great age of operative Masonry, and at its close the building corporations began to decline in power, until in England and Germany especially the movement miscalled the Reformation killed out ecclesiastical architecture, and church building as a fine art practically ceased.

In the fourteenth century the merchant guilds, which organized an entire industry, became decentralized, and a new system of craft guilds gradually arose, organizing different branches of each industry. This change of organization was due to a profound change of thought among the people, which was to lead to the great stirring of the Renaissance and the growth of national consciousness in the different countries. It is at this period that the Old Charges of our ancient operative Brn.

first appear, and they were written down as the Freemasons became gradually disorganized, in order to preserve the older oral records from oblivion.

THE OLD CHARGES

These Old Charges reflect in no small measure the ignorance of the time in matters of geography and chronology, but they nevertheless contain an account of the broad outline of Masonic descent from Egypt, through Judaea, into Europe; and it would certainly be difficult to suppose that they were fabricated by mere operative builders who had nothing of hidden mystery to transmit. I give below a brief summary of the Dowland manuscript, which is fairiy representative of the tradition common to all. It is reproduced from Hughan's *Old Charges* (1872), and is quoted from Mackey's *Encyclopaedia*.[29]

The legend begins with an account of Lamech and his four children, who founded all the sciences of the world before the flood. These sciences were engraved on two pillars, one of which was later found by Hermes, who taught its contents to the people. Nimrod is next mentioned as having employed Masons at the building of the Tower of Babel, and as having given them their first Charge. Next Abraham and Sarah are said to have taught the seven sciences to the Egyptians, and especially to a "worthy Scoller that hight Ewclyde". The latter was commissioned by the king to teach Masonry to a large number of children of "the lord and estates of the realm". The legend passes then to David, who, when he began the temple of Jerusalem, learned the Charges and manners of Masons from Egypt and gave them to his people. Solomon continued the building of the temple after David's death, sent for Masons from all lands, and confirmed the Charges given by his father. There is no reference to the legend of the 3° in any of the Old Charges before the second edition of Anderson's Constitutions, published in 1738, except that Aynon, the son of Iram, is mentioned as being the "chiefe Maister" of all Masons, and "Master of all his gravings and carvinge and of all other manner of Masonrye that longed to the temple". The legend, in defiance of all chronology, then states that, "one curious Mason that hight Maymus Grecus," who had been at the making of Solomon's temple, taught Masonry to Charles Martel of France. Since the latter died in A.D. 741, the former

---

[29]Art. *Legend of the Craft.*

would have been about seventeen hundred years old, unless we are to understand that the Charge assumes that he had reincarnated!

A legendary account is given of S. Alban's work for Masons in the third century, and especially of his institution of General Assemblies. He is also said to have obtained for them a Charter, to have given them Charges, and to have arranged for better pay. Later, Athelstan is said to have built many abbeys and towers, and to have "loved well masons". His son Edwin, who loved them still more, held an Assembly at York and gave them a Charter. All the old writings were collected at this period, "some in Frenche, and some in Greek, and some in English, and some in other languages; and the intent of them all was founden all one". These old writings were digested into the York Constitutions which resulted from this Assembly of A.D. 926. It is from this source that we draw the material now embodied in the Old Charges.

9

The Transition from Operative to Speculative

THE REFORMATION

THE dawn of a new era was heralded by the Renaissance of classical learning and culture in the fifteenth century, a time of immense creative activity, of the bursting of bonds, of the liberation of a new and vital spirit of freedom, the direct result of which was what it is the fashion to call the Reformation. The cause of this change and reconstruction was a general reaction against the spirit of the Middle Ages.

The Renaissance originated in that longing for emancipation from the shackles of the past which is probably felt by every new generation, and which now and then, favoured by special conditions, succeeds in realizing its ideals. . . . The ideals in this case were joy and liberty and personality, liberation from mediaeval asceticism, mediaeval priestcraft, mediaeval dogma; liberation from the anathema that had rested on the natural rights of man—on freedom of thought and on moral judgment; liberation from traditional law and self-constituted authority, and the restoration to the individual of intellectual aud moral self-rule.[1]

One of the factors which helped to bring about this great revival of learning was the overthrow of the Eastern Empire by the Muhammadans, the capture of Constantinople and the conquest of Greece,

---

[1]Cotterill. *History of Art,* Vol. i, p. 390.

driving all who possessed the means to take refuge in Italy. Many scholars came to Italy at this time, bringing with them precious manuscripts of the old Greek writers; and the restoration of classical learning, classical building and classical art is the most notable feature of the Renaissance. The invention of printing made possible a wider diffusion of learning, and a wave of creative enthusiasm swept over Europe, leaving its mark upon the art, literature and philosophy of the age, and indeed making all things new.

It was obvious to the thinking men of the period that a reform of the Church was essential, for corruption and abuses of all kinds had crept into her sanctuaries. At first an attempt was made towards a broader view of Christian doctrine from within the Roman Church, and scholars, such as Ficino, the Platonists of Italy, Erasmus, and Sir Thomas More, sought to reinterpret Christianity in the light of the philosophy of Plato and Plotinus. But this attempt failed; and, in consequence, the Reformation took place outside the Church in the sixteenth century. It was an attempt to purify the Church from her abuses, to bring her teachings into closer harmony with the new ideas; but it must be admitted that it did little to improve matters from the spiritual point of view, even though it won freedom of belief and liberty for the individual intellect to search for the truth in its own way. For so great was the ignorance and bigotry of the reformers that they cast aside the good with the evil, and framed a theology more intolerable than that of Rome, while to a great extent rejecting her sacramental and contemplative treasures.

THE REAPPEARANCE OF SPECULATIVE MASONRY

After the Reformation in England ecclesiastical architecture practically ceased as an activity of the guilds, and the operative Lodges fell into decay since their work was no longer needed. But while the Reformation thus injured operative Masonry, it made Europe safe for the re-emergence into comparative publicity of the speculative art. The guilds had always accepted rich and influential patrons, and there was nothing new in the introduction of theoretic Masons into the Lodges. Some have denied the possibility of any speculative Masonry existing before the revival; but speculation was the rule rather than the exception in all the guilds, not only the Masonic, and in that devotional age workmen of all trades might be found moralizing upon the instruments of their labour.

But between the period when operative Masonry was at the height of its power and inspiration and the revival of the speculative art at the beginning of the eighteenth century, there was a dark period in which the light of Masonry, both operative and speculative, seemed almost extinguished. Many of the operative Lodges had lost nearly all trace of ritual workings, and had forgotten the traditional secrets of building no less than the ancient secrets of the building symbolism. It is to this period of darkness and decay as well as to the O. not to write those secrets, that we may attribute the paucity of records referring to the mystery-tradition among so many of the old operative Lodges; but by the guidance of the Great Ones this was nevertheless definitely preserved, and transmitted from various sources into our modern Craft.

THE FIRST MINUTES

It is during this post-Reformation period, when the old Lodges had almost forgotten the glory of their heritage, both operative and speculative, that we first find actual minutes of Lodge Meetings. These minutes show the condition into which the Craft had fallen at the time; they are, as we should expect, almost silent upon all questions of ritual, secrets and symbolism, although there are occasional indications which point to the concealment of a hidden tradition. It is in this period also that the first public references to the secrets of the Freemasons occur in contemporary literature; and we are able by means of them to trace to some extent the gradual emergence of the speculative Mysteries.

SCOTTISH MINUTES

The oldest Lodge Minute extant at the present time is contained in the records of the Lodge of Edinburgh, Mary's Chapel, No. 1 upon the roll of the Grand Lodge of Scotland, and is dated 1598. We know that it had been the custom from the earliest times for the operative Lodges to "accept" nonoperative Brethren; but the first authentic record of this is contained in the same archives, which state that John Boswell of Auchinlech was admitted in the year 1600.[2] The signature of Boswell, a facsimile of which is given in Murray-Lyon's admirable *History,* is followed by his mark, a cross within a circle—a symbol often used by the Brn. of the Rosy Cross, and bearing a profound

---

[2]*History of the Lodge of Edinburgh,* D. Murray-Lyon, p. 53.

meaning in connection with their Mysteries. One of the earliest references to the Rosy Cross in Great Britain occurs in Scotland and in connection with Masonry; for in Henry Adamson's *The Muses' Threnodie* (dated Perth, 1638) we find the words:

> For what we do presage is riot in grosse,
> For we are brethren of the Rosie Cross,
> We have the Mason Word and second sight.
> Things for to come we can fortell aright.

The Rosicrucian Manifestos, which are the first literary memorials of the order (c. 1614), were not translated and published in English until 1652, when Thomas Vaughan, the celebrated alchemist and mystic, who wrote under the name of Eugenius Philalethes and has now become an Adept of the White Lodge, undertook the task;[3] so as early as 1638 Masonry was associated both with the Rosicrucian Brotherhood and with the occult power known as second sight. The connection of the Rosy Cross with Masonry belongs to our next chapter.

The *Mason Word* is the only secret alluded to in early Lodge Minutes in Scotland. What it was is still unknown, although there are curious indications emanating from two writers who did not belong to the Craft. The Rev. George Hickes, afterwards Dean of Worcester, describes it about 1678 as "a secret signall masons have thro'out the world to know one another by". Robert Kirk in 1691 says that it is:

Lyke a Rabbinical Tradition, in way of Comment on Jachin and Boaz, the two Pillars erected in Solomon's Temple (I. Kings vii, 21), with ane Addition of some secret signe delyvered from Hand to Hand, by which the know and become familiar one with another.[4]

So far had the Craft forgotten its traditions in Scotland that it seems clear that only one degree existed, so far as the communication of secrets was concerned. The Mason Word was revealed to Apprentices, under a "Great Oath," and it is probable that a Charge was read, but there is no other indication of ritual procedure. The attainment of the grade of Fellow of the Craft or Master was merely a question of age and skill, and it is ordered in the Schaw Statutes of 1598 that admis-

---

[3] *The Brotherhood of the Rosy Cross*, A. E. Waite, p. 375.

[4] Gould. *Concise History*, p. 183.

sion to it should take place in the presence of Apprentices, thus precluding any secrets peculiar to the Degree.[5] As the years passed by more and more non-operatives were admitted into the Scottish Lodges, until the speculative element entirely predominated.

ENGLISH MINUTES

An indication of the secret transmission of speculative masonry is found in the Lodge of the Acception attached to the Masons' Company of London, whose records go back to 1356.[6] We first hear of that Lodge in 1620-21, when it was clearly a body distinct from the Company, for the King's Master Mason, Nicholas Stone, though Master of the Company in 1633, and again in 1634, was not enrolled among the "Accepted Masons" until 1639.[7] Persons not belonging to the Company were also eligible for admission, although from them a higher fee was demanded for the privilege of initiation. Elias Ashmole, the celebrated student of alchemy, who collected certain texts upon this abstruse science in his *Theatrum Chemicum Britannicum,* was initiated into a non-operative Lodge at Warrington in Lancashire in 1646.[8] In 1682 he received a summons to attend a Lodge at Masons' Hall in London— which was almost certainly the Acception—and was present at the initiation of six candidates, two of whom were not members of the Masons' Company.[9]

Elias Ashmole has sometimes been cited as the real founder of speculative Masonry, and also as a Bro. of the Rosy Cross; the latter suggestion is possible, although no evidence exists upon the point, but the former cannot of course be accepted by those who hold that Masonry has descended from the ancient Mysteries. A speculation is put forward by Bro. A. E. Waite in a recent book, connecting the Acception with Robert Fludd, the great English Rosicrucian Philosopher (1576-1637). He says:

---

[5]*History of the Lodge of Edinburgh.* D. Murray-Lyon, p. 10.

[6]Gould. *Concise History,* p. 105.

[7]Gould. *Concise History,* p. 111.

[8]*Ibid.,* p. 112.

[9]*Ibid.,* p. 116.

However and whenever it arose, my thesis is that the Acception may have included a group of Hermetic Students, of which there were many at the period; that Fludd drew them together or took his place among them; and that—after his manner and the manner of the Rosy Cross—they began to speak of spiritual building in a Hall of Masons, of a Hermetic Art in stone; and that therefore they may have contributed something to our own unfinished sketch of figurative building.[10]

Among the records of the Acception was a *Book of Constitutions* "which Mr. Fflood gave".

In the Harleian MSS., No. 2054, a rough memorandum of date 1665 is found, containing the following sentence, which looks like notes of an Obligation, used probably in the Chester Lodge:

There is seu^{r}all word and signes of a free Mason to be revailed to y^u wch as y^u will answ: before God at the great and terrible day of Iudgm^t y^u keep Secret and not to revaile the same to any in the heares of any pson w but to the M^{rs} and fellows of the said Society of free Masons so helpe me God, xt."[11]

Dr. Robert Plot in his *Natural History of Staffordshire* (Chap. iii), published in 1686, refers to the admission of Masons, "which cheifly consists in the communication of certain *secret signes,* whereby they are known to one another all over the *Nation.*" He also speaks of "a large *parchment volum* they have amongst them containing the *History* and *Rules* of the craft of *masonry.*"[12] In the Aubrey MSS. of the *Natural History of Wiltshire* Dr. Plot refers to the adoption of Sir Christopher Wren as a Freemason.[13] The Minutes of Lodge Antiquity No. 2, the old Lodge which met at the Goose and Gridiron, dated 1723, refer to a set of candlesticks which "its worthy old Master, Sir Christopher Wren" presented to the Lodge.[14]

The "old Lodge at York City" was in a flourishing condition in 1705, but there is no documentary evidence to show its earlier history,

---

[10]*Emblematic Freemasonry,* p. 43.

[11]*Ibid.,* p. 115.

[12]*Emblematic Freemasonry,* p. 119.

[13]*Ibid.,* p. 120.

[14]*The Builders,* Vol. x, No. 2, p. 55.

though a *Logium Fabricae* is mentioned in the Fabric Rolls of York Minster in 1352. From 1705, and perhaps before, the York Lodge was exclusively the home of speculative or symbolical Masonry. The earliest minutes preserved are in a parchment roll dated 1712-1730. The greater number of meetings are described as *Private* while a few are referred to as *General Lodges,* although Candidates were apparently admitted at both. New members were ''Sworne and Admitted''—the only documentary trace of any ritual working.[15] As we shall see, the York Lodge proclaimed itself the ''Grand Lodge of All England'' in 1725, eight years after the foundation of the Grand Lodge of England, and only a few months after the Grand Lodge of Ireland was formed; it lingered somnolently until the closing years of the eighteenth century, when it seems to have been silently absorbed into the bosom of its rivals. Anderson in his Constitutions of 1738 refers to Grand Lodges which derived from other sources than the Grand Lodge of England, and gives them definite recognition:

But the *old Lodge* at York City, and the *Lodges* of Scotland, Ireland, France, and Italy, affecting Independency, are under their own *Grand Masters,* though they have the same *Constitutions, Charges, Regulations,* etc., for substance, with their Brethren of *England.*[16]

This is a significant statement, for Lodges ''affecting independency,'' one of which is admittedly ''old,'' do not take kindly to innovations from outside their ranks. If any proof is required that Masonry was not the invention of Anderson, we have it here in his own words.

Two of Steel's essays in *The Tatler* in 1709 and 1710 refer to the existence of signs and tokens among the Freemasons. In the Minutes of the Old Lodge at York and of Mary's Chapel at Edinburgh there is evidence of the proving of Brn. before they were admitted to the Lodge, the latter entry referring to no less a person than Dr. Desaguliers, who in 1721 was found qualified in all points of Masonry by his Scottish Brn.—an incident showing identity of secrets between the Scottish and the English Lodges.[17] The same gradual transition from operative to non-operative membership took place in the English

---

[15]Gould. *Concise History,* p. 122.

[16]Gould. *Concise History,* p. 197.

[17]*History of the Lodge of Edinburgh.* D. Murray-Lyon, p. 159.

as in the Scottish Lodges, and it was this infiltration of educated and cultured men which made possible the momentous events of 1717.

IRISH MINUTES

Irish Masonry presents certain difficulties of research; for it was a point of honour among Irish Masons in the eighteenth century to destroy all documents, warrants, certificates, Lodge registers and minute books, rather than that they should pass into the hands of outsiders.[18] Dr. Chetwode Crawley states that there was a speculative Lodge of the English type at Doneraile in 1710-12, which used methods of initiation not to be distinguished from those perpetuated at the revival. Into this Lodge Elizabeth St. Leger, the famous lady Mason, was initiated, and it must have worked at least two degrees. Dr. Crawley remarks:

This last deduction will require a good deal of explaining away on the part of those Brethren who hold that, because early Scottish operative Lodges suffered the ritual to dwindle into the merest mode of recognition, the early English speculative Lodges cannot have worked more than one degree.[19]

This period of transition forms the connecting link between the old dispensation and the new. The day of operative Masonry as practised in the mediaeval Lodges was over; that of speculative Masonry as we know it to-day had not yet begun. No longer was there need of secrecy; the dread of death and torture no longer compelled the servants of the Hidden Light to take refuge in the workshops of the builders in stone. Freedom of thought, freedom of speech, freedom of action had at last been won. And as in the twilight that precedes the dawn we may discern the faint mysterious outlines of some lovely landscape hidden beneath the robe of darkness, till, as the light of the rising sun glows stronger and yet stronger, they are clothed with richer colour and beauty; so in this age of twilight we may glimpse in the outer world the dim shadows of the Hidden Mysteries as they emerge from their long night of secrecy and silence into the freedom of the day, and the Royal Art is seen once more of men.

---

[18]Dr. Chetwode Crawley. *A. Q. C.*, xvi, 69.

[19]*A. Q. C.*, viii, 55.

THE GRAND LODGE OF ENGLAND

The only extant record of the founding of the Premier Grand Lodge of the world occurs in the second edition of Dr. Anderson's Constitutions, published in 1738. No minute of Grand Lodge itself has been traced before the year 1723.[20] The following is part of the account therein given of this important event in the history of Craft Masonry:

After the Rebellion was over, A.D. 1716, the few *Lodges* at *London*... thought fit to cement under a *Grand Master* as the centre of Union and Harmony, viz., the *Lodges* that met,

1. At the *Goose* and *Gridiron* Ale-house in St. *Paul's Church-yard.*

2. At the *Crown* Ale-house in *Parker's Lane,* near *Drury-Lane.*

3. At the *Apple-Tree* Tavern in *Charles Street, Covent Garden.*

4. At the *Rummer* and *Grapes* Tavern in *Channel-Row,* Westminster.

"They and some old Brothers met at the said *Apple-Tree,* and having put into the Chair the *oldest Master* Mason (now the *Master* of a *Lodge),* they constituted themselves a *Grand Lodge* pro Tempore in *Due Form,* and forthwith revived the Quarterly *Communication* of the *Officers* of lodges (called the GRAND LODGE), resolv'd to hold the *Annual* ASSEMBLY and Feast, and then to chuse a GRAND MASTER from among themselves, till they should have the Honour of a *Noble Brother* at their Head." The Grand Lodge was according formed on S. John the Baptist's Day 1717, with Anthony Sayer as the First Grand Master.[21]

Bro. Calvert has demonstrated that the first three Lodges were probably composed of operative Masons, and numbered about fifteen Brethren each, while the fourth Lodge had a roll of seventy members and was *the* speculative Lodge, to which all the leading men of the Craft belonged in the early days, including Payne, Anderson and Desaguliers, and a large and influential body of noblemen.[22]

At first very little seems to have been done, and it does not appear that the original founders of the Grand Lodge had the least idea of starting a world-movement; but with the advent of the Duke of

---

[20]Gould. *Concise History,* p. 204.

[21]Gould. *Concise History,* p. 201.

[22]A. F. Calvert. *The Grand Lodge of England,* cited in *The Builders,* Vol. x, p. 84.

Montague to the Grand Master's Chair in 1721, the Society rose into fame and success at one bound.

The first task was the compilation and 'digesting' of the Old Gothic Constitutions, which as we have seen had been handed down in the Lodges from operative times; and this was done by Anderson in 1721. The Constitutions were printed in 1723, and a subsequent and somewhat altered edition in 1738, when the speculative system was firmly established under Grand Lodge auspices. George Payne, the second Grand Master, drafted the regulations, Anderson 'digested' the general subject matter after 'a new and better manner,' Dr. Desaguliers, the third Grand Master, wrote the Preface and Dedication, and the fourth Grand Master, the Duke of Montague, ordered the book to be printed after its formal approval by the Grand Lodge.[23]

Perhaps the most important feature of these Constitutions is the definite removal of all religious barriers to membership in the Order. Our ancient operative Brn. had, of course, been Christians and Catholics; but now the universality of the Mysteries was again to be demonstrated by the excision of all sectarian limitations. The language in which this was expressed is not happy; but it is possible that some inspiration may have been given upon this point, for it was certainly in accordance with the policy of the White Lodge. Masonry is indeed the heart of all religions, and should be bound definitely to none; although every Mason is at liberty to profess whatever faith may be most congenial to him, since they are all facets of the truth.

THE RECOMPOSITION OF THE RITUALS

Much debate and controversy has taken place among Masonic writers with regard to the origin of our modern speculative rituals, of which there is no documentary trace before the revival in 1717. That there was a definite Masonic Ceremonial in existence at this time we learn from Dr. Stukely, who tells us that "his curiosity led him to be initiated into the mysterys of Masonry, suspecting it to be the remains of the mysterys of the antients".[24] He was initiated into the Order on January 6th, 1721, and says: "I was the first person made a freemason for many years. We had great difficulty to find members enough to perform the

---

[23]*Ibid.*, p. 205.

[24]Gould. *Concise History*, p. 54.

ceremony.''[25] The Manningham Letters also offer testimony that the rituals of speculative Masonry belong to an earlier period than 1717. Dr. Manningham, Deputy Grand Master of the Grand Lodge of England, writes in 1757 of:

One old Brother of Ninety, who I conversed with lately; this Brother assures me He was made a Mason in his youth, and has constantly frequented Lodges, till rend'red incapable by his advanc'd Age, and never heard, or knew, any other Ceremonies or Words, than those us'd in general amongst us; such Forms were deliver'd to him, and those he has retain'd.[26]

This testimony is significant, for a Mason ninety years old in 1757 would have been fifty years of age in 1717, so that if he was initiated in his youth, our ceremonies must date at least from the last half of the seventeenth century. It will be remembered that the judgment of R. F. Gould is precise upon this matter:

If we once get beyond or behind the year 1717, *i.e.*, into the domain of ancient Masonry, and again look back, the vista is perfectly illimitable, without a speck or shadow to break the continuity of view which is presented to us.[27]

The decay of the operative Lodges, noted earlier in this chapter, had a disastrous effect upon the ancient ritual which had been handed down orally from Lodge to Lodge and from Master to Master from the days of the Roman Collegia. No word of it might ever be written, and it had to be learnt by heart by the Masters and officers of the Lodges. By the time, however, that we reach the days of the revival, this oral tradition had become much corrupted, and although the ancient ritual actions were still remembered, the words accompanying them had degenerated into mere verbal jargon, often quite unintelligible to those who recited it. One example will be sufficient to indicate the state of affairs. Several inns in England are named ''The Goat and Compasses,'' and as it stands the phrase has no meaning, unless it be taken to refer to the perennial fable of the ''riding of the goat''. The real derivation is from the words ''God encompasses us,'' degenerated into ''Goat and Compasses''. It was into a somewhat analogous state that the whole ritual had fallen in the days of Anderson

---

[25]Gould. *Concise History,* p. 223.

[26]*Ibid.*, p. 249.

[27]R. F. Gould. *A. Q. C.* xvi, 30.

and Desaguliers, who after the founding of the new Grand Lodge set to work to bring order out of chaos.

They proceeded to collect and revise all the workings known to them, clothing the skeleton of the ritual in the eighteenth century English so familiar in our ears to-day. On the whole their task was well carried out, and although many losses had occurred before 1717, the portion which Anderson brought with him was fairly representative of the general chaos. Anderson was clearly not a man of genius, though he did his best, and it may well be a matter of regret that the stilted language of that dullest of dull periods should have been chosen to clothe the ancient Mysteries rather than the inspired and stately English of a century before. But taverns are not conducive to spiritual inspiration, and it was in taverns that this rebirth of the Mysteries took place.

Two and Three Degrees

At first it would appear that only two degrees were worked, for the Constitutions of 1723 (Regulation xiii), speak of "Apprentices," and of "Masters and Fellow-Craft" who could only be made in Grand Lodge "unless by a Dispensation".[28] This rule was repealed in 1725, when Grand Lodge enacted that "the Master of Each Lodge, with the Consent of his Wardens and the Majority of the Brethren, being Masters, may make Masters at their discretion".[29] There is in this same year a mention of three degrees in the working of the "Grand Lodge of All England" at York, when a speech was delivered by Dr. Francis Drake, Junior Grand Warden, in which he mentions E. A., F. C., and M. M. R. F. Gould holds that the "Apprentice Part consisted of what we now know as the 1° and 2° and that the Master's Part" was our 3°, containing the legend of Hiram.[30]

He considers it settled beyond dispute

Not only that what we now call the Third Degree existed before the era of Grand Lodges, but that, having passed through a long decline, its symbols had become corrupted, and their meaning (to a great extent) forgotten, when the step itself—then known as the "Master's Part"—is first heard of (i.e.,

---

[28] *The Constitutions of Freemasons* (Bi-centenary Ed.), p. 61.

[29] *A. Q. C.*, xvi, p. 38.

[30] *A. Q. C.*, xvi, p. 36.

unequivocally referred to) in any print or manuscript to which a date can be assigned (1723).[31]

It seems probable that the original workings may have been compressed into two degrees, and the subsequent division into three degrees may well have been a rearrangement of the material in accordance with ancient tradition. Evidence for the working of three grades of Masonry occurs as early as 1725 in London in the *Transactions of the Philo-Musicae et Architecturae Societas* in which certain brethren are recorded as "regularly passed Masters," "regularly passed Fellow-Crafts" and "regularly passed fellow Craft and Master," although it is not clearly known exactly what took place.[32] By 1738 the procedure in the Lodges seems to have been generally similar to that known among us to-day.

OPPOSITION

That there was at first some distrust and dislike of the new movement, upon the part of older Masons, is certain. In the second edition of the Constitutions (1738) Anderson tells us that in 1720:

At some *private* Lodges, several very valuable *Manuscripts* (for they had nothing yet in print) concerning the Fraternity, their Lodges, Regulations, Charges, Secrets, and Usages (particularly one writ by Mr. *Nicholas Stone, the Warden of Inigo Jones)* were too hastily burnt by some scrupulous Brothers, that these Papers might not fall into strange Hands.[33]

We know that there were other Lodges not at first included in the Grand Lodge, and it may well be that certain of the older Brn. viewed the new venture with suspicion, and destroyed their records to prevent them from falling into the hands of innovators. There is a suggestion, too, that other traditions were preserved elsewhere in greater fullness, as we shall see in connection with the schism of the "Antients". But although the Grand Lodge was inaugurated humbly enough, it soon began to attract attention under the Duke of Montague, and its success as a movement was immediately established.

THE SUCCESSION OF I.M.s

The succession of I.M.s was preserved under the new dispensation, although there is little trace in London of a definite degree in the sense

---

[31]Gould. *Concise History,* p. 223.

[32]*Ibid.,* p. 228.

[33]*A. Q. C.,* xvi, p. 33. See *ante,* page 246.

of ritual working. Such a degree was part of the authorized working of the "Ancients" in 1751, though it was not adopted by the "Moderns" until 1810.[34] The actual power, however, was transmitted by the act of installation which forms the essential part of the sacrament, and we learn from the "Manner of Constituting a New Lodge according to the ancient Usages of Masons" given in the Constitutions of 1723, that after the new Master had submitted to the Charges of a Master "as Masters have done in all ages," the Grand Master shall "by certain significant Ceremonies and ancient Usages, install him".[35]

THE GRAND LODGES OF YORK, IRELAND AND SCOTLAND

But although the impulse towards revival clearly originated in London with the erection of the Grand Lodge of England, the Apple-Tree Tavern was not the only temple of the Mysteries. Other Lodges existed both in England and the sister-kingdoms, and other equally valid streams of tradition began to emerge in different centres. York was for unnumbered years a powerful and hallowed sanctuary of speculative Masonry; and the "old Lodge" at York proclaimed itself a Grand Lodge in 1725. It is even possible that it may have called itself such before, for there is written testimony in 1778 from the then York Grand Secretary to the effect that the Grand Lodge at York antedated the Lodge of London by twelve or more years.[36]

It is clear that ancient York workings existed, and that something of their tradition, passing through Irish and "Ancient" Masonry, is with us to-day, blended with the traditions inherited from Anderson. York has a glamour about its ancient walls like that which surrounds Kilwinning and the sanctuary which was Heredom; to York also we must look for one of the guardian-centres of our Mysteries.

It is clear from a study of Irish Masonry and that of the "Ancients," which was so closely allied to it, that more was handed down from the past than the three Blue degrees; for the latter on their own showing are not complete without the symbolism preserved for us in the Holy Royal Arch and other similar degrees, which did not, it would seem, emerge in the South. The first mention of the Holy Royal Arch comes from Youghal in Ireland in 1743; the second emanates from

---

[34]Gould. *Concise History*, p. 225.

[35]*The Constitutions of Freemasons* (Bi-centenary Ed.), p. 72.

[36]A. E. Waite. *Emblematic Freemasonry*, p. 59.

York in 1744. The "Ancients," though they had nothing to do with the "Grand Lodge of All England" at York, nevertheless persistently refer to themselves as York Masons, thus claiming kinship with the York tradition.

On the other hand, Murray Lyon shows that the records reveal no traces of ritual procedure or of speculative Masonry as we know it to-day until after the foundation of the Grand Lodge of England in 1717, and that the speculative ritual was derived from England after that event. No evidence exists to show that Lodge Kilwinning, the second Lodge in Scotland according to the Schaw Statutes, whose extant Minutes go back to 1642, ever worked any degrees other than those belonging to Craft Masonry, either before or after the formation of the Grand Lodge.

A Past Master of Lodge Canongate Kilwinning draws my attention to a serious mistake which I made in *The Hidden Life in Freemasonry* (p. 119) in describing that historic Lodge as founded in 1723. He says:

Lodge Canongate Kilwinning No. 2 received a Charter from the Mother Lodge at Kilwinning in Ayrshire (now known as Lodge Mother Kilwinning No. 0) dated 20th December, 1677, and recorded in the Minutes of Kilwinning Lodge on that date.

The Lodge history tells us that

At the beginning of the eighteenth century the Lodge numbered amongst its members the foremost noblemen and gentlemen of Scotland who were devoted to the Stuart cause.

The unsuccessful rising in 1715 sent those who had escaped death on the battlefield into exile: and during the confusion attendant on those times, the whole early records of the Lodge were lost or destroyed, and no trace of them can now be found. At length the survivors, a small but trusty band, met about the beginning of 1735 and resumed the meetings.

The earliest Minute in preservation is dated 13th February, 1735, and begins:

Cannongate, Feby. ye 13th A.D. 1735 A.M. 5735.
The Lodge having met according to adjournment do appoint....

The Lodge is never closed, but adjourned to the next fixed day of meeting.

Most Lodges install on S. John the Evangelist's Day, 27th December.

Lodge Canongate Kilwinning installs on S. John the Baptist's Day, 24th June. The earliest reference in the Minutes of this (or any Scottish) Lodge to the admission of Master Masons is on 31st March, 1735.

I apologize for the error in my previous book, and will see that it is corrected if a second edition should be needed.

The Grand Lodge of Ireland appears to have come into being in 1725, and the Irish rituals are clearly derived from a somewhat different line of tradition from those preserved in Southern England, being indeed closely allied with the York workings. The Grand Lodge of Scotland was formed in 1736; and here again we find marked differences of ritual and even of secrets, though there is no evidence on the physical plane to show whence this distinctive Scottish Masonry is derived. It is from these three Premier Grand Lodges, and from the Grand Lodge of the Ancients, now amalgamated with the Grand Lodge of England, that all Anglo-Saxon Masonry, and probably much of Continental Masonry also, has sprung. The details of their workings may differ in non-essentials, but the same hallowed Mysteries were the heritage of all, and through them have penetrated into all the world "to be a light to those who sit in darkness" and "to guide their feet into the way of peace".

THE "ANCIENTS"

As a further indication that the Grand Lodge of England had not inherited the only tradition current in the United Kingdom, we find the schismatic Grand Lodge of the "Ancients" formed in 1751 in London, under the title of the "Grand Lodge of England according to the old Institutions". The researches of Mr. Henry Sadler into the archives of the Grand Lodge prove that the establishment of this body was due to the activity of a number of Irish Masons resident in London.[37] They claimed affinity with the York tradition, though not with the York Grand Lodge; and it is clear that they differed considerably from the Modern or regular Grand Lodge of England. Their Grand Secretary, Lawrence Dermott, says:

The Ancients under the name of Free and Accepted Masons according to the old Institutions, and the Moderns under the name of Freemasons of England,

---

[37]Gould. *Concise History,* p. 252.

though similar in name, yet differ exceedingly in makings, ceremonials, knowledge, Masonic language, and installation, so much that they have always been, and still continue to be, two distinctive societies totally independent of each other.[38]

Furthermore he tells us something of the nature of such differences:

A Modern Mason may safely communicate all his secrets to an Ancient Mason, but an Ancient cannot with like safety communicate all his secrets to a Modern Mason without further ceremony. For as a Science comprehends an Art (though an Art cannot comprehend a Science), even so Ancient Masonry contains everything valuable among the Moderns, as well as many other things that cannot be revealed without additional ceremonies.[39]

There is little doubt that these differences consisted of changes in the 3°, the degree of I. M., and the Holy Royal Arch; and they are clearly the result of the inheritance of a different stream of Masonic tradition. It is almost certain that the Moderns did make innovations in the ritual; they seem to have exchanged the words of the First and Second Degrees, because of the exposures contained in Samuel Pritchard's *Masonry Dissected,* which had an enormous sale in England and on the Continent, and the old order is still preserved in Continental Masonry, especially in Lodges working what is known as the French Rite.

THE HOLY ROYAL ARCH

The first mention in contemporary records of the Holy Royal Arch occurs at Youghal in Ireland in 1743; and we hear of it again in 1744 in Dr. Dassigny's *"Serious and Impartial Enquiry into the cause of the Present Decay of Freemasonry in the Kingdom of Ireland,"* in which he tells us of the existence of an Assembly of Royal Arch Masons at York—from which city the degree was introduced into Dublin; that it was known and practised in London "some small space before"; and that the members thereof were "an organis'd body of men who have passed the chair".[40]

We have already seen how in ancient days the Royal Arch was associated with the 3°, as the Mark was with the 2°; and both these

---

[38]Quoted. *loc. cit.*

[39]*Ibid.*, p. 256.

[40]Quoted. *loc. cit.* p. 199.

items of ceremonial appear to have been included in that corpus of tradition which reached Anderson in 1717 or thereabouts, and to have been worked in private in certain of the Lodges from time immemorial, although they do not seem to have been formally sanctioned by the Grand Lodge. The first exoteric mention of the Mark Degree occurs in the Minute-Book of a Royal Arch Chapter in Portsmouth in 1769.[41] A careful study of existing rituals of both these degrees shows that considerable differences occur in English, Scottish and Irish workings; and it is clear that in their case also many lines of tradition were handed down. Bro. A. E. Waite refers to a ritual of the Old York Mark Lodge in his possession, which differs almost completely from any of our present workings.[42] It is not difficult to account for differences of ritual between "Ancients" and "Moderns," when we consider the number and variety of traditions handed down throughout the ages.

THE UNITED GRAND LODGE

In 1813 the two rival Grand Lodges of England formally united, and thenceforward the United Grand Lodge of England has been the governing body of Craft Masonry in that country. At the union an amalgamation took place between the two lines of tradition, and English Craft Masonry is indebted to Ireland and to York as well as to the Apple-Tree Tavern for its methods of working. According to the Articles of Union already noted it was agreed upon that for the future

Pure Antient Masonry consists of three degrees, and no more, viz., those of the Entered Apprentice, the Fellow Craft, and the Master Mason (including the Supreme Order of the Holy Royal Arch). But this Article is not intended to prevent any Lodge or Chapter from holding a meeting in any of the Degrees of the Orders of Chivalry, according to the Constitutions of the said Orders.[43]

In such wise the Masonic tradition became fixed, and it remains the same in essentials to-day.

CRAFT MASONRY IN OTHER COUNTRIES

It is commonly held that Masonry was introduced into France from England about 1732, though some think that it came in seven years

---

[41]Quoted. *loc. cit.*, p. 263.

[42]*Emblematic Freemasonry*, p. 62, note.

[43]*A. Q. C.*, xvi, 63.

earlier under Jacobite auspices. In reality it antedates that era altogether, for Masonic tradition of some sort had existed in France from time immemorial, and when King James II took refuge at Clermont Abbey in 1688 he found a Masonic centre there which he tried unsuccessfully to use for political purposes. Whether the English rite which was brought in at the date above-mentioned linked itself in any way with the indigenous Masonry is uncertain—there is no evidence upon the point—but French Masonry has diverged very considerably from the English workings.

The symbolic or blue degrees of the Ancient and Accepted Scottish Rite appear in many ways to preserve a fuller tradition, and they probably represent another line of descent, for they employ the ancient Chaldaean method of seating the three principal officers in an isosceles triangle. As in the regular Grand Lodge of England prior to 1810, there is no degree of I. M. worked on the Continent, except in bodies deriving authority from the Grand Lodge in London. The elected Master is placed in the Chair without ceremony, as in the older English working. The Grand Lodge of Scotland recognized the ceremonial degree only in 1872. It was derived from sources accessible to the "Ancients," possibly from York. Certain of the signs of the degree are found on the walls of Egyptian temples, and when its inner or occult side is studied, installation into the Ch.: of K.:S.: is found to have formed part of the genuine and immemorial tradition of the Mysteries.

Masonry is said to have appeared in Germany in 1733, though the first known Lodge was established in Hamburg in 1737; in Sweden it dates from 1735; while Dutch Masonry was inaugurated in 1731, when the Duke of Lorraine was initiated at the Hague by Dr. Desaguliers.[44] It was introduced into America before 1733, when the first Lodge holding written authority from the Grand Lodge of England was established in Boston.[45] It was in reality practised in America before the date of the founding of Grand Lodge, being carried thither by some of the earlier settlers. Many Lodges were constituted with Scottish, Irish and "Ancient" Warrants, which accounts for the many variations to be found in American workings. In America to-day there

---

[44]Gould, *Concise History,* p. 306.

[45]*Ibid.,* p. 333.

are over fifty Grand Lodges with a membership of at least two millions, many of whom also belong to various high degree Obediences.[46] There are nine Grand Lodges in Canada, with a hundred and twenty thousand members, and seven Grand Lodges in Australasia, with seventy-five thousand members.[47] Craft Masonry flourishes likewise in many other countries, and is unquestionably one of the greatest powers for good in the world in this twentieth century.

---

[46]*Ibid.*, p. 345.

[47]*Ibid.*, pp. 348, 349.

10

Other Lines of Masonic Tradition

THE STREAM OF SECRET SOCIETIES

IN the name of the Christ, the Lord of love and compassion, that body which called itself His Church and professed to follow Him had established a reign of terror throughout Europe, and plunged into a mad orgy of cruelty and unbridled wickedness such as the world has rarely seen even among the most degraded savages. It was this desperate condition of affairs that made necessary the intentional confusion of the inner truths of Freemasonry with the trade secrets of the operative guilds; but that was not the only method adopted by the Powers behind to carry on the tradition of the Light through those days of more than Cimmerian darkness. There were also certain societies, secret or semi-secret, which existed for the express purpose of perpetuating a noble and pure teaching.

Just because they had to work so warily and so quietly it is not easy to find traces of the activity of these organizations; but a very earnest Mason, Mrs. Isabel Cooper-Oakley, has devoted years of patient and laborious original research in many parts of Europe to the study of this subject, and has published the results of her toil in *Traces of a Hidden Tradition in Masonry and Mediaeval Mysticism*. From that book I extract the following list of mystical societies, interspersed with a few names of individual mystics:

In the third century we find Manes, the widow's son, the link for all of those who believe in the great work done by the "Sons of the Widow" and the Magian Brotherhood.

In the fourth century the central figure for all occult students is the great Iamblichus, the forerunner of the Rosicrucians.

From the third to the ninth century the following organizations and sects appear; Manichaeans; Euchites; Dionysian Artificers; Ophites; Nestorians; Eutychians, and the Magistri Comacini, of whom we may read in Llorente's *History of the Inquisition,* and in Professor Herzario's *I Maestri Comacini.* This author says: "In this darkness which extended over all Italy, only one small lamp remained alight, making a bright spark in the vast Italian necropolis. It was from the *Magistri Comacini.* Their names are unknown, their individual works unspecialized, but the breath of their spirit may be felt all through those centuries, and their name collectively is legion. We may safely say that of all the works of art between 800 and 1000 A.D., the greater and better part are due to that brotherhood—always faithful and often secret—of the *Magistri Comacini.*"

In the tenth century we find still the Manichaeans and the Euchites; also the Paulicians and the Bogomiles.

Eleventh century: the Cathari and Patarini, condemned by the Roman Church, both derived from the Manichaeans; the Paulicians with the same tradition, also persecuted; the Knights of Rhodes and of Malta; Scholastic Mystics.

Twelfth century: the Albigenses appear, probably derived from Manichaeans who settled in Albi; the Knights Templars, publicly known; the Cathari, widely spread in Italy; the Hermetists.

Thirteenth century: the Brotherhood of the Winkelers; the Apostolikers; the Beghards and the Beguinen; the Brothers and Sisters of the Free Spirit; the Lollards; the Albigenses, crushed out by the Catholic Church; the Troubadours.

Fourteenth century: the Hesychasts, the precursors of the Quietists; the Friends of God; German Mysticism, led by Nicholas of Basle; Johann Tauler; Christian Rosenkreutz; the great Templar persecution; the Fraticelli.

Fifteenth century: the Fratres Lucis at Florence, also the Platonic Academy; the Alchemical Society; Society of the Trowel; the Templars; the Bohemian Brothers, or Unitas Fratrum; the Rosicrucians.

Sixteenth century: the Rosicrucians became widely known; the Order of Christ, derived from the Templars; Cornelius Agrippa of Nettesheim, in connection with a secret association; Saint Teresa; S. John of the Cross; Philippe Paracelsus; the Fire Philosophers; Militia Crucifera Evangelica, under Simon Studion; the Mysteries of the Hermetic Masters.

Seventeenth century: the Rosicrucians; the Templars;, the Asiatische Brüder; Academia di Secreti, at the home of John Baptista Porta; the Quietists, founded by Michael de Molinos; and the whole group of Spanish mystics.

Eighteenth century: the Fratres Lucis, or the Knights of Light; the Rosicrucians; the Knights and Brothers Initiate of St. John the Evangelist from Asia, or the Asiatische Brüder; the Martinists; the Theosophical Society, founded in London, 1767, by Benedicte Chastamer, a mystic Mason; the Quietists; the Knights-Templars; some Masonic bodies.

The various sects and bodies here detailed should not be understood as belonging exclusively to the century under which they appear in the above classification. All that this list is intended to convey is that such sects were more markedly prominent during the century in which they are placed.[1]

Yet again Mrs. Cooper-Oakley writes with deep appreciation of the work done by the Troubadours:

From the death of Manes, A.D. 276, there was an intimate alliance—even a fusion—with some of the leading Gnostic sects, and thence do we derive the intermingling of the two richest streams of Oriental Wisdom: the one, directly through Persia from India; the other, traversing that marvellous Egyptian period, enriched by the wisdom of the great Hermetic teachers, flowed into Syria and Arabia, and thence with added force—garnered from the new divine powers made manifest in the profound mystery of the blessed Jesus—into Europe, through Northern Africa, finding a home in Spain, where it took deep root. From this stock sprang into full flower that richness of speech and song for which the Troubadours will live for ever, Manichaeans who sang and chanted the Esoteric Wisdom they dared not speak.

Next we see them dispersed in sects, taking local names—separated in name only, but using the same secret language, having the same signs. Thus, everywhere they journeyed, and no matter by what name they were called, each knew the other as a "widow's son," bound together on a Mystic Quest, knitted—by virtue of a secret science—into one community; with them came from the East a chivalric ideal, and they chanted of love and sang of heaven: but the love was a Divine Love, and their heaven was the wisdom and peace of those who sought the higher life.[2]

I have taken two long extracts from Mrs. Oakley's book, because it is the only one of which I know which treats in any detail of these little-known sects. Among them two stand out as better known or at

---

[1]*Op. cit.*, pp. 27-9.

[2]*Ibid.*, p. 124.

any rate more fully discussed than the others, and both of them have to a considerable extent influenced our modern Masonic rituals, especially those of the higher degrees. These two are the Knights Templars and the Brethren of the Rosy Cross.

THE KNIGHTS TEMPLARS

The Order of the Knights Templars, called also the Poor Knights of Christ and of the Temple of Solomon, was founded in 1118 by Hugues de Payens (Hugo de Paganis), a Knight of Burgundy, and Godefroid de St. Omer, a Knight of Northern France, in order to protect the pilgrims who flocked to the Holy Land after the First Crusade. Baldwin I, King of Jerusalem, allotted to those two knights and six others who joined with them quarters near the site of Solomon's Temple, whence their name Templars was derived.

Nine years later Hugues de Payens visited Europe with the object of placing the new Order upon a more secure foundation and of gaining recognition and a Rule from the Pope. He secured the enthusiastic support of S. Bernard, the great Abbot of Clairvaux, and in 1128 a Rule, which was drawn up for them by S. Bernard himself, was approved for the Knights Templars by the Council of Troyes. It was not, however, until 1163 that Pope Alexander III issued the charter of the Order, and its organization was fully established.

The Order of the Temple in the days of its glory consisted of various grades. The Knights (fratres milites) formed its most important section, at least from the military point of view; at their reception they were pledged to observe the three evangelical counsels of poverty, chastity and obedience,[3] like the members of all other religious orders throughout the Church. The Knights, who were often of high birth, were each entitled to three horses, a squire and two tents. Married men also received, but only on condition of bequeathing one half of their property to the Order. No women were admitted.

Besides these there was also a body of clergy (fratres capellani)—Bishops, priests and deacons—who were under the same vows as the Knights, and by special dispensation owed obedience to no superior, ecclesiastical or civil, except the Grand Master of the Temple and the

---

[3] *The Reception of a Templar.* Bro. E. J. Castle, K. C. in *A. Q. C.*, Vol. xv, p. 163.

Pope. It was laid down that the confessions of brethren of the Order should only be heard by these special clergy; and thus their secrets were guarded inviolate. There were also two classes of Serving Brothers, those bearing arms (fratres servientes armigeri), and the menials and craftsmen (fratres servientes famuli and officii).

At the head of the whole organization stood the Grand Master; next in rank came the Seneschal of the Temple, and the Marshal, the supreme authority in military affairs; and the Order was administered in Provinces under a number of Commanders. After the fall of the Latin Kingdom, the Headquarters of the Order were moved from Jerusalem to Cyprus, and Paris became the chief Templar centre in Europe.

The influence wielded by the Templars grew rapidly. They fought gallantly in the various Crusades, and also became the great international financiers and bankers of the age, thereby amassing vast riches. It is reckoned that before the middle of the thirteenth century they possessed nine thousand manors in Europe alone. The Paris Temple was the centre of the world's money market, and their influence and wealth in England also were very great. In the later part of that century they are said to have drawn a revenue amounting to nearly 2,500,000 in our money, more than that of any European kingdom or state of that time.[4] At this period the Templars were believed to number between 15,000 and 20,000 Knights and Clergy; but in attendance upon these there was a veritable army of squires, servants and vassals. Their influence may be estimated from the fact that members of the Order were summoned to the great Councils of the Church, such as the Lateran Council of 1215 and the Council of Lyons of 1274.[5]

The Knights Templars brought back to the West a set of symbols and ceremonies belonging to the Masonic tradition, and they possessed certain knowledge which is now given only in the degrees of the Ancient and Accepted Scottish Rite. The Order was thus one of the repositories of the Hidden Wisdom in Europe in the twelfth and

---

[4]*Quelques Reflexions sur les Origines de la Franc-Maconnerie Templiere,* par le Grand Commandeur du Supreme Conseil de Belgique (Count Goblet d'Alviella). Bruxelles, 1904, p. 8.

[5]See also *Encyclopaedia Britannica,* Art. *Templars,* from which much of the above information is derived.

thirteenth centuries, although the full secrets were given only to the few; alone, therefore, among the religious Orders, their ceremonies of reception were conducted in strict privacy. As was but natural in such an age, the most evil and horrible practices were attributed to the Order because of this secrecy, and stories were told which had absolutely no foundation whatever in fact.

In the Templar form of what we now call the 18°, the Most Wise Sovereign was an ordained priest or Bishop, and the bread and wine which was consecrated in open Chapter in the course of a splendid ceremony was a veritable Eucharist—a wonderful blending of the Egyptian with the Christian sacrament.

THE SUPPRESSION OF THE TEMPLARS

The suppression of this great and powerful Order forms one of the darkest blots upon the tenebrous history of the Roman Catholic Church. The reports of the French trial were published by Michelet, the great historian, in 1851-61 and an excellent digest of the evidence given both in France and England is contained in a series of articles which appeared in 1907 in *Ars Quattuor Coronatorum* (xx, 47, 112, 269). We can give here but a brief outline of what took place, referring those who wish for a more detailed account to the sources quoted, and to the general literature of the subject.

Philip the Fair, King of France, was in desperate need of money. He had already debased the coinage, had arrested the Lombard bankers and the Jews, and after confiscating their wealth upon a trumped-up charge of usury—a thing abhorrent to the mediaeval mind—had expelled them from his country. Then he determined to get rid of the Templars, who had lent him large sums, and since the Pope, Clement V, owed his position to the intrigues of Philip, the matter presented little difficulty. His task was rendered easier, too, by the accusations brought against the Order by the ex-knight Esquiu de Floyran, who had a personal interest in the matter, and pretended to reveal all manner of evil things—blasphemy, immorality, idolatry and the worship of the devil under the form of a black cat. This traitor is still execrated in some of the Masonic rituals, together with one Noffo Dei of Florence, who, however had nothing to do with the matter.

These charges were accepted by Philip with delight, and on Friday, October 13th, 1307, all the Templars throughout France were arrested without warning on behalf of the most infamous tribunal that has ever existed, a collection of demons in human form called in ghastly mockery the Holy Office of the Inquisition, which at this time held plenary jurisdiction in this and other countries of Europe. The Templars were horribly tortured, so that many died, and the remainder confessed in set terms whatever the Church required. The interrogations were concerned chiefly with the alleged denial of Christ and the spitting on the cross, and in a minor degree with certain grave charges of immorality. A study of the evidence reveals the entire innocence of the Templars and the diabolical ingenuity of the familiars of the Holy Office, who kept them separated without adequate defence or proper consultation, and circulated among them lying rumours that the Grand Master had confessed to the Pope that there were evils in the Order. The brethren were cajoled, bribed and tortured into confessing crimes they had never committed, and they were treated with the most fiendish cruelty.

Such was the "justice" of those who bore the name of the Lord of Love in the Middle Ages; such the compassion which was shown to His faithful servants, whose only crime was their wealth, lawfully won for the Order, and not for themselves. Philip the Fair obtained his money; but what karma, even in a thousand lives of suffering, could ever be sufficient for so vile a wretch? The Roman Church has doubtless many good deeds to its credit; but can all of them put together ever cancel such incredible wickedness as this?

The Pope desired to destroy the Order, and called a Council at Vienne in 1311 for that purpose, but the Bishops refused to condemn it unheard. The Pope, therefore, abolished the Order in private Consistory on November 22nd, 1312 (5312 A.L.—a date still commemorated in a striking fashion in our high-grade rituals), although he admitted that the charges were not proved. The riches of the Temple were to be transferred to the Order of S. John: but it is certain that the French portion found its way into the coffers of King Philip.

The last and most brutal act of this stupendous tragedy occurred on the 14th of March, 1314, when the venerable Grand Master of the Temple, Jacques de Molay, and Gaufrid de Charney, Preceptor of Normandy, were publicly burned as relapsed heretics before the great cathedral of Notre Dame. As the flames closed round him the Grand Master summoned the King and the Pope to meet him within a year before the judgment-seat of God, and both Pope and King were dead within twelve months.

THE PRESERVATION OF THE TEMPLARS' TRADITION

The destruction of the Order of the Temple did not, however, involve a complete suppression of the teaching enshrined within it. Certain of the French Knights Templars took refuge with their brethren of the Temple in Scotland, and in that country their traditions became mingled to some extent with the ancient Celtic rites of Heredom, thus forming one of the sources from which the Scottish Rite was later to be evolved. Traditions of vengeance upon the execrable King and Pope and the Traitor passed down throughout the ages, and were interwoven with the Egyptian tradition corresponding to our Black Masonry, culminating in what we now call the 30°.

It is not difficult to see how such a confusion might arise, especially among those who did not fully understand the inner meaning of the Egyptian teaching, and how a particular and temporary idea of vengeance might be blended with the philosophical doctrine of the meaning of evil and retribution and its place in the divine plan. It is these traditions of vengeance, however little understood, that form the basis of our 30° ritual, although in modern days the tendency has been to soften the harsh outlines as far as possible, to expunge all ideas of physical revenge, and even, as in the French rites, to delete all reference to the Templars and their wrongs.

Other streams said to be from the Order of the Temple are claimed as genuine by their modern representatives, but without sufficient reason. The French Ordre du Temple alleged a direct succession from Jacques de Molay, and produced in support thereof the celebrated Charter of Larmenius (which is usually considered a forgery); in any case the Ordre du Temple had no connection with modern Masonry. The Strict Observance, though it claimed to perpetuate Templar lines of thought, never, I believe, held its rituals to be of ancient origin, for these clearly belong to the eighteenth century. The modern Military and Religious Order of Knights Templars does not claim direct descent, though it may well embody certain genuine traditions. Its ritual is beautiful, and it appears to have been one of those rites which have been taken up by the H. O. A. T. F. and used. The real rites of the Templars have not survived, though it would no doubt be possible to reconstruct them, and certain traditions about them have passed down and become incorporated into various modern degrees.

THE ROYAL ORDER OF SCOTLAND

The most important of the bodies inheriting part of the Templar tradition is the Royal Order of Scotland, though it is in reality the result of the interaction of several lines of Masonic descent. As I have said on page 124, the doctrines which the Knights Templars brought with them from France when their Order was suppressed in their native country were intermingled with those of more than one of the existing Scottish rites. Those who founded it, or at least developed its teaching, appear to have been thoroughly eclectic, for in addition to the two sources above indicated they seem to have assimilated a certain amount of material from the Culdees, and also from the Jewish tradition, though using the symbology of the Second Temple. Ramsay quotes in connection with it the Jewish legend of the sword and trowel; and it is with the sword in one hand and the trowel in the other that the Brn. of the Royal Order still take their O. I have already referred to its curious old rhymed ritual, which bears internal evidence of antiquity, and teaches the search for a lost word which is eventually found in Christ.

The Order consists of two degrees, the first that of HRDM or Heredom, and the second of RSYCRS or the Rosy Cross. The degree of HRDM is divided into two parts, the Passage of the Bridge, and the Admission to the Cabinet of Wisdom. It has certain resemblances to some of the degrees of the Ancient and Accepted Scottish Rite. Its form has been very grossly corrupted to make it agree with the most extravagant form of modern protestantism, with references to the blood of Jesus, to the lamb and the book, etc. The quest for the Word is analagous to that undertaken in the Rose-Croix, though the degrees are quite different. Our 18° has little to do with the symbolism of the Royal Order, although the purpose of the two rites is the same. The 46° of the Rite of Mizraim (Sovereign Prince Rose-Croix of Kilwinning and of Heredom) has a close resemblance to the ritual of the Royal Order, bearing some of the signs and much of the essential meaning. Of all those bodies which may be thought of as developing into what afterwards became higher degrees, this Royal Order of Scotland was the first to formulate itself definitely, though little is heard of it in the outer world; and it may be taken as the primary type of the Scots degrees.

THE BROTHERS OF THE ROSY CROSS

The mysterious Order of the Rosy Cross still remains something of a problem to the student. The glamour of the Rosicrucian Philosophy has not yet passed away, and an enormous mass of controversial literature has gathered about the Order, many students affirming that it never existed at all, and that its famous manifestos were but an elaborate hoax played upon Europe by a few unscrupulous jesters; others say that the Society did exist, but that it was no more than an obscure Lutheran sect which thus cleverly advertised its opinions; others, again, think that it was a genuine school of wisdom, in which the deeper knowledge of life's secrets was given to the few who were prepared by long discipline to receive it.

THE LITERATURE OF ROSICRUCIANISM

The Order of the Rosy Cross was first made known to Europe by the publication in 1614 of the *Fama Fraternitatis of the Meritorious Order of the Rosy Cross, addressed to the Learned in General and the Govenors of Europe.* This was, according to mediaeval custom, bound up with another treatise: *A Universal Reformation of the Whole Wide World, by order of the God Apollo, is published by the Seven Sages of Greece, and some other Litterati.* Some have thought this latter to be a Rosicrucian pamphlet, but in reality it is a translation from the *Ragguagli di Parnasso* of Boccalini, and probably, as Michael Maier held, had no connection with the Order at all.[6]

The *Fama Fraternitatis* contains a description of the traditional life of Christian Rosenkreutz (b. A.D. 1378), the founding of the Order of the Rosy Cross, and his death and burial. This is followed by a highly symbolical account of the discovery of the Tomb of C.: R.: C.: by Brn. "of the third order and row of succession"; and finally the resolution of the Head of the Order that it should now be proclaimed to the Western world is narrated, and an invitation issued (in five languages) to the learned of Europe to join the Fraternity. It closes with the statement that

---

[6]A. E. Waite. *The Real History of the Rosicrucians*, p. 35.

Although at this time we make no mention either of our names or meetings, yet nevertheless everyone's opinion shal assuredly come to our hands, in what language so ever it be, nor any body shal fail, whoso gives but his name, to speak with some of us, either by word of mouth, or else, if there be some lett, in writing.[7]

This extraordinary document was followed in 1615 by another striking pamphlet, the *Confessio Fraternitas R. C. ad Eruditos Europae*, which was bound up in a Latin work entitled: *Secretioris Philosophiae Consideratio Brevio a Philippo a Gabella, Philosophiae studioso, conscripta*. In the *Confessio*, which is divided into fourteen chapters, we have a guarded account of the aims of the Society, the knowledge of nature's secrets contained within its different grades, the dawn of a new age of regeneration, and a consequent appeal to all those who had the welfare of mankind at heart, and who cared nothing for the folly and selfishness of the "ungodly and accursed goldmaking" mentioned in the *Fama*, to join the Order and partake of its privileges:

We affirm that we have by no means made common property of our arcana, albeit they resound in five languages within the ears of the vulgar, both because, as we well know, they will not move gross wits, and because the worth of those who shal be accepted into our Fraternity will not be measured by their curiosity, but by the rule and pattern of our revelations. A thousand times the unworthy may clamour, a thousand times may present themselves, yet God hath commanded our ears that they should hear none of them, and hath so compassed us about with His clouds that unto us, His servants, no violence can be done; wherefore now no longer are we beheld by human eyes, unless they have received strength borrowed from the eagle.[8]

The *Confessio* is clearly written by one deeply versed in genuine occult lore, and contains a veiled but unmistakable promise that real knowledge will be given to the earnest and unselfish aspirant.

A year later a third pamphlet was published at Strasburg called *The Chymical Marriage of Christian Rosenkreutz*, supposed to have existed in MSS. as early as 1601-2. It is dated Anno 1459, and commences with the following significant warning:

Arcana publicata vilescunt, et gratiam prophanata amittunt. Ergo: ne margaritas objice porcis, seu asino substernere rosas.[9]

---

[7]*Fama Fraternitatis*, quoted *op. cit.*, p. 83.

[8]*Confessio Fraternitatis*, quoted *op. cit.*, p. 90.

[9]"Published secrets become valueless, and things profaned lose their grace. Therefore cast not pearls before swine, nor strew roses before an ass." *Op. cit.*, p. 99.

—showing clearly that it was meant to be taken in a mystical sense. It is a long and cryptic account, lit with gleams of humour, of the initiation of Christian Rosenkreutz into the Mysteries of the Rosy Cross, commencing from his invitation, or awakening to the inner life, and ending with his final triumph or regeneration as a Knight of the Golden Stone. This is the most curious of all the Rosicrucian documents, and it will repay the close study necessary to its comprehension; for within it are contained some of the deepest secrets of spiritual alchemy.

The authorship of these pamphlets has always been a matter of speculation. They have all been attributed to Johann Valentine Andreas, a cultured and travelled German scholar of the seventeenth century, who was much interested in secret societies, and was a follower of the doctrines of Paracelsus. The arguments for and against his authorship are very ably given by Bro. A. E. Waite in his *Real History of the Rosicrucians,* and in his recent work, *The Brotherhood of the Rosy Cross,* in which, however he may mistake, in our opinion, as to the real purpose and aims of the original Order (the existence of which he denies) he has nevertheless brought together a mass of valuable facts which throw a good deal of light upon the whole question. Andreas acknowledges the *Chymical Marriage,* although he calls it a *ludibrium* or jest; from his later works he seems to have turned against the Order of the Rosy Cross, and started a new Society of his own. It is extremely unlikely, however, that Andreas was the author of the *Fama* and the *Confessio.*

These three documents raised an indescribable storm of curiosity all over Europe. Numbers of students wrote open letters applying to be admitted into the Order, and setting forth their qualifications; but none of these seem to have been openly answered. A multitude of pamphlets appeared, especially in Germany, some attacking the Society, and others no less valiantly defending it; while many charlatans arose, claiming to be Brethren of the R. C., and relieving the credulous of their superfluous money. The most noted of the opponents of Rosicrucianism was Andreas Libavius of Halle, who wrote three treatises against the Order, in the last of which, "though posing as a critic, he advises all persons to join the Order, because there is much to be learned and much wisdom to be gained by so doing."[10]

On the Rosicrucian side we may note the *Echo of the God-illuminated Brotherhood of the Venerable Order R.C.,* published in 1615, and

---

[10] *The Real History of the Rosicrucians,* p. 252.

supposed to have been written by Julius Sperber of Anholt, in which
he asserts that the Rosicrucians possessed deep wisdom, although only
a few had been accounted worthy to partake of it. The *Echo* claimed
to embody absolute proof that the statements of *Fama* and *Confessio*
were possible and true, that the facts had been commonly familiar to
certain God-fearing people for more than nineteen years, and that they
were on record in secret writings.[11] Another pamphlet published in
1617, the *Fraternitatis Rosatae Crucis Confessio Recepta*, declares that
it requires much study and careful research, as well as personal
sacrifice, to become the possessor of transcendental secrets.[12]

But the literature of the Rosy Cross was by no means confined to
pamphlets. A system of philosophy was put before Europe through
their mediation, a philosophy which bears a striking resemblance to
that of the theurgic Neoplatonism of the third and fourth centuries of
our era. Many great names are associated with the Order; among them
was Michael Maier, who died in 1622, after writing the *Silentium post
Clamores* (1617); the *Symbola Aureae Mensae* (1617), and the *Themis
Aurea* (1618)—all of which expound and defend Rosicrucian and
alchemical philosophy. Thomas Vaughan, although not an actual
member of the Society, was in close sympathy with its tenets, and
translated into English the *Fama Fraternitatis* and the *Confessio*. There
were Robert Flood, a great English Rosicrucian philosopher, author
of the *Tractatus Apologeticus*, the *Tractatus Theologo-Philosophicus*,
and other works; "Sincerus Renatus," or Sigmund Richter, who
published in 1710 the curious work, *The Perfect and True Preparation
of the Philosophical Stone, according to the secret of the Brotherhoods
of the Golden and Rosy Cross*, with which is included the *Rules of
the above-mentioned Order for the initiation of new Members;* and,
lastly, the author of the *Secret Symbols of the Rosicrucians of the Sixteenth and Seventeenth Centuries*, a rare book containing a number
of occult engravings which enshrine much inner teaching.

THE TRADITIONAL HISTORY OF THE ROSICRUCIANS

The traditional history of Christian Rosenkreutz is contained in the
Fama Fraternitatis, but it obviously cannot be accepted literally as it

---

[11]*The Brotherhood of the Rosy Cross*, p. 254.

[12]*The Real History of the Rosicrucians*, p. 256.

stands. It is clearly intended to bear an allegorical and mystical meaning, like all the traditional histories in the mystic schools; and, although
certain historical facts may well be woven into its structure, they can
only be subordinate to the living truth its author has sought to convey.
Origen clearly states the principle always used in the Mysteries in his
De Principiis:

Where the Word found that things done according to the history could be
adapted to these mystical senses, he made use of them, concealing from the
multitude the deeper meaning; but where, in the narrative of the development
of supersensual things, there did not follow the performance of those certain
events which were already indicated by the mystical meaning, the Scripture
interwove in the history the account of some event that did not take place,
sometimes what could not have happened; sometimes what could, but did not.[13]

This is one of the methods by which the secret teachings are guarded
from the profane, who throw them aside, thinking that as history they
are inaccurate and uninteresting, and so completely miss their deeper
meaning.

The *Fama Fraternitatis,* which admittedly contains only a tradition,
written down long after the events recorded had taken place, tells us
how C.: R.: C.: was born in A.D. 1378, of poor but noble parents,
and how he entered a monastery at a very early period of his life.
While still quite young, he is said to have journeyed to Cyprus with
a Brother P.A.L., who died there. He then crossed to Palestine, and
came into touch at the age of sixteen with the wise men of Damcar
in Arabia,

Who received him not as a stranger (as he himself witnesseth), but as one
whom they had long expected; they called him by his name, and shewed him
other secrets out of his cloyster, whereat he could not but mightily wonder.[14]

There he learnt Arabic, translated into Latin the book M., which
he afterwards brought to Europe, and in which Paracelsus was said
to have been interested; and thence he travelled to Egypt and to Fez,
to become acquainted with the "Elementary Inhabitants, who revealed
unto him many of their secrets".

---

[13]Origen, Bk. IV, Chap. i, 15 (Ante-Nicene Library Ed.).

[14]*Fama Fraternitatis,* quoted in *The Real History, etc.,* p. 67, from which
translation the citations following are also taken.

From Fez the Founder of the Order is said to have crossed into Spain, where he offered his knowledge to the learned, but "to them it was a laughing matter". He therefore returned to Germany, his own native country, determining gradually to begin there the foundation of the brotherhood that was destined to reform Europe. He chose three brethren out of his own monastery to be the first Rosicrucians; and later increased the number to eight, binding them by certain definite rules.

The brethren then went forth to the world, leaving only two of their number to remain with the head of the Order. In due time, Christian Rosenkreutz died, and was buried very secretly in the tomb prepared for him, his resting-place remaining unknown even to members of the fraternity.

At a later period, a seeming accident revealed the door of the tomb, upon which was written in great letters: "Post cxx Annos Patebo"— "After a hundred and twenty years I will come forth." In the midst of the tomb there shone a blazing star, and upon the altar in the centre of the vault these significant words were engraved: "A. C. R. C. Hoc universi compendium unius mihi sepulchrum feci" — "I have made this my tomb a compendium of the universe." Beneath the altar was found "a fair and worthy body. . .with all the ornaments and attires. In his hand he held the parchment called T., the which next unto the Bible is our greatest treasure, which ought not to be delivered to the censure of the world." Various other objects were discovered— "looking-glasses of divers virtues, little bells, burning lamps, and chiefly wonderful artificial songs'—and most important of all, the secret Book M. and other volumes, including certain of those of Paracelsus, the philosopher and chemist of the sixteenth century.

Such is the traditional history of Christian Rosenkreutz, as contained in the documents of the Order. The form in which the story is cast shows that it is obviously not intended to be an historical narrative. It is clearly designed as an allegory to express certain hidden truths to those whose eyes are opened, even though historical details are probably contained within it.

THE HISTORY OF THE ORDER

Despite the assertions of scholars and the absence of corroborative evidence, Christian Rosenkreutz did indeed found the Order of the Rosy Cross, and he was in fact an incarnation of that mighty Master of the Wisdom whom we revere to-day as the H. O. A. T. F. He was born in 1375, three years before the date given in the *Fama*, and was sent, when quite young, to a lonely monastery on the borders of Germany and Austria, where he received his education and training. Like many such communities in the Middle Ages, this monastery preserved a secret tradition, and its monks, who devoted themselves to meditation, were possessed of genuine spiritual and occult knowledge. Here Christian Rosenkreutz studied those deeper secrets of nature of which chemistry is but the outer shell, that alchemy which is concerned primarily with the transformation of the lead of the personality into the gold of the spirit, and only secondarily with the transmutation of metals and the manufacture of jewels. Christian Rosenkreutz now began to travel, and after passing through Germany, Austria and Italy, finally reached Egypt, where he was welcomed by the Brethren of the Egyptian Lodge of that White Brotherhood to which in past lives he had belonged.

In Egypt Christian Rosenkreutz was received into all the degrees of the Egyptian Mysteries, which had been preserved by the White Lodge in direct succession from the hierophants of old; and through him we may trace one of the most important of the lines of succession which eventually became incorporated into the Ancient and Accepted Scottish Rite. Among other things he adapted, and translated into Latin from the Egyptian, that Ritual of the Rosy Cross to which we have already referred, and this became the prototype of the Ceremony of Perfection worked in the Sovereign Chapters of Co-Masonry to-day.

On his return from Egypt Christian Rosenkreutz founded the Order of the Rosy Cross, choosing here and there a brother who was worthy to be brought into touch with the secret Mysteries of Egypt and the profound occult knowledge which they enshrined. The Order was always extremely limited in numbers, some thirty or forty at most, but it had an enormous effect upon the secret tradition in Europe, and indeed formed a Western school through which the White Lodge might be directly reached. In later days a portion of its teaching and ritual passed into less exclusive hands, and it is through one of these semi-exoteric bodies that the Rose-Croix Ritual was transmitted into the keeping of the Council of Emperors of the East and West.[15]

---

[15]See chapter xi.

During its passage through many hands ignorant of its true meaning that Ritual has suffered much distortion, being on the one hand
blended with protestant Christianity, as in English and American workings, or rationalized beyond recognition under the auspices of the
Supreme Council of France. In our Co-Masonic Order we have the
great privilege of using, by order of the H. O. A. T. F., an English
translation of His original Latin ceremonial and I think that we may
say without exaggeration that it is one of the most stately and beautiful
rituals of the Rose-Croix in existence.

The Rose-Croix, as we have said before, is essentially a degree of
Christhood, concerned with the awakening of the Christ mystical within
the heart, the hidden Love which is the heart of the mystic rose, and
which can only be known when the heart is laid upon the Cross of
Sacrifice; but it was not originally intended to be an appendage to
Christianity, as it has now become in England, but rather an independent sacramental channel through which the Lord of Love may pour
down His Blessing upon initiates of every faith, for it was founded
thousands of years before the birth of the disciple Jesus in Palestine.
Thus although it is the Christ, the Second Person of the Blessed Trinity,
who is adored in the Rose-Croix, the Christ whose Love is outpoured
in the Sovereign Chapters of Heredom, in our Co-Masonic Ritual we
speak of Him only as the Lord of Love, and do not bind our Brn.
especially to the doctrines of the last great faith which He founded
in person on earth; for He is the Lord of all religions alike, and the
Rose-Croix is no less His than the glorious sacraments of the Christian
Church which He Himself gave two thousand years ago.

The original Order of the Rosy Cross still exists in utter secrecy,
and, although it is unknown in the outer world, its Mysteries are yet
handed down on the physical plane, and it still preserves the ancient
secrets of healing and magic which its M. W. S. brought in the fifteenth
century from the Egyptian Lodge. Only very few, and those high
Initiates of the White Lodge from whence it came, are admitted to
its House of the Holy Spirit. Many have claimed and still claim to
belong to it, but it is quite independent of the many Orders and
Societies, both open and secret, which bear its hallowed name in the
twentieth century. In Masonry, however, we inherit some portion of
its ritual, though but little of its hidden lore, and the sacramental powers
of the Rosy Cross yet shine through certain of our high grades in the

Ancient and Accepted Scottish Rite. There is thus good reason why modern Masons have claimed affinity with the Rosy Cross, and why it has exercised so fascinating an influence over the minds of men since it was first heard of in the seventeenth century.

It is the nearest approach to "a higher degree" that existed in ancient Egypt; in fact, we may say that to all intents and purposes it *was* a higher degree, though it never called itself so. I have explained in *The Hidden Life in Freemasonry* that in Egypt thousands of years ago there were three Grand Lodges which differed from all the rest in their objects and workings, and that it was these three Lodges which, at certain stated times every year, undertook the duty of flooding the land with spiritual force by means of the magnificent ritual of *The Building of the Temple of Amen*.[16] When the Brn. were performing that holy duty they showed their solidarity with ordinary Masonry by opening in the 1° and raising the Lodge as quickly as possible to the 3° before commencing their wonderful work; on the comparatively rare occasions when they had to admit a candidate carefully selected from one of the Craft Lodges, they did *not* open in Blue Masonry at all, but plunged straight into this ceremony of the Rose-Croix.

The ritual had to be modified somewhat in the eighteenth century to bring it into harmony with the system of higher degrees which it had then been thought well to adopt; the list and explanation of those degrees were added, and also the reference to Jerusalem. The Word, which in modern Masonry has degenerated into mere initials, was then in itself a living "word of power," pregnant with deepest meaning, though a double scheme of initials was also used. All this needed and received the most skilful attention when the translation from Egyptian into Latin was made; one cannot but admire the marvellous ingenuity which, while changing the language, yet contrived to keep practically intact the sound, the form, and an elaborate triple set of meanings, one within the other. The eighteenth century additions have considerably lengthened the ceremony, but they are congruous with the older part, so that it still retains its transcendent beauty; and all the principal features of the degree—the rose, the cross, the cup, the sacrament— are precisely the same as they were thousands of years ago.

---

[16]*The Hidden Life in Freemasonry*, p. 290.

11

The Scottish Rite

ORIGIN OF THE RITE

THE origin of the Ancient and Accepted Scottish Rite of 33°, or rather that of the Rite of Perfection or of Heredom of 25° out of which it was evolved, has been one of the most obscure Masonic problems; practically nothing is known about it by scholars, since no authentic contemporary evidence is preserved in available documents or publications. This silence need cause but little wonder to the student who has followed us so far, for, like many other activities both in politics and religion, the high-grade Masonry of the early eighteenth century was *intended* to be kept secret, and the secrecy was preserved by committing nothing to writing and leaving no trace on the physical plane. I cannot expect that my statements will be accepted by Masonic scholars who pin their faith to documents alone, but I shall nevertheless give a brief account of what actually took place, supplying corroborative evidence whenever possible from reliable historians, so far as their works are available to me. This book is written in Australia, far away from the chief centres of Masonic life and learning, and I have consequently had to depend largely upon the resources of my own library. If I had access to a larger selection of Masonic volumes I should no doubt be able to find other fragments of valuable testimony.

THE JACOBITE MOVEMENT

There has been a persistent tradition among Continental writers upon Masonry that the Jacobites had much to do with the development of the higher degrees of the eighteenth century; and, as Bro. R. F. Gould points out, colour is lent to this view by the fact that the earliest names mentioned in connection with Freemasonry in France are those of well-known adherents of the Stuarts, although he himself rejects the hypothesis for lack of sufficient evidence.[1] We have the direct and personal testimony of Baron von Hund, the founder of the Rite of the Strict Observance, given in 1764, that he himself was received into the Order of the Temple in Paris in 1743 by ''an unknown Bro., the Knight of the Red Feather, in the presence of Lord Kilmarnock[2]. . .and that he was subsequently introduced as a distinguished Brother of the Order to Charles Edward Stuart, the Young Pretender''.[3] From papers found after his death it is clear that von Hund regarded the Knight of the Red Feather as Prince Charles himself. The life of von Hund shows him to have been a man of stainless honour who had made great sacrifices for the cause which he had at heart; and although it has been said that in 1777 Prince Charles denied to an emissary of the Strict Observance[4] that he had ever been a Freemason, such an official démenti is not unknown even to-day in political circles, and perhaps we need not attach great importance to it.

The Scottish adherents of King James II, who followed him into exile after the landing of the Prince of Orange in 1688, brought to the English Court at S. Germains (which had been placed at the disposal of the King by Louis XIV) those ancient rites of Heredom and Kilwinning, intermingled with the Templar tradition, to which we have already referred. When King James II fled from England he took refuge at the Jesuit Abbey of Clermont, which had attached to it a College of Clermont in Paris, founded by Guillaume du Prat, Bishop of

---

[1]Gould. *Hist. Freem.*, III, 78.

[2]At that time Grand Master of the Grand Lodge of Scotland, and Master of Lodge Kilwinning on his election to that high office in 1742. *Ibid.*, p. 53

[3]*Ibid.*, p. 101.

[4]*Ibid.*, p. 110.

Clermont, in 1550.[5] There, most unexpectedly, the King found a Masonic centre, working rites which had been handed down in France from a remote past. An intermingling of two traditions thus took place, and it was at this period—many years before the revival in 1717—that certain of the ceremonies which are to-day included in the Ancient and Accepted Scottish Rite were first put together.

It is probably this fact which gave birth to that other recurring tradition that the Jesuits were connected with the development of high-grade Masonry on the Continent; and it is from this indigenous French tradition, of which another branch had found its way into the Compagnonnage, that the rituals of French Craft Masonry—so different from the English—were derived. A further intermingling with the English tradition transmitted through Anderson no doubt took place after 1717.

King James conceived the idea of trying to use Freemasonry to assist him in his endeavour to regain his throne; but this attempt failed, for, though they sympathized with the King, the Masonic authorities staunchly refused to abandon their traditional neutral policy, or to allow the Order to become a cloak for political intrigue. The Jacobite influence nevertheless left its traces upon this part of Masonry, and in the Ancient and Accepted Scottish Rite the 14° is still called, under some Obediences, Grand Scottish Knight of the Sacred Vault of James VI, though its older name was Grand, Elect, Ancient Perfect Master.[6] Baron von Hund spoke the truth when he claimed to have met Prince Charles in Paris in 1743, and he seems to have inherited certain lines of succession which afterwards became the heart of the Rite of the Strict Observance. After the Battle of Culloden in 1746, which practically destroyed the Jacobite movement, the connection of the Stuarts with Masonry was dropped, and it seems probable that Baron von Hund himself composed the Latin Rituals of the Strict Observance, which played a considerable part in German Masonry in the eighteenth century.[7]

---

[5]*The Catholic Encyclopaedia* (1913), Vol. xiv, p. 88.

[6]A. E. Waite. *Secret Tradition in Freemasonry,* Vol. I, p. 125.

[7]Gould. *Hist. Freem.,* III, 101.

THE ORATION OF RAMSAY

After the year 1740 "Scots Degrees" sprang up in all parts of France,[8] and their creation and development are largely attributable to the celebrated Oration delivered in 1737 in the Provincial Grand Lodge of England in Paris by the Chevalier Ramsay; although the first published reference to a "Scotch Masons' Lodge" occurs as early as 1733 in London.[9]

Ramsay was born in 1681 or 1682 at Ayr near Kilwinning (though he does not seem ever to have joined that ancient Lodge). He was converted to Catholicism by Archbishop Fenelon, whose *Life* he wrote and with whom he continued to live till his death in 1715. After that he acted as tutor to the two sons of the rightful King James III in Rome. He was unquestionably a learned man, a deep student both of ancient and modern history, a D.C.L. of Oxford University and, like many other prominent Freemasons of the period, a Fellow of the Royal Society. He never appears to have taken much interest in Masonry, though he wrote to Cardinal Fleury, the Prime Minister of France, in 1737 asking his protection for the Freemasons, and stating that their ideals were very high and most useful to religion, literature and the state. He died in 1743.

But although Ramsay never did much work for Masonry, the Oration which he delivered in 1737 before the Provincial Grand Lodge of England in Paris, of which he was Grand Chancellor and Orator, had a profound influence upon French Masonry. It was a tolerably good Oration, but nothing very extraordinary. None the less it appears to have given just that impetus that was needed to set the French high-grade movement in activity, and ever afterwards the makers of high grades looked to Ramsay as their pattern and ensample.

He proclaimed the ideal of Masonry to be a Universal Brotherhood of cultured men, a Spiritual Empire that would change the world. He refers to the three degrees, and calls them Novices or Apprentices, Fellows or Professed Brothers, Masters or Perfected Brothers—a slightly different set of titles which may refer to a different stream

---

[8]*Ibid.*, p. 92.

[9]R. F. Gould, *A.Q.C.*, XVI, 44.

of tradition. These are required to practise respectively the moral virtues, the heroic virtues and the Christian virtues.

According to him, Masonry was founded in remote antiquity and was renewed or restored in the Holy Land at the time of the Crusades. It has affinities with the ancient Mysteries, especially those of Ceres at Eleusis, Isis in Egypt and others. The Crusaders adopted a set of "ancient signs and symbolical words drawn from the well of religion," which were intended to distinguish Crusader from Saracen, and were concealed under strict pledges of secrecy. The intimate union between the Crusading Masons and the Knights of S. John of Jerusalem is the reason why the Blue degrees are called S. John's Masonry. The returning Crusaders brought Lodges of Masonry to Europe, and from thence they were introduced into Scotland, where "James, Lord Steward of Scotland, was Grand Master of a Lodge established at Kilwinning, in the West of Scotland in 1286, shortly after the death of Alexander III, King of Scotland, and one year before John Baliol mounted the throne".

Ramsay goes on to explain that by degrees our Lodges and rites were neglected almost everywhere, but nevertheless they were preserved in all their integrity amongst those Scotsmen to whom the kings of France confided during many centuries the safeguarding of their royal persons. He allows that "Great Britain became the seat of our Order, the conservator of our laws and the depository of our secrets". Many of our rites and usages which were contrary to the prejudice of the reformers were changed, disguised or suppressed. Thus it was that many Brn. forgot the spirit and retained only the shell of the outer form. Masonry however is to be restored to its pristine glory in the future.

The rituals of these Scots Degrees are varied, but one chief idea underlies them all—the discovery in a vault by Scottish Crusaders of the long-lost and ineffable Word, during the search for which they had to work with the sword in one hand, and the trowel in other.[10] This same symbolism of the sword and the trowel is mentioned in Ramsay's speech, in which he derives Freemasonry from the patriarchs and the ancient Mysteries through the Scottish crusaders; and they are further mentioned both in the present ritual of the Royal Order of Scotland, in which the candidate takes his O. with a sword in one

---

[10]*Hist. Freem.*, III, p. 92.

hand and a trowel in the other,[11] and in a quotation from that ritual occurring as early as 1736 in print at Newcastle.[12] We hear of two Scottish degrees being received by Baron C. Scheffer, the first Grand Master of Sweden, in 1737,[13] and we may perhaps suggest—though in opposition to the theory held by most Masonic writers—that the oration of Ramsay, although it may have helped to popularize Scottish Masonry, was in reality an effect rather than the cause of the introduction of high-grade Masonry on the Continent, which was all the time being quietly directed from behind by the H.O.A.T.F.

The Scots Masters claimed extraordinary privileges in the French Craft Lodges, and these were formally recognized by the Grand Lodge of France in 1755.[14] They wore distinctive clothing, remained covered in a Masters' Lodge, claimed the right to confer the Craft degrees with or without a ceremony; and eventually the Scots Lodge actually appointed the W. M. of the corresponding Craft Lodge without consulting the Brn. over whom he was to rule. They further usurped the privilege of the Grand Lodge and issued warrants of constitution. One of the most important of these is the Mere-Loge-Ecossaise of Marseilles, said to have been constituted in 1751, which worked a number of degrees not belonging to what afterwards became the Scottish Rite, but later incorporated—at least as far as their titles are concerned—in the Rite of Memphis of 96°. These Scots Lodges or still more, the Royal Order of Scotland from which they arose, form the first public manifestation of the movement for creating high degrees which reached such a fervour of activity in the latter half of the eighteenth century.

THE CHAPTER OF CLERMONT

Our main channel of descent lies behind the Scots Lodges, and first appears indubitably in the outer world in the Chapter of Clermont, commonly thought to have been founded by the Chevalier de Bonneville

[11]A. E. Waite. *Secret Tradition in Freemasonry,* Vol. I, p. 404.

[12]*A.Q.C.,* XV, 186.

[13]Gould. *Concise History,* p. 300.

[14]Gould. *Hist. Freem.,* III, p. 95.

in 1754,[15] but in reality a continuation of that same Order of the Temple into which Baron von Hund was received in 1743, which was derived from the Scottish courtiers exiled at S. Germains and from the College of Clermont. According to Thory (who, however, wrote sixty years after the event) this Chapter was based on the three degrees of Blue Masonry, the Scots or S. Andrew's Degree, and worked three higher grades—5, Knight of the Eagle or Select Master; 6, Illustrious Knight or Templar; 7, Sublime Illustrious Knight.

In the later form in which it emerges in 1754 both Jacobite and Jesuit connections had been dropped, and the succession, together with certain ceremonial degrees, probably including a form of the Kadosh, had passed into the hands of distinguished French noblemen, courtiers, military officers, and the *elite* of the professions.[16] It was in this Chapter of Clermont and in the Council of the Emperors of the East and West into which it was transformed in 1758, that the colossal work of casting the ancient traditions into a ceremonial rite was to a great extent performed; and it is in these two bodies, which were yet one body, that the immediate origin of our Ancient and Accepted Scottish Rite is to be found.

THE COUNCIL OF EMPERORS

The Council of Emperors was composed largely of men of noble birth and high culture who were also deep students of the secret science, learned in various traditions of the wisdom which had been handed down along so many lines in the past. They had inherited not only the Clermont Rites and the Scottish lines of Kilwinning and of Heredom, but other traditions derived directly from both Templar and Rosicrucian sources, together with the powers of the Egyptian rite to which we have previously referred. They were men of wide knowledge, but also apparently of overweening pride, like so many of the nobles of the *ancien regime;* and the drawing together of this body of noblemen was one of the attempts made by the emissaries of the White Lodge to prepare them for the great changes which should have been accomplished, had not their pride been so great, without the horrors of the French Revolution.

---

[15]*Ibid.*, p. 94.

[16]*Ibid.*, p. 95.

A definite commission appears to have been given to them by the H. O. A. T. F., the Master the Comte de S. Germain Himself, to mould all these various traditions, which He had caused them to inherit, into a rite which should express to some extent the power for good of the Egyptian succession in a form suited to a more modern age. These orders they proceeded to carry out as faithfully as possible, and the result of their labours was the Rite of Perfection or of Heredom of twenty-five degrees, all of which are still contained in our modern Ancient and Accepted Scottish Rite.

The Council of Emperors received much inspiration from the H. O. A. T. F., although not necessarily on the physical plane, and it must have been far easier to influence such a body of men than the frequentors of those Georgian taverns which were the first temples of the English Mysteries after the great revival in 1717. But, as with many other attempts to synthesize a number of traditions by a committee of revision, the Council of Emperors was hampered in its work by the necessity of including less important materials which had come into the hands of certain of its members. The result is seen in the inclusion of several almost meaningless intermediate degrees, which still belong to the Scottish Rite, but are seldom or never worked among us.

A certain marriage of traditions took place in the case of the 18°, for the great ritual of the Rosy Cross used for the perfecting of the Rosicrucian and Egyptian Brethren, though shorn already of much of its ancient splendour, was blended with the old Mithraic Eucharist handed down in the Rites of Heredom, to form the source of our modern workings of the Rose-Croix. The Emperors' Ritual of the 30°, then called the 24°, Grand Commander of the Black and White Eagle, Grand Elect Kadosh, reflected far more efficiently the Egyptian teachings of Black Masonry than those which have to-day reached us through the hands of many editors, who were ignorant of their true meaning. The highest Degree among them was the 25°, now our 32°, called Most Illustrious Prince of Masonry, Grand and Sublime Knight Commander of the Royal Secret; and the Tracing Board of the 32°, often little understood, reflects their original plan of union with the Hidden Light through the passing of many rites of initiation.

There was no degree of Sovereign Grand Inspector-General, for the 33° as such did not yet exist; but the wonderful powers which now belong to that high rank were conferred upon their Grand Inspectors, chosen from among the Prince Masons of the 25°; and the great white Angels who wear the insignia of the KING were linked with these, even as they are linked with the Brn. of the 33° to-day. The crimson Angels of the Rosy Cross likewise attended their Sovereign Chapters, and many other glorious powers which are ours to-day were theirs also. Thus the Council of Emperors represents the first real attempt ever made to incorporate the full Egyptian inner tradition into a ceremonial form; and as such it is an important landmark in the history of Masonry.

Almost all the splendid teaching given by the great Master the Comte de St. Germain, by Pere Joseph and Cagliostro, and other emissaries of the White Lodge, was swept into oblivion in the colossal tragedy of the French Revolution. The Rite of Perfection of twenty-five degrees was carried into Great Britain, and handed down among the Templar Encampments long before the advent of the Supreme Councils of the Scottish Rite which derived their authority from Charleston. Most of the Brn. of the old Rite joined the new Obediences as soon as they were formed; but there exists to-day one line of tradition at least, in part derived from those old Templar Encampments, which has never been incorporated in the Supreme Councils of England, Scotland and Ireland. There was also a perpetuation in France, which later amalgamated with the French Supreme Council.[17]

STEPHEN MORIN

The scene of our story now shifts to the New World; for it was there that the change from the Rite of Perfection of 25° into the Scottish Rite of 33° took place. In 1761, three years only after its foundation, the Council of the Emperors of the East and West granted a patent to one Stephen Morin "to establish perfect and sublime Masonry in all parts of the world," constituting him a Grand Inspector of the Rite of Perfection. The patent authorized him to "form and establish a Lodge in order to admit to and multiply the Royal Order of Masons in all the perfect and sublime degrees," and gave him power to create other Inspectors. The original of this document has not yet been found, and the world knows of it only from the copy preserved in the Golden Book of the Comte de Grasse-Tilly, founder of the Supreme Council 33° of France. Bro. R. F. Gould, however, has a right intuition in the

---

[17]Gould. *Hist. Freem.*, p. 164.

matter, for he "is by no means prepared to deny its authenticity," and a complete transcription of it is given in his *History of Freemasonry*.[18] It is signed by Chaillon de Joinville, Prince de Rohan, Brest-de-la-Chaussee, Comte de Choiseul, and others of the Council of the Emperors. In 1761, Stephen Morin arrived in San Domingo, where he commenced the dissemination of the rite, and appointed many Inspectors both for the West Indies and the United States.[19]

He was unfortunately by no means an ideal Channel for spiritual force, and although he certainly transmitted to his American Brn. the Egyptian succession of powers, he was sometimes not in possession of the fullness of the power himself. At times he rose splendidly to the occasion, and showed signs of distinct advancement; I have watched him during the consecration of a Chapter of the high degrees magnificently overshadowed by the H.O.A.T.F. Himself and the great white Angels. But it cannot be denied that he had many faults, among others a passion for amorous intrigues; and not infrequently the greater part of his spiritual heritage was withdrawn, leaving him the mere seeds of the succession to transmit to others. The reports of his misdoings were so numerous and persistent that at one time the Council of Emperors actually withdrew his patent; but posts were slow in those days, and before the withdrawal reached him the Council had already cancelled it, and fully reinstated him.

Stephen Morin was also unfortunate in his choice of lieutenants, for in many cases these were Jews of not very good repute; and it is through these somewhat soiled hands that we must trace the Rite of Perfection during the next forty years. The rite passed through a period of obscuration, when the degrees were shamelessly sold to any who would buy their titles, and the inner meaning of the ceremonies was almost forgotten. But although the splendid occult knowledge of the Emperors was lost and the rites became shorn of most of their power, the seeds of the succession still passed down—until a higher class of egos was guided into the rite and a new era began. The rite was established at Charleston in 1783 by Isaac da Costa, who was created Deputy-Inspecter of South Carolina by Moses Hayes. It will be seen that a succession is definitely claimed by the authorities of the rite.

---

[18]III, p. 125ff.

[19]Mackey's *Encyclopaedia*. Art. *Scottish Rite*.

Frederick the Great

It was during this period of obscuration that the curious myth of Frederick the Great arose among the Jews, probably in order to enhance the commercial value of the degrees; and it was apparently really believed that the King of Prussia was the Supreme Head of the Rite, for in the Minutes of the Grand Lodge of Perfection in Albany (New York), founded in 1767, the Lodge is required, on September 3rd, 1770, to prepare its report for transmission to Berlin. We find also in 1785, one year before the king's death, a letter addressed to Frederick by a certain Solomon Bush, Deputy Grand Inspector of North America, asking for recognition of a Lodge which he had consecrated.[20] It was afterwards alleged that Frederick the Great, on his death-bed, ratified the Grand Constitutions of 1786 containing the laws that still bind the Scottish Rite, and that he constituted the 33° in person, delegating his powers as a Sovereign of Masonry to nine Brn. in each country. The original Grand Constitutions were in French, but in 1834 a Latin version of them alleged to have been signed by Frederick himself was accepted as genuine by the Supreme Council of France; but this is now on all sides admitted to be a forgery.

The truth is that Frederick took no active part in the Rite of Perfection, that he neither ratified the Constitutions nor created the 33°; and indeed to-day the majority even of the Supreme Councils are prepared to waive the claim that they derive their authority from Frederick the Great, whose interest in Masonry (at any rate in later years) was but of the slightest. The grand constitutions nevertheless remain the law of the Rite in all Supreme Councils deriving lawfully from Charleston, and Albert Pike believed them to be genuine. As it is certain that Frederick had nothing to do with the Rite, I fear we must regretfully conclude that both the fourth and the fifth documents in de Grasse-Tilly's *Golden Book*—the alleged *Constitutions of 1762* and the *Grand Constitutions of 1786*—were forgeries. It would seem that they were sent over from Europe, perhaps in response to a demand from the Jewish interest; and the fact that Dr. Dalcho's father was an officer in the Prussian army who had served with great distinction

---

[20]*Note Historique sur le Rite Ecoss.: Anc.: et Acc.:* Par le Souv.: Gr.: (Count Goblet d'Alviella) p. 7.

under Frederick the Great may well have disposed the Doctor the more readily to accept these remarkable documents.

THE CHARLESTON TRANSFORMATION

The second great transformation of the high degrees, though it was on a far smaller scale than the first, took place at Charleston before 1801. We learn from the *Circular* of Dr. Dalcho that

On the 31st of May, 1801, the Supreme Council of the Thirty-Third Degree for the United States of America was opened, with the high honours of Masonry, by Brothers John Mitchell and Frederick Dalcho, Sovereign Grand Inspectors-General; and in the course of the present year (1802) the whole number of Grand Inspectors-General was completed, agreeably to the Grand Constitutions.[21]

Such is a brief account of the formation of that which called itself the Mother Supreme Council of the World, from which, indeed, all other Supreme Councils of the world spring, with the exception of a few survivals of other lines of descent. It is clear from archives in the possession of the Mother Supreme Council that up to the eve of its formation the *only* degrees worked were the 25° of the Rite of Perfection.

The formation of the new Rite was inspired and directed by the H.O.A.T.F. Himself, and the extra eight degrees which then appeared were but rearrangements of the old twenty-five degrees of the Rite of Perfection. Now that more advanced egos had come into possession of the degrees, a fuller manifestation of the power behind was permitted; and since then the Scottish Rite, though its rituals have been altered in various countries and in various interests, has become the most important and splendid of all Masonic Obediences.

THE SPREAD OF THE SCOTTISH RITE

We may here refer back to the third document in the *Golden Book,* the patent granted to De Grasse-Tilly by the new Supreme Council 33° in Charleston in 1802, only a few months after its formation, which certifies that he has been tested in all the degrees of the Rite and authorizes him to erect Lodges, Chapters, Councils and Consistories

---

[21]Quoted in Mackey's *Encyclopaedia*. Art. *Supreme Council.*

in both hemispheres, creating him Sovereign Grand Commander of a Supreme Council for the Antilles for life. It is signed by Dalcho, De la Hogue and others, who all describe themselves as Kadosh, Prince of the Royal Secret, Sov. Gr. Inspector 33°.

The Scottish Rite was introduced by the Comte de Grasse-Tilly into France (1804); from France it passed into Italy (1805), Spain (1811) and Belgium (1817). In 1824 the Supreme Council for Ireland was formed with jurisdiction over the official degrees of White Masonry only, because of the previous existence of Chapters and Lodges of Rose-Croix and Kadosh belonging to the old Rite of Perfection. The Supreme Council of England and Wales was formed in 1845, and that of Scotland a year later.

In America in 1812 a working jeweller named Joseph Cerneau established in Boston what he called a Sovereign Grand Consistory of the United States. Cerneau possessed the necessary succession, and so was able to pass on the actual powers; but as he had no mandate from the Council of Emperors the Charleston Supreme Council denounced his proceedings as irregular, and themselves appointed a Supreme Council for the Northern Jurisdiction a year later. Supreme Councils deriving from Cerneau still exist, though they are not recognized by bodies holding the Charleston succession. Both lines, however, are valid.

The rite has spread into almost all countries of the world, and does an incalculable amount of good to thousands upon thousands of Brn., even though but few derive from it the full possibilities of spiritual advancement which lie behind it. But to be brought, however unconsciously, into touch with so holy an influence must unquestionably uplift and bless even the least sensitive; and some touch of its hidden glory is conferred upon all.

12

The Co-Masonic Order

THE RESTORATION OF AN ANCIENT LANDMARK

THE Co-Masonic Order is distinguished from the rest of the Masonic world by the admission of women to Masonry on equal terms with men. In this it is introducing no innovation into the body of Masonry, but rather restoring one of the ancient landmarks which was forgotten during the confusion of the Mysteries with the operative Masonry of the Middle Ages. In both Egypt and Greece, as we have seen, women were admitted to the Mysteries, and were able to penetrate into the inmost sanctuaries as well as men. The officials of the masculine Craft are for the most part against their admission to-day. They have been most strongly impressed, and quite rightly so, with the paramount importance of keeping the rituals and customs unchanged; but they quite wrongly regard the admission of women as a serious departure from ancient usage. Co-Masons are equally urgent in their respect for the traditions; but in this matter they prefer to follow the older custom, which has also the added merit of being logical and fair. Since reincarnation is a fact, there is no difference between the ego or soul of a man and that of a woman; and we do not see any reason why in a particular birth, because he happens in the course of his evolution to occupy a woman's body, that ego should be deprived of the advantages of initiation into the sacred Mysteries of Masonry.

THE SUCCESSION OF CO-MASONRY

The Co-Masonic Order derives its succession of Sovereign Grand Inspectors-General of the 33° from certain Brn. belonging to the Supreme Council of France, founded by the Comte de Grasse-Tilly in 1804. In his booklet, *Universal Co-Freemasonry: What is it?*, the Very Illustrious Bro. J. I. Wedgwood, 33° gives the following account of its foundation, which he derives from the official minutes of the Supreme Council published in Dr. Georges Martin's *Etude de la Franc-Maconnerie Mixte et de son Organisation*, and from *Transaction No. 1* of the Dharma Lodge, Benares:

Our own Order of Universal Co-Freemasonry, or, to give it its French title, *L'Ordre Maconnique Mixte Internationale*, is the first Masonic body which has aimed at establishing a world-wide order to which women should be admitted on equal terms with men. Its career began in the year 1882. There existed a body styling itself *La Grande Loge Symbolique Ecossaise de France*. It consisted of various Craft Lodges which had broken loose from the Supreme Council in France and constituted themselves into a Grand Lodge. It was only anticipating what the other Craft Lodges under the Supreme Council did in 1894-97, when they organized themselves into the now existing Grand Lodge of France, and absorbed into themselves, with one exception, the Lodges of *La Grande Loge Symbolique Ecossaise de France*. This latter body, with which we are concerned, almost at once received recognition from the Grand Orient of France . . .

The principle which this particular schism espoused was that of the autonomy of Craft Lodges, summed up in the phrase *Le Macon libre dans la Loge libre*—a principle sound enough in the main, but, it may at once be confessed, obviously not capable of application outside certain wide limits. Still, it has always received much recognition in France, ever since French Masonry broke away from the parent English stem. One of the Lodges holding from this body was called *Les Libres Penseurs*, and met at Pecq, a little place in the Department of Seine et Oise. This Lodge—belonging to a then recognized Masonic Obedience—decided to initiate a woman, a certain Mdlle. Maria Deraismes, a well-known authoress and lecturer, noted for her service to humanitarian and feminist movements. They did so, in the presence of a large assembly, on January 14th, 1882. The Right Worshipful Master, Bro. Houbron, 18°, justified their experiment as having the welfare and highest interests of humanity at heart, and as being a perfectly logical application of the principle of 'A Free Mason in a Free Lodge'. The Lodge was of course suspended for putting the family motto into practice . . .

For some time Sister Maria Deraismes did nothing in the way of extending to others the Masonic privileges she had received. Eventually she yielded to the persuasions of friends, and notably of Dr. Georges Martin. This latter gentleman was a member of the Lodge *Les Libres Penseurs* when Mdlle. Deraismes was initiated. He gave her his staunch support and the benefit of his wide Masonic experience throughout her Masonic career. Upon his retirement from political life—he had been a Senator—he devoted his energies to the helping of humanity through our Order. . .On March 14th, 1893, Sister Deraismes initiated a number of ladies, in the presence of Dr. Martin, and on April 4th of the same year *La Grande Loge Symbolique Ecossaise de France, Le Droit Humain,* came into being. . . .

In 1900 the new Grand Lodge, with a view to extending its ramifications into other countries, found it desirable to work the higher degrees. Aided, therefore, by Brethren in possession of the 33° the body was raised from a Craft Grand Lodge to a Supreme Council of the Ancient and Accepted Scottish Rite. Mme. Marie Martin, the close friend and collaborator of Mdlle. Deraismes, succeeded upon the death of the latter to the leadership of the movement, Dr. Georges Martin holding the office of *Grand Orateur,* and she occupied her exalted position with distinction, with dignity, and with utter devotion, until her demise in 1914.

There are Lodges in France, Belgium, England, Scotland, India, Australia, South Africa, America (over 100), Holland, Java, Switzerland, and Norway.

We need add only a few words about the movement in England. The first of our English lady members to enter the Order was our highly esteemed Sister Francesca Arundale. Mrs. Annie Besant, feeling that a Masonic movement open to men and women alike could be made a powerful force for good in the world, who had been offered initiation by Mdlle. Deraismes, learned of the continuance of the Order from Miss Arundale, and sought initiation in Paris. She was subsequently created Vice-President Grand Master of the Supreme Council and Deputy for Great Britain and its Dependencies. The first Co-Masonic Lodge was consecrated in London in September, 1902, by the grand Officers of the Supreme Council, under the title of Human Duty, No. 6.[1] (See Plates X and XI, following p. 178.)

With the advent of Dr. Annie Besant to the leadership of the Order in the British Empire, the direct link between Masonry and the Great White Lodge which has ever stood behind it (though all unknown to the majority of the Brn.) was once again reopened; and the H. O. A. T. F. has taken a keen personal interest in its development. The ancient English and Scottish succession of Installed Masters, Installed Mark Masters and Installed First Principals of the Holy Royal Arch of Jerusalem was introduced into Co-Masonry by sympathetic

---

[1]*Op. cit.,* p. 25 ff.

Brn. from the masculine Obediences, and these degrees now form part of our British Co-Masonic workings. (Plate XII, following p. 178.)

THE CO-MASONIC RITUALS

In 1916, by order of the H. O. A. T. F., the ritual of the Craft degrees was finally revised in accordance with their ancient occult meaning, this ritual being based upon the English and Scottish workings. Certain features, such as the recognition of the elementals and the three symbolical journeys, were introduced from the French Craft rituals worked under the auspices of the Ancient and Accepted Scottish Rite— with further modifications from occult sources. This ritual was approved by the H. O. A. T. F. Himself, who deigned to work it in His own Lodge, afterwards making certain suggestions, which were of course immediately adopted.

In 1923 He further most graciously authorized an English translation of His Latin ritual of the Rose-Croix, to be worked in those Sovereign Chapters R   C who desired to make use of it. The celebration of this ceremonial has enormously quickened the occult strength of our Chapters; and though as yet we cannot hope to equal the old Egyptian working, we are able to some extent to call down and pour forth upon the world the splendid powers of the Rosy Cross.

In 1925 the H.O.A.T.F. was kind enough to allow the use of a Mark Ritual which had been brought into line with the inner meaning of the degree; and in the same year He directed that a ritual of the Holy Royal Arch should be prepared, embodying certain suggestions which He Himself had deigned to make. Thus step by step the whole working is being revised in accordance with the ancient knowledge, and the way to the restoration of the Mysteries is being prepared.

THE FUTURE OF MASONRY

Masonry must surely have a wonderful part to play in the civilization of the future. Not for naught have the old hallowed rites been preserved in secret and the immemorial powers of the Mysteries transmitted throughout the ages to our modern world of the twentieth century; for we stand to-day on the threshold of a new era, which will be heralded by the coming forth once more of the World-Teacher, the Lord of Love Himself, who taught in Palestine two thousand years ago. We have seen that human evolution takes place according to a cyclic law; race succeeds race, and subrace follows subrace according to the plan of the Great Architect of the Universe, working in this world through that White Lodge which is the guardian of humanity. The time has come for the blossoming of a new subrace, the sixth of our great Aryan race, and it is already beginning to appear in North America, Australia and other lands. In that subrace, as in all the others, there will be egos of different temperaments; some no doubt will seek their inspiration in the liberal forms of Catholic Christianity, but others will find themselves attracted to the philosophic and ceremonial teaching formerly given in the Mysteries of Egypt which are the heritage of the Masonic brotherhood.

The coming of the World-Teacher has always in the past marked a revival or an inauguration of the Mysteries. Thoth in Egypt, Zoroaster in Persia, Orpheus in Greece—each of these mighty Messengers of the White Lodge, who were yet one Messenger appearing under different names and in different forms, left behind Him a glorious rite of initiation to lead men to His feet after He had gone. That great Teacher of mankind passed from human sight as Gautama the Lord Buddha; but the sceptre of the Lord of Love was placed by the spiritual KING in the hands of His successor, whom to-day we revere as the Lord Christ, whose coming we await with hearts filled with longing love.

He, too, will surely take the sacred vessels of the Mysteries and fill them anew with His own wonderful life; He, too, will mould them according to the needs of His people and the age in which they live. For the influence of the sixth ray, the ray of devotion which inspired the Christian mystics and the glorious Gothic architecture of the Middle Ages is passing away, and the seventh ray is beginning to dominate the world—the ray of ceremonial magic which brings the especial co-operation of the Angelic hosts, of which Masonry itself with its many coloured pageant of rites is a splendid manifestation. Thus in the coming days when the Lord of Love who is our Most Wise Sovereign and the Prince of Sovereign Princes will visit yet again His holy sanctuaries—guarded throughout the ages by His great Disciple, the Prince-Adept of the seventh ray and the Master of our Craft—we may look for a restoration to the worthy, and to the worthy alone, not only of the full splendour of ceremonial initiation, once more to be a true vehicle of the Hidden Light, but also of that secret wisdom of the Mysteries which has long been forgotten in the outer Lodges and Chapters of the Brotherhood.

Such surely is the destiny that awaits our beloved Order in the future; such the splendour that will transfigure the Craft in the years that are to come, until within its temple walls once more is raised—not only in symbol but in actual fact—the ladder which stretches between earth and heaven, between men and the Grand Lodge above, to lead them from the darkness of the world to the fullness of light in God, to the Rose which ever blossoms at the heart of the Cross, to the Blazing Star whose shining brings peace and strength and blessing to all the worlds.

TRANSMUTEMINI, TRANSMUTEMINI DE LAPIDIBUS MORTUIS IN

LAPIDES VIVOS PHILOSOPHICOS

S...M...I...B...

APPENDIX I

THE DEGREES OF THE RITE OF PERFECTION

COMPARED WITH THOSE OF

THE ANCIENT AND ACCEPTED SCOTTISH RITE

LIST OF TWENTY-FIVE DEGREES

WORKED BY THE

COUNCIL OF EMPERORS OF THE EAST AND WEST

1758

LIST OF DEGREES OF THE RITE OF PERFECTION	LIST OF CORRESPONDING DEGREES OF THE ANCIENT AND ACCEPTED SCOTTISH RITE
1° Apprentice	Entered Apprentice
2° Companion	Fellow Craft
3° Master	Master Mason
4° Secret Master	The same
5° Perfect Master	,,
6° Intimate Secretary	,,
7° Intendant of the Buildings	8°
8° Provost and Judge	7°
9° Master Elect of Nine	The same
10° Master Elect of Fifteen	Illustrious Master Elect of Fifteen
11° Illustrious Elect Chief of the Twelve Tribes	Sublime Knight Elected
12° Grand Master Architect	The same
13° Knight Royal Arch	Royal Arch of Enoch

List of Degrees of the Rite of Perfection	List of Corresponding Degrees of the Ancient and Accepted Scottish Rite
14° Grand Elect, Ancient Perfect Master	Grand Scottish Knight of the Sacred Vault (of James VI)[1] or Sublime Mason
15° Knight of the Sword or of the East	The same
16° Prince of Jerusalem	,,
17° Knight of the East and of the West	,,
18° Knight Rose-Croix	Sovereign Prince of Rose-Croix
19° Grand Pontiff or Master *ad Vitam*	Grand Pontiff or Sublime Scotch Mason
20° Grand Patriach Noachite	21° Noachite or Prussian Chevalier
21° Grand Master of the Key of Masonry	20° Venerable Grand Master of Symbolic Lodges
22° Prince of Libanus, Knight Royal Arch alternatively Royal Axe[2]	The same
23° Knight of the Sun, Prince Adept, Chief of the Grand Consistory.	28°
24° Illustrious Chief Grand Commander of the White and Black Eagle, Grand Elect Kadosh	30°

[1] This is clearly a later title, and in the Master the Count's list the degree is given as Grand Elect, Perfect and Sublime Mason.

[2] This is obviously a confusion in sound, the word being *Hache* or Axe. Count Goblet D'Alviella has pointed out both in this connection and in that of the Royal Arch that the names in French show that they are not of French origin. The French would be *Chevalier de l'Arche Royale*, not *du Royale Arche*, had the degrees originated in France. It seems quite possible that this may be true of the Royal Arch of Enoch, and that the *Royale Hache* may have been made to agree.

List of Degrees of the Rite of Perfection	List of Corresponding Degrees of the Ancient and Accepted Scottish Rite
25° Most Illustrious Sovereign Prince of Masonry, Grand Knight, Sublime Knight Commander of the Royal Secret	32°

The Brn. of the highest degree were termed the Council of the Emperors of the East and West, Sovereign Prince Masons, Substitutes-General of the Royal Art, Grand Surveillants and Officers of the Grand Sovereign Lodge of S. John of Jerusalem; and the rite which they worked was called the Rite of Perfection or of Heredom.

There was also an Office or Rank of Grand Inspector, though there was no degree of Sovereign Grand Inspector-General until the beginning of the nineteenth century.

On the formation of the Mother Supreme Council at Charleston in 1801, eight further Degrees were added to the 25° to make the total of 33°. It is supposed that these were drawn from Continental sources. Most of them were previously worked under a Grand Chapter of Prince Masons in Ireland. They received the approval of the H.O.A.T.F.

These are:

23° Chief of the Tabernacle
24° Prince of the Tabernacle
25° Knight of the Brazen Serpent
26° Prince of Mercy
27° Sovereign Commander of the Temple
29° Grand Scottish Knight of St. Andrew
31° Grand Inquisitor Commander
33° Sovereign Grand Inspector-General

APPENDIX II

TABLE OF PRINCIPAL MASONIC

EVENTS FROM 1717

Note

The history of Freemasonry, and more especially of its higher degrees and what are called the side degrees, during the eighteenth and nineteenth centuries is so extraordinarily confused and questionable that I think it is advisable to arrange its principal events in chronological order, in tabular form, and in parallel columns, tracing its development in England, on the Continent of Europe, and in North America respectively. The organization whose story we are trying to follow is after all a *secret* organization; it moves steadily on its way in the privacy of its Lodge rooms, and it is only rarely and as it were by accident that any reference to it or to its proceedings appears in the light of day. Little wonder that accounts are scrappy, and difficult to reconcile one with another; we are dealing with sporadic and largely accidental manifestations, and no outer indication has before been given, so far as I know, to the inner clue which makes all the confusion clear. That clue is of course the existence of the H.O.A.T.F., who is acting all the time for Masonry the part popularly assigned to Providence—watching over it, guiding its activities in this direction or that, stimulating it where it needs stimulation, bringing it to the surface in one place, and letting it sink out of sight in another, and seeing that, in one way or another, its existence is maintained and its light ever kept burning. He is the true Hidden Life in Freemasonry to whom my previous volume referred; it is His energy flowing through it which has kept this wonderful body alive; while He continues to inspire it, we need have no fear for its future.

TABLE OF PRINCIPAL MASONIC EVENTS FROM 1717

DATE	GREAT BRITAIN	FRANCE	AMERICA
1717	Foundation of the Grand Lodge of England	Clermont Degrees and Rites of Heredom practised privately.	Masonry of various rites existing but unorganized, introduced by settlers.
1722	First reference to degrees higher than Blue Degrees. Robert Samber.[1]		
1723	References to the Arch and Mark of a Master in *A Mason's Examination*, published in *The Flying Post*.		

[1] In Robert Samber's Dedication in an Hermetic Tract entitled "Long Livers" appearing in 1722 under the pseudonym of Eugenius Philalethes, Junior, and addressed to members of the Grand Lodge of England, we find what many have thought to be an allusion to higher degrees. Samber distinguishes between those "who are not far illuminated" and those "who have greater light," who are "of the higher class," and "are illuminated with the sublimest mysteries and profoundest secrets of Masonry"; and he speaks to those Masons of the higher degree which is found "behind the veil". Bro. A. E. Waite, who has deeply studied the alchemical tradition, holds that these quotations refer rather to progress in the secrets of alchemy; yet even if that be so, the remarks are of interest, only five years after the foundation, in a tract actually dedicated to the Grand Lodge.

Date	Great Britain	France	America
1729	Ephraim Chambers in *Cyclopaedia* referred to Masons "who have all the character of Rosicrucians".		
1732		Introduction of the English tradition of Craft Masonry	
1733	First mention of a Scotch Mason's Lodge in Dr. Rawlinson's List of Lodges. Also in same List the first mention in print of a Master Mason's Lodge was made.		A Lodge of S. John founded in Boston.
1735	Oration of the Provincial Grand Master of Durham quoting twelve verses on the use by the Jews of the Sword and Trowel; now used in the rhymed ritual of the Royal Order of Scotland.		
1737		Baron Scheffer, first Grand Master of Sweden, received the Three S.	

Year			
1738	Anderson's Book of Constitutions (Second Edition) published.	First condemnation of Freemasons by Papal Bull *In Eminente.* Duc d'Antin succeeded Lord Derwentwater as Grand Master of France. John's Degrees in Paris, and also two Scottish Degrees. Chevalier Ramsay's famous Oration in Paris gave an impetus to high-degree movement in France.	A Master's Lodge established in Boston.
1740	An itinerant peddler of the Royal Arch degree is said to have propagated it in Ireland, claiming that it was practiced in York and London.	Rise of Scots Lodges in all parts of France. Many rituals existed, exceedingly diverse in character. Chief theme the Recovery of a Lost Word in a Secret Vault by Scottish Crusaders. Scots Masters claimed extraordinary privileges in Blue Lodges.	
1741		Masons of Lyons are said to have introduced the Kadosh Degree, but there is no direct evidence of this.	

Date	Great Britain	France	America
1743	Stirling Rock Royal Arch Chapter of Scotland has Minutes dating from this year. First decisive reference to Royal Arch in Ireland in contemporary report of proceedings of a Lodge at Youghal.	Baron von Hund was received into the Order of the Temple by "the Knight of the Red Feather," and presented to Prince Charles Edward Stuart in Paris.	
1744	Dr. Dassigny's *Serious and Impartial Enquiry* referred to an Assembly of Royal Arch Masons at York, whence the degree was introduced into Ireland. Known and practised also in London "some small space before," and described as "an organized body of men who had passed the Chair".		
1746	Regulation of fees at Swalwell Lodge for the admission of Harodim; cf.		

the first degree of the Royal Order, *i.e.*, HRDM. the second being RSYCRS.

Five Brn. made Scots Masons in the Old Lodge at Salisbury.

1751	Formation of the Grand Lodge of the "Ancients" who accused the "Moderns" of having altered the ritual and changed the landmarks.	About this date was founded the Mere-Loge Ecossaise, working a number of degrees not belonging to our Scottish Rite. Marseilles. This was probably descended from a Scots Lodge which had assumed the right to constitute other Lodges. Among these degrees we find Rosecroix and the degree of Knight of the Sun. These do not appear before 1765, however, and were probably taken from the Emperors. Certain of the other degrees all found in the Rite of Memphis.
1753		Under date December 22, the Minutes of Fredericksburg Lodge,

Date	Great Britain	France	America
			Virginia, are said to contain the earliest known record of the Royal Arch degree in actual working.
1754		Foundation of the Rite of the Strict Observance, claiming unknown Superiors, said by its founder to derive from Prince Charles Edward Stuart in 1743, and hence from the Scottish Templars. This system very popular in Teutonic Masonry.	
		Foundation of the Chapter of Clermont, said to have worked Templar Degrees superimposed upon the Scots Degrees. Composed of high members of the nobility.	
		College de Valois of Knights of the East. Composed of bourgeois.	

Year		
1755		May have worked ten degrees. In rivalry to Chapter of Clermont. Grand Lodge of France recognized the privileges claimed by Scots Masons.
1757	Scots Lodges and Degrees of Masonic Chivalry condemned by Grand Lodge, Maningham Letters, as innovations.	
1758		Under the direction of the H.O.A.T.F. the Chapter of Clermont was expanded into the COUNCIL OF THE EMPERORS OF THE EAST AND WEST. This was composed of some of the highest nobility of the country. It worked the Rite of Perfection or Heredom; a list of its degrees will be found in Appendix I.
1761	The Grand Lodge of All England at York revived. Said to have recog-	Stephen Morin received from the COUNCIL OF THE EMPERORS the

DATE	GREAT BRITAIN	FRANCE	AMERICA
	nized Templars and Royal Arch besides Blue Degrees.	rank of Inspector-General and a commission to establish the Rite of Perfection in America.	
1763			Stephen Morin founded the Rite of Perfection in San Domingo.
1766		A Chapter of True and Ancient Rose-Croix Masons was established at Marburg, Germany, by F.J.W. Schroder.	
1769	Earliest known reference to the Mark Degree occurs in the Minute Book of a Royal Arch Chapter in Portsmouth.		
1770			Stephen Morin created a Council of Princes of the Royal Secret 25° at Kingston, Jamaica.

		(Period of the Jews)
1772	Louis Claude de S. Martin created Knight of the Rose-Croix by Martines de Pasqually, at Bordeaux.	Morin conferred the rank of Inspector-General upon Franklin of Jamaica, he in turn upon Moses Hayes of Boston, and he upon Spitzer of Charleston. All these Inspectors met at Philadelphia to confer the Inspectorship upon Moses Cohen of Jamaica, who in turn gave it to Isaac Long.
1777	A Grand Chapter of the Royal Arch established in London.	
1786	Institution by the Grand Orient of France of the French Rite of 7°, the highest being Rose-Croix. The Rite of Perfection absorbed into the Grand Orient.	
	At some period during the latter half of the eighteenth century the Rite of Perfection was taken to England, and worked in Templar Conclaves. (Yarker gathered up the threads of this succession in his Supreme Council 33°).	
	These were also introduced into Ireland before the formation of the	

DATE	GREAT BRITAIN	FRANCE	AMERICA
1791	Mother Supreme Council at Charleston, and were worked under a Grand Chapter of Prince Masons and Templar Grand Conclave. The degrees of Kadosh and Rose-Croix were thus already in possession when the Supreme Council of Ireland was introduced.	THE REVOLUTION. Rite of Perfection disappeared from public view.	At some time during this period the myth of the formation of the 33° by Frederick the Great arose and the alleged Grand Constitutions of 1762 and 1786 were produced. Who was originally responsible for these is not known, but there is clearly no foundation for them, though they were widely accepted as genuine.
1796			Isaac Long conferred the Inspectorship upon Comte de Grasse Tilly,

Year		
1801	A Scottish Rite of 33 ° is said to have been formed in Paris.	founder of the Supreme Council of France, upon his father-in-law, De la Hogue, and a number of others.
1802		Formation of the MOTHER SUPREME COUNCIL OF THE WORLD at Charleston. Eight degrees were added to the 25 of the Rite of Perfection. De Grasse Tilly and De la Hogue formed a Supreme Council 33° in Port-au-Prince.
1804	Formation of the Supreme Council 33° of France by De Grasse-Tilly in Paris. This body underwent various vicissitudes, but is now flourishing.	
1805	(Supreme Council of Italy formed).	
1810	The Degree of Installed Master sanctioned by the Regular Grand Lodge	Patent said to have been granted by Lechangeur to Marc Bedarride for

DATE	GREAT BRITAIN	FRANCE	AMERICA
1914	The Rt. Rev. J. I. Wedgwood received the degrees of Prince Patriarch Grand Conservator 33°, 95° of the Rite of Memphis; Absolute Grand Sovereign 33°, 90°, of the Rite of Mizraim; and Sovereign Grand Inspector-General 33° of the Ancient and Accepted Scottish Rite (Cerneau) by Yarker in person.		

Index

Abraham, 1

Acception, Lodge of, 145-46

Act of Union, Solemn, 3

Adam, 1

Adamson, Henry, 143

Adept, 48

Adonis, Mysteries of, 102

Aeneid, 102

Aether of space, 84

Agamemnon, 54

Ages, Dark, Masonry emerging from, 12

Akashic records, 8

Akoustikoi, 98

Alban, S. 139

Albigenses, 161

All Souls' Festival, 35; and death of Osiris, 35

Alone to the Alone, the, 6

Alviella, Count Goblet d', 188

Amen-Ra, 17

Amen, ritual of, 73; temple of, 177

Amenta, 34

America, Masonry introduced into, 158; higher degrees in, 186-87

Amset, 21

Ancient and Accepted Scottish Rite, 12, 27, 39, 178; intermediate degrees of, 12;

powers of higher degrees of, 27, 39

"Ancients," 153-56

Anderson, Dr., 1, 146, 148-49, 150-51

Anderson's Constitutions, 138

Andreas, Johann Valentine, 171

Angel of Presence of H.O.A.T.F., 43

Angels assist in ceremonial, 10, 23, 24; called at Consecration, 23; great white, 43-44; of 18° and 33°, 185; of K.H., 42; of N.S.E. and W, 22; of Rose-Croix, 40-41; overshadowed Morin, 186; worshipped as gods, 20

Animal deities, 19

Animals, embalming of, 19; symbolize Deity, 19, 20

Ankh, 55

Anthropological school, 3, 4

Antiquity, and Christopher Wren, 145; Lodge, 145

Aphrodite, 83; corresponds to Lakshmi, 84

Apis, bulls of, 19, 22

Apollo, Phoebus, 83; originally Orpheus, 83; Pythian, 84

Apple Tree Tavern, 148, 153

Apron, Masonic in Crete, 60, 61

Apuleius, 27, 33; and Mysteries of Isis, 27, 28; and Mysteries of Osiris, 33

A.Q.C., 147, 150, 151, 163; and 3°, 151; and fixing of tradition, 157

Arch, Holy Royal, 39; correspondence to, in Egypt, 39; intuition developed in, 40

Architect, Ptah as, 20

Architects, attached to Roman Legions, 109; colleges of, 109-10

Architects, Four Crowned Martyrs and, 109; Mysteries spread by, 109

Architecture, connected with Mysteries, 106; due to Comacini, 127; Gothic, 135; Ionic order of, 107; orders of reflect thought-form, 107; Romanesque, 128

Arhat compared to M.M., 48

Arimathaea, Joseph of, 119

Arthur, King, 122

Articles of Union, 157

Artificers, Dionysian, 101

Arundale, Miss F., 193

Aryanization of Egypt, 16

Ashmole, Elias, 144

Asiatische Bruder, 162

Aspects of Deity, 19

Ass, roses strewn before, 170

Assembly at York, 139

Astarte, 69

Astral plane and the Mysteries of Isis, 31-32; depicted in Mysteries, 29-30; Initiate efficient worker on, 46; tests on, in Mysteries, 29-30

Athelstan, account of, in Old Charges, 138-39; Masonry in reign of, 123

Athene, Pallas, 82

Atlantean conquest of Egypt, 16, 17

Atlantis, Story of, 17

Attis, rites of, 72

Augustine, S., 128

Australasia, masonry in, 159

Authentic history of Egypt, 15; interpretation, 3; records, 2-3; school, 2-3

Author's recollection of Masonry in Egypt, 15

Axe, double-headed, 51

Babylon, the Captivity in, 71

Bacchus, Platonic solids and, 94; top or whirling atom of, 94; toys of, 94-95

Balder, 121

Baldwin I, 163

Banqueting, 13

Baptism, derived from Mysteries, 32; symbol of Second Initiation, 46

Basle, signs on town hall at, 129

Bast, cats of, 19

Beasts, four, of Revelation, 21; symbolism of, 22

Beauty, the One, 81; cult of Greece, 81-82

"Bees," priestesses of Eleusis, 85

Begemann, Dr., 2

Benares, Dharma Lodge, 192

Bernard S. and Templars, 163

Besant, Bro. Annie, 193

Bhagavad Gita, 20

Birth, Mystic, 46; of Horus, 46

Black Masonry, 39, 41-42 and vengeance, 41, 167

Blood of Jesus, 168
Blue degrees of Scottish Rite, 169
Boniface S., 132
Book of Constitutions, 1, 144, 148; and Premier Grand Lodge, 148
Book of Splendour, 74
Book of the Dead, the, contains spiritual teaching, 31; written in secret language, 3
Boswell, 142
Brahma, four-faced, 22
Bridge, Passage of the, 168
Brito, 51
Brother Book, 132
Brotherhood, Great White, 25; directs evolution, 113; Egypt auxiliary center of, 25; headquarters in Central Asia, 25; subsidiary Lodges of, 25
Brotherhood of Masters, 7
Brotherhood of the Rosy Cross, The, 143, 171
Brothers of Horus, 20
Budge, Sir E. A. Wallis, 16, 21, 35
Builders, mediaeval, 3; associated with Mysteries, 107
Building of pyramid, 26; spiritual, done by Masonry, 106-7
Bull, of Mithra, 22; symbol of aspect of Deity, 19
Bulls of Apis, 19
Byblos, 35

Cabinet of Wisdom, 168
Caduceus or thyrsus, 93; Ida and pingala symbolized in, 94; Kundalini and, 94
Caesar, Julius, landing of, 8

Cagliostro, 186
Canada, Masonry in, 159
Canopy of heaven, 21
Cardinal points, 21
Castle, E. J., 163
Cathedrals, Masonic signs upon, 4, 133
Cats of Bast or Pasht, 19
Celestial worker in metals, 20
Celtic Mysteries, 118-24; Iona and, 122
Centre of Great White Lodge, Egyptian, 25
Ceremonial magic, 6
Ceremonial of Freemasonry antedates 1717, 3
Ceremonies, Masonic, channels of spiritual power, 9-10; contain instruction given in Mysteries, 25, 29-30; symbolize inner worlds, 9-10
Ceremony of 3°, 69; of raising, 38; of Fourth Initiation, 46-47; of Misraim of 3°, 70; of Osiris, 38, 70
Cerneau, 190
Chaldaean, arrangement of officers, 13, 106, 158; descent of Mysteries, 68; rites among Essenes, 72-73; ritual and Star Angels, 106
Charges, Old, 138
Charles, Edward, Prince, 179, 180
Charleston, rite established at, 187, 189
Charney, Gaufrid de, death of, 166
Cheetham, 33
Cheops, 15
Chephren, 15

Cherubim, described by Ezekiel, 21

Christ and Holy Eucharist, 72-73; and Mithraic Eucharist, 73; indwelling, 37-41

Christ, love of, and 18°, 48-49

Christian Creed, The, 47

Christian Fathers, 78; and pagan Mysteries, 79

Christian Mysticism, 115

Christian teachings, 47; and Egyptian ritual, 47

Christianity, and Mysteries, 113-14; Celtic, 119-20; Intolerance of, to Mysteries, 113; introduced into Britain, 119; neglects Mysteries, 115

Churches and Masonic signs, 132-33

Churchward, Bro. Albert, 4

Cicero, initiate of Mysteries, 79

Civilization of Egypt, 18

Clairvoyance, quotation from, 8

Clairvoyance, Hierophant, 86; and tests of, 31-32

Clement, S. and Mysteries, 114

Clermont, Abbey of, 158; Chapter of, 183-84; James II at, 158

Coire Cathedral and Masonic signs, 129

Colleges of Architects, 109-10; abolished A.D. 378, 109; attached to Roman Legions, 109; centre at Eboracum, 110; Comacine Masters descended from, 127; Four Crowned Martyrs and, 109; Masonic Lodges correspond to, 109; Mysteries spread by, 109; retired to Isola Comacina, 127

Collegia, Roman, 72; and Masonic tradition, 106-7; buried city and, 187; Numa founded, 107; ritual handed down orally, 150; tradition of, passed into guilds, 111

Columns, three in Minoan temple, 57; Mycenaean models of, 58

Comacine guild, 128; and analogies to Masonry, 128-29; and K.S.'s knot, 129; and Masonic symbols, 129; inherited Mysteries of Collegia, 128

Comacine guilds, Masonic signs on buildings by, 127; Masters, 127, 129, 161; work of, at Coire Cathedral, 129

Co-Masonic Order, 191; succession of, 192

Co-Masonry, history of, 192-94; Deraismes Mdlle. and, 192-93; rituals of, 194

Compagnonnage, 130-31, 180; *Livre du,* 130; Sons of Solomon and, 131; three divisions of, 131

Concise History of Freemasonry, 3, 144, 146, 148, 149, 150, 152, 153, 155, 158

Consecration of Lodge, 23-24; maize instead of corn at, 24

Constitution of universe, symbolized in Masonry, 10

Constitutions, Book of, 1; and religious barriers, 149; Old Gothic, 149

Continent, Scottish rite introduced on, 190

Cooper-Oakley, Mrs. 160

Coptos, 35

Corn, 24; scattered in north, 23; wine, oil and salt at consecration, 23-24

Correspondences between three degrees, 48

Cotterill, 135, 140

Council, of K.S. and Mysteries, 68, 69, 70; founded modern working, 70; Mother Supreme, 189

Councils, Supreme, 186; deriving from Charleston, 188; formed, 189-90

Craft degrees, 12; confused with operative guilds, 111, 118; descended from Egypt and Judaea, 118; essence of Jewish Mysteries, 72; Mark and Arch associated with, 72

Crawley, Dr. Chetwode, 2, 147

Cretan race, 53; Minos founder of, 53

Crete, apron used in, 60; buildings in, described, 52

Crete, civilization as great as Egyptian, 53; civilization of, 52; cross as symbol in, 60; divided into three, 50; double-headed axe in, 51; doves used as symbols in, 58; Father-Mother worshipped in, 51; Kings of, High Priests, 51; labyrinth symbolized Path in, 51; Masonic signs and symbols in, 61-62; Minoan shrines of, 59; Minoan temples of, 57; Mysteries of, 50-62; open air, worship in, 51; pottery of, 52; religious worship in, 55-56; sacred rocks in, 51; three columns in Temple of, 57; throne room at Knossos in, 55, 56-57; sacred tree in, 51

Critias, 53

Cross as symbol in Crete, 60

Crowned Martyrs, four, 23, 109; Patron Saints of Comacini, 129; Stonemasons venerated, 132; Strasburg Constitutions and, 132

Crusaders, 182

Crypt, excavated Minoan, 101

Culdees, 118-23

Culloden, battle of, 181

Dadouchos, 85

Dalcho, Dr., 188-89

Daitya and Ruta, 16

Dark Ages, Masonry emerging from, 12; Masonry and, 111

Dassigny and Royal Arch, 156-57

De Iside et Osiride, 35

Death, life after, taught in Mysteries, 24, 25, 29

Degree, Eighteenth, 40; inner power conferred by, varies, 11

Degree, First, and Eleusinian Mysteries, 85; education given in Egyptian, 30

Degree, First, inner Mysteries of, 31; open to thousands, 31; or Lesser Mysteries, 31

Degree, Second, 31; and Eleusinian Mysteries, 90; F.C. corresponds to, 32; inner Mysteries of, 31

Degree, Third worked in 1725, 152; reflects Fourth Initiation, 46

Degree, Thirtieth, 41, 42

Degree, Thirty-first, 42

Degree, Thirty-third, 11, 42, 44

Degrees, certain, of greatest value, 12; duality of, of Egyptian Mysteries, 31

Degrees, higher, powers of, derived from Mysteries, 27; not organized as such in Egypt, 117

Degrees, Mark and Arch, 12

Degrees, no higher, in Egypt, 39; of Black Masonry, 39, 41, 42; Royal Arch, 39, 40; sacramental power introduced into, 11; symbolize plane of nature, 10; two, worked until 1725, 151; worked in Co-Masonic Order, 12

Deity, aspects of, symbolized by animals, 19, 20; manifestations of One, 40

Demeter, 83; corresponds with Uma, 83

Demigods, myth of, 16, 17

Dermott and "Ancients", 155-56

Desaguliers and compilation of rituals, 150-51; and Grand Lodge, 149

Devarajas, Four, 21, 22, 24

Devotion, channel for, 20; and Gothic architecture, 137; and Middle Ages, 136

Diktynna, 51, 55-56

Diocletian, Emperor, 109

Diodorus, Siculus, 16, 34

Dionysian Artificers, 101

Dionysus, 83; and consecration of an egg, 101; Mysteries of, 101, 102; s...and p...w employed in mysteries of, 101

Divine Kings, 15, 16-17

Documents, Masonic, research into, 2

Doneraile, Irish Lodge at, 147

Double-headed axe, 51, 55-56

Dove, and Mycenaean relics, 57-59

Dowland manuscript, 138-39

Druidic Mysteries and Kabiric correspondences, 121; compared to other rites, 120-21; influenced by Mysteries of Ireland, 121; Reincarnation and, 121; traced to Orpheus, 121

Dutch Masonry, 158

Dynasties, Atlantean, 15

Egyptian, 15

E.A. compared to Mystery of Isis, 48; compared to probationer, 48

Early German Architecture, 133

East and West, Mysteries of, 123; Council of Emperors of, 124

Easter Festival and Osiris, 33

Eboracum or York, 188

Education given in Mysteries, 24, 29-31

Edwin and York Assembly, 139

Egypt, Aryanization of, 16; Atlantean conquest of, 16-17; centre of spiritual illumination, 25; civilization of, 18; Freemasonry in, 6,000 years ago, 15; Gods of, 18; Grand Lodges in, 177; greatness of, and the Mysteries, 25; Jews in, 64-65; Negroid domination of, 16

Egyptian Dynasty, first, 15; empire, first, 15; Gods, 17, 18-19; history, antiquity of, 15-16; method of arranging officers, 13

Egyptian Mysteries, 15-49; Jews adopted, 65; visited by Rosencreutz, 175

Eighteenth Degree and Royal Order, 168; and Templars, 165

Eighteenth Degree, Angels of, 40; correspondence to, in Egypt, 39; few passed beyond, in Egypt, 41; Love outpoured in, 40-41; M.W.S. of, 41; reflects Christhood, 48

Elements, Rulers of the, 20-22, 23-24

Eleusinian Mysteries, 84-96

Eleusinian succession, 96

Embalming, 19-20

Emblematic Freemasonry, 153

Emperors, Roman, initiated into Mysteries, 95; of E. and W. 175

Empire, first Egyptian, 16

Encyclopaedia, A New, 73

Encyclopaedia Britannica, 105

Epoptae, 153

Erasmus, 141

Eschenbach, Wolfram von, 122

Essenes celebrated daily Sacrament, 73; inherited Chaldaean rites, 72; inherited Mithraic Eucharist, 72; Jesus lived among, 72

Ethical truth given to world in the Mysteries, 26; taught in the Mysteries, 26

Eucharist, Holy, 73; based on Mithraic, 72-73

Eumolpidae, 80-81, 84

Eusebius, 119-20

Evolution, God's plan for man, 112

Evans, Sir Arthur, 50, 53, 60; quoted, 54, 56-57, 61

Events from 1717, table of, 201

Excavations in Crete, 54

Ezekiel, four beasts of, 21-22, 66; and Jewish Mysteries, 65

F.C. Degree, 48; compared to Initiate, 48; compared to Mysteries of Serapis, 48; Greater Mysteries, and, 32; S...n used in Mysteries, 33

Father-Mother worshipped in Crete, 51

Fawn skin or nebris, 88

Feather, Knight of the Red, 179

Feminine Aspect of Deity, 18, 20, 51; and the "Virgin Sea,"

83-84; worshipped in Crete, 51, 55

Fertility cult, 69

Findel, J.F., 2

Flame, Lords of the, 9

Flight of alone to Alone, 6

Flood, great, 16

Fludd, Robert, 144-45, 172

Follow the King, 18; the Light, 18

Form and life, 12

Forty-sixth degree and Royal Order, 168

Foucart, 78, 80-81

Four Beasts, 21-22

Four Crowned Martyrs, 24; Patron Saints of Comacini, 129; Stonemasons venerated, 132; Strasburg Constitutions and, 132

Four Rulers of elements, 20-22, 24

Fourth Initiation, 46, 48

France, Masonry introduced into, 157-58

Fratres Lucis, 161

Frederick the Great, myth of, 188-89

Freemasonry, history of, a colossal undertaking, 1

Freemasonry, Lexicon of, 28

Freemasons, Travelling, 126

Friday, Good, 34; and death of Osiris, 34

Future of Masonry, 194-96

F...p...o...f, 38, and Mysteries of Osiris, 38

Gavel of Master, 55

German Stonemasons, 132-33; and Masonic signs on architecture, 133

Germany, Masonry introduced into, 158

Gizeh, pyramids of, 15

God, the Supreme, 20; geometrizes, 95; Name of, 40

Goddess of love and beauty, Hathor, 20

Gods, Egyptian, 17, 18-19; Greek, 81-84

Golden Book, The, 186, 188, 189

Golden Fleece of Jason, 90

Good Friday, and death of Osiris, 34

Goose and Gridiron, 145; Lodge Antiquity met at, 145; Premier Grand Lodge met at, 148

Gothic architecture, rise of, 135; change from Romanesque to, 137; inspired by H.O.A.T.F., 135, 137; intended to arouse devotion, 137; travelling Masons and, 137

Gothic Constitutions, Old, 149

Goths and Vandals, 113

Goulas, 50

Gould, R.F., 2, 3, 132, 133, 143, 144, 148, 149, 151-52, 158, 179, 186-87

Grail, Holy, 94, 122

Grammar included secret language, 30-31

Grand and Royal Lodge, 71

Grand Guild of Steinmetzen, 133

Grand Inspector Inquisitor Commander, 42

Grand Lodge of All England, 146; worked three degrees, 151

Grand Lodge of England, 146, 149; Duke of Montague and, 149; first four Lodges of, 148; Premier, 148

Grand Lodge of Ancients, 155; of Ireland, 155; of Scotland, 155; of York, 153

Grand Lodges, pronouncement as to higher degrees, 3, 5; union of rival, 157

Grand Master, Duke of Montague, fourth, 148-49; Desaguliers, third, 149; Manningham, Deputy, 150; Payne, second, 149; Sayer, first, 148

Grasse-Tilly, Comte de, 186, 188, 189; and Co-Masonry, 192

Great Mother, 51

Greece, Mysteries of, 78-102; Dionysus, the Logos in, 83; Path of Holiness and, 95

Greek gods, Angels sometimes ensouled, 82; Aphrodite, 83-84; Apollo, Phoebus, 83; channels of divine blessing, 81; Demeter, 83; Dionysus, 83; Hera, 82-83; Pallas Athene, 82; Persephone, 83; resembled national Angels, 82

Greeks, ancient, 53

Greek mythology, 81; love of beauty, 81-82

Gregory the Great, 128

Guild Masons, 126

Guilds, English, 133

Guilds Operative, 3; Church did not persecute, 111; Free Masons accepted into, 111; Mediaeval, 77; tradition and terminology of, 111

H.O.A.T.F., 11; and Co-Masonry, 194; and Rose Croix, 176; Angel of Presence of, 43; inspired Charleston changes, 189; inspired Emperors of E. and W., 185; is now

Hierophant of Mysteries, 43;
Masonry in hands of, 12;
overshadowed Morin, 187;
pours forth power, 13-14;
revived high degrees, 183;
teaching given by, 186
Hagava, 70
Hakina, 70
Hallows or Hiera, 84; carried in
procession, 88-89; reverence
paid to, 88, 89
Hapi, 21
Harrio-Jubal-Abi, 70
Hathor, 20
Hawk, 19
Hagia Triada, sarcophagus of, 58
Heaven-world, 90
Heaven, canopy of, 21
Hera, 82-83
Heredom, 122-23; and Lord of
Love, 176; degree of, 168
Heredom of 25°, 178, 185; rite
of, 39
Heremda, 70
Heresy and orthodoxy, 13
Hermes Trismegistus, 10
Herodotus, 26, 34
Heroes Greek, 16-17
Hidden Life in Freemasonry, The,
10, 11, 15, 16, 24, 25, 48, 63,
70, 106-07, 110, 177; and
Kilwinning Lodge, 154
Hickes, Rev. George, 143
Hidden Light, 15, 17, 26, 39, 43
"Hidden Paths of Nature and
Science", 32
Hidden Work in Masonry, 13
Hiera, 84
Hieroceryx or herald, 85
Hieroglyphics, grammar included,
30
Hierophant, of Mysteries, 39;

H.O.A.T.F. is now, 43; makes
links for 33° Mason, 43; seat
of, in Minoan shrine, 57, 59
Hierophants of Eleusis, 84, 86;
Eleusinian women, 85
High Priests, the Pharaohs as,
17-18; Kings of Crete also, 51
Higher degrees, 3; authority upon,
5; not organized as such in
Egypt, 117
Hippolytus, 91-92
Hiram, King of Tyre, 67-69; and
Chaldaean descent, 68; father
of, 69
Hiram Abiff, 68-71
Historian, Manetho the, 16
Historian, Masonic, 2
Historical research, occult, 7-9
History of Art, 135, 140
History of the Lodge of
Edinburgh, 142, 146
Holiness, Path of, 26
Holy Grail, 94
"Holy, Holy, Holy", 21
Holy Royal Arch, 3; and King
Josiah, 72
Holy Royal Arch and 3° of Jewish
Mysteries, 72; and Zerubbabel,
72; associated with 3°, 156-57;
at York, 156; first mention of,
153; second mention of,
153-54, 156
Holy Spirit, Ptah, 20
Horus, 17-18, 36; and power of
33°, 44; birth of, 46; brothers
or children of, 21, 24;
followers of, 16; indwelling,
41; Star shone at birth of, 46
HRDM-RSYC, 124; and Royal
Order of Scotland, 124
Hughan, W.J., 2
Hund, Baron von, 179

I.M., 38-39; "Ancients" and ritual of, 152-53; apex of Mysteries, 38; became hierophant, 38; constitution of 1723, 153; great progress of, 38; power of, transmitted by installation, 153; receives ancient Egyptian power, 39; succession of, from Egypt, 71; succession of, preserved, 152-53

I.M. degree, Grand Lodge of Scotland and, 158; on Continent, 158; signs of, on Egyptian temples, 158

Illumination, Egypt centre of, 25

India, Masonic secrets in, 4

Inge, Dean, 115

Initiates, alone received power of 33°, 44; thousands of, in Mysteries, 88

Initiation, Fifth, 48-49; symbolized by Ascension, 48

Initiation, First, 46; and Mysteries of Serapis, 48; called birth of Horus, 46; compared to F.C., 48; opens out emotional nature, 46

Initiation, Fourth, 46-48; ceremony in Egypt, 47-48; symbolized by Passion and Resurrection, 46-48

Initiation, hall of, excavated, 56

Initiation, Masonic, ceremony of, 9-10, 28-29; described in Lexicon, 28-29; preparation for, 28; reflects true Mysteries, 9-10; symbolizes evolution, 26

Initiation, Second, 46; and temptation in wilderness, 46; expands mental body, 46; symbolized by baptism, 46

Initiation, symbolism of, 45; tests of, 46

Initiation, Third, 46; symbolized by Transfiguration, 46

Initiation, true, power of 33° almost equal to, 44; masonry preparation for, 10; qualifications for, 45

Initiations, five great, 7, 27, 45; Masonry reflects, 26

Initiator, The One, 49

Initiatory rites, Masonic signs in, 4

Inner Light, 17

Inner Mysteries, 31-32; of Isis, 31-32; of Osiris, 38

Innovations, Continental, 3

Inquisition, History of the, 161

Intuition, growth of, in Rose-Croix, 41; in Royal Arch Degree, 40

Iona, 120, 122-23

Ireland, Grand Lodge of, 155

Irish Lodge at Doneraile, 147; Elizabeth St. Leger initiated into, 147; rituals allied to York, 155

Isaiah, 65-66

Isis, 17, 18-19; the moon, 37; Angels of 33°, represent, 43; the eternal Mother, 44; influence of, 19, 20; inner Mysteries of, 31-32

Isis, Mysteries of, 27, 29, 31; compared to E.A., 48; compared to probationer, 48

Isosceles triangle, 13; officers arranged in, 13

J.H.V.H., 74-76; Adonai substituted for, 76; became Jehoshua, 76; symbolism of, 76

Jackal, deity with head of, 21

Jacobite movement, 179-80, 184

Jason, fleece of, 90; symbolism of, 90

Jacques de Molay, 132

Jacques, Maitre, 132

James II and Masonry, 158, 179

James III, 181

Jehovah, 75-76

Jeremiah, 65-66

Jesuits and Masonry, 180, 184

Jesus, Initiate of Egyptian Lodge, 45; lived among Essenes, 72

Jewish form of Masonry, 110; Christianity and, 110; Comte de S. Germain and, 110; intentionally adopted, 110

Jewish migrations, 63-65

Jewish Mysteries, 63-77

Jews and Morin, 187

Jews in Egypt, 64

John, S., 21-22, 69

Jonah, 69; and death and resurrection, 69; and F.C.H.S. at Ravello, 129

Joseph, Pere, 186

Journeymen, operative, of France, 132

Jubal, 70

Jupiter, fourfold, 22

Justice, divine, 7, 23; and Black Masonry, 41-42

K.H., 41, 42, 184, 185, 190

Kabbala, the, 10, 73-75; *Sepher ha Zohar,* text of, 74; *Sepher Yetzirah,* text of, 74; translation of, into Latin, 74

Kabbala Denudata, 74

Kabbalism, 73-77; close similarity to Masonry, 73; students of and Masonry, 73

Kabeiroi, Mysteries of, 102

Kali Yuga, 42

Karma, 7, 23; Black Masonry studied, 41-42; Osiris and Lords of, 36

Kestha, 21; Keryces, 84

Khafra, 15

Khufu, 15

Kilwinning and Ramsay, 181; date of founding, 154; earliest Minutes of, 154; in 1286, 182; Minutes of 1642, 154; rites of, 123; worked Craft degrees only, 154

King Arthur, 122

King, follow the, 18

King of the World, 43; adumbrated in 33°, 49; 33° Mason linked to, 43

Kings, divine, 15, 16-17

Kirk, Robert, 143

Knossos, 50, 56-58

Knot, King Solomon's, 129

Kore or Persephone, 83; and Eleusinian Mysteries, 85

Krater or cup, 94

Labrys, 51; and sacral knot, 55; emblem of God, 55; gavel derived from, 55

Labyrinth, 51; based on fact, 54; built for double-headed axe, 51, 56; symbolized difficulty of Path, 51

Lakshmi corresponds to Aphrodite, 84

Lamb and book, 168

Lamech, 70

Lanfranc, Archbishop, 134

Language, Mystery, 30-31

Last Supper, 133; Apostles and Masonic signs, 133

Law of eternal justice, 7, 23
Lexicon of Freemasonry, 28
Leyland-Locke MS., 97
Life and form, 12
Light, follow the, 18; gone to the, 18; Hidden, 17, 39, 40
Light, inner, 17; look for the, 18; "that lighteth every man", 17
Light on the Path, 45
Lipika, 22
Llorente's *History of Inquisition,* 161
Lodge, Antiquity No. 2, 145
Lodge, consecration of, 3; at York, 145-46
Lodge, Great White, 7-8, 25, 43; Egypt centre of, 25; stands behind Masonry, 25, 27, 45
Lodge Minutes, research into, 2
Lodge of the Acception, 144-45
Lodges, operative, 3; Freemasonry derived from, 3
Logos and myth of Osiris, 38; descent of, 38, 40; the Word or, 76
Lord of Love, reflected in 18°, 48
Lost Word, 75
Love, divine, 40; and Rose-Croix Degree, 40-41; Lord of, reflected in 18°, 48; poured forth in Mysteries, 41

M.M., 33; and mystery of Osiris, 33, 48; compared to arhat, 48; degree of, reflects Fourth Initiation, 46
M.W.S., 41
Mackey's *Lexicon, 28; Encyclopaedia,* 70, 187
Magic, ceremonial, 6; of Eleusinian Mysteries, 88-95
Magistri Comacini, 161

Maitre Jacques, 132; Soubise, 132
Maize, ineffective at Lodge consecration, 24
Manes, 16, 162
Manetho, Egyptian historian, 16
Manichaeans, 161-62
Manningham letters, 150
Manu, 15, 63-65; reflected in 30°, 48-49
Man: Whence, How and Whither, 16, 18, 53, 64, 80
Mark Degree, 72; and 2° of Jewish Mysteries, 72; associated with 2°, 156
Mark Degree, difference of working, 157; first mention of, 157; tradition of, 157
Marseilles, Lodge at, 183
Martel, Charles, 134, 138
Martin, Dr. Georges, 192-93; Mme. Marie, 193
Martyrs, Four Crowned, 24; patron saints of Comacini, 109; patron saints of Masonry, 109; Stonemasons venerated, 132; Strasburg Constitution and, 132
Mary's Chapel at Edinburgh, 146
Masonic symbols in Crete, 61; signs on Churches, 129, 132; signs in Crete, 62
Masters, Brotherhood of, 7
Masters and the Path, The, 45, 48, 96; Initiation described in, 45
Mathematikoi, 99
Maymus Grecus, 138
Mead, G.R.S., 96
Mediaeval builders, 3; guilds, 77
Memphis and Mizraim, 12; ceremonies of, manufactured, 12
Memphis, rite of 96°, 183

Mena, 26

Menkaura, 15

Mental plane, 8; and Mysteries of Serapis, 32, 33

Metals, celestial worker in, 21

Minotaur based on fact, 54

Minos, King, 53, 54; Masonic temple in throne room of, 59; palace of, 56; throne room of, 56-57

Minoan temple, 57; apron used in, 60; civilization, 53, 55; doves on roof-beams in, 57-58; Masonic symbols found in, 61; shrines, 59; symbol of cross in, 60; rites, 55; three columns in, 57-58

Minutes, earliest extant, 3, 142; Mason word alluded to in, 143; of Old Lodge at York, 145; research into, 2

Mithra, 37; bull of, 22

Mithraic Eucharist, 73; Mysteries, 103-11

Mizraim, ceremony of 3° of, 70

Models, Minoan terra-cotta, 57-59

Molay, Jacques de, 132; death of, 166-167

Molinos, Michael de, 162

Montague, Duke of, 148-49

Moon, symbol of, 19; and 33° power of Isis, 44

More, Sir Thomas, 141

Morin, Stephen, patent of, 186-87

Morte d'Arthur, 122

Mosiac pavement in Crete, 59

Moses, 1; founded Jewish mysteries, 65; "learned in wisdom of Egyptians", 64

Mother, Eternal, 17, 18, 20; Isis, the, 44

Mother God, 51; worshipped in Crete, 51; tree sacred to, 51, 55

Murray-Lyon, David, 2, 3, 142, 146

Muses' Threnodie, The, 143

Mysteries, Christian Fathers and, 114; Christianity and, 113-14; Christians intolerant to, 113; Jewish, 63-77; occult truth kept secret in the, 114; of Adonis or Tammuz, 102; of Attis and Cybele, 102; of Crete, 50-62; of Dionysus, 100-2; of Eleusis, 84-85; of Greece, 78-102; of Kabeiroi, 102; of Osiris, 33-38; of Serapis, 32-33; of the East and West, 122; Pagan and Christian, 33; Theodosius issued edict against, 116; withdrawn, 116

Mycenaean relics, 57-59; civilization, 54; columns, 59-60; Minoan source of, 58

Mycerinus, 15

Mysteres d'Eleusis, Les, 78, 80-81, 85

Mystic death, 38; birth, 46; way of, 6-7

Mystical Four, 22; school, 5-6

Myth of sun-god, 35, 37

Mythology, Greek, 81-82

Myths, Egyptian, 15, 35-37

Name, of God, 39-40; Adonai substituted for, 76; found in Royal Arch, 40; Jehovah used as, 76; JHVH regarded as, 75-76; Loss of Divine, 75; Symbolism of, 76-77

Nebris or fawn skin, 88

Nebuchadnezzar, 71

Nekys, 16

Nephthys, 20

Nile, 26, 37

Numa, King, 72; adopted Mysteries of Dionysus, 108; an Initiate of White Lodge, 108; and Roman Collegia, 72, 107; Dionysian Artificers and, 108

Numbers, science of, 97-98; and Pythagorean School, 97-99; and higher mathematics, 98-99

O., The, 134

Oath, great, 143

Occult Chemistry, 95

Occultism defined, 6

Occultist, knowledge of, 7; way of, 6

Officers of Mysteries, 38; position of, 13; transmit power, 38

Occult, Path, stages of, 45-48; records, 8; research, 8-9, 73; school, the, 6

Occult training, 87

Oil, poured in west, 23

Oliver, Dr. 1-2

Omer, S., 163

Omnific word, 76

One, Initiator, the, 49; the many are, 40

Operative guilds, confused with speculative Masonry, 111; declined after Reformation, 141; in Middle Ages, 125; Masonry derived from, 3; not persecuted by Church, 111

Operative Masonry, 125-39

Oral tradition, 150; and Roman Collegia, 150

Order, Royal, of Scotland, 124

Origen, and Mysteries, 114-15, 173

Origins of Freemasonry, 1-4; and Roman Collegia, 72; antiquity of, 3; attributed to Kabbala, 73; based on Old Testament, 1; legends of, 1; traced to Egypt, 4; traced to mediaeval builders, 3; traced to operative Lodges, 3; traced through Jewish rites to Egypt. 73

Orpheus, 79; Mysteries of, 80

Orpheus, by G.R.S. Mead, 96

Orphic Schools, 80

Orthodoxy and Heresy, 13

Osirified, 37

Osiris, 17-18; and Mysteries of Serapis, 33; and traditional history, 71; Angels of 33°, represent, 43; astronomically the sun, 37; death and resurrection of, 34; legend of, 35-36; meaning of legend of, 37-38; Mysteries of, 33-38; regarded as Nile, 37; the divine Father, 44; the Hidden Light, 26; "Thou art", 73; typifies descent of Logos, 38

Osiris, Mysteries of, 33-38

Outline History of Freemasonry, 102

Palace of Minos at Knossos, The, 54, 56-59, 60

Pallas Athene, 82

Papyri, secret language used in, 30

Papyrus of Ani, 32

Paracelsus, 161, 175

Parvati corresponds to Hera, 83

Pasht, cats of, 19

Path, the, 7, 26; Mysteries preparation for, 44; probationary, 7; stages of occult, 45-47

Patriarchs before flood, 2

Patron saints of Craft, 38; and fertility cult, 69; Four Crowned Martyrs, 109

Paul, S. 37; "I travail in birth", 37

Pavement mosaic in Crete, 59-60

Payens, Hugues de, 163

Payne, and Grand Lodge, 148

"Pearls before swine", 171

Pelasgians, 53

Perfection, Rite of, 39, 178, 185, 186, 189, 197

Persecution by Church, of Masonry, 115-16; of Mysteries, 116

Persephone, 83; or Kore, 83, 85

Peru, civilization of, 113

Phaedo, The, 78-79

Phaestos, palace of, 59; similar to Masonic Temple, 59

Pharaoh also high priest, 17; and Jewish Mysteries, 68; as Crowned and Anointed Sovereign, 43; as Sovereign Grand Inspector-General, 43; daughter of, 68; reason for embalming, 19-20; treatment of Jews by, 64-65

Philae, temple of, 33; and body of Osiris, 33

Philo, 76; expounded Word of God, 76

Physikoi, 99; mental 8, 33; and Greater Mysteries, 33

Pike, Albert, 189

Pillars of the House, 58

Ptolemaic period, 16

Plane, astral, 29, 30, 31-32

Planes of nature, in Masonic ceremonies, 10

Plato, 53, 78

Plot, Dr. Robert, 145

Plotinus, 6

Plutarch, 35, 37, 107

Polurheni, 50

Porphyry, 85

Poseidonis, 16

Position of officers, 13

Pottery, Cretan, described, 52

Power, sacramental, 10; and officers in Mysteries, 38; in higher degrees, 39; Masonic sometimes withdrawn, 11, 13-14; of 33°, 45; spiritual, conferred in Masonry, 11; transmitted by officers, 38

Powers behind Freemasonry, 13

Preliminary trials, 28

Premier Grand Lodge, 148

Premier Grand Lodges, 155

Preparation for initiation, 28

Principles in man symbolized, 10

Probationary path, 7, 48; symbolized in Masonry, 10

Processions and Mystery ceremonial, 88-89; to Eleusis, 89-90

Proclus on Mysteries, 79

Progress, method of human, 6

Proserpine, 27

Ptah, Master Architect, 20

Purification for initiation, 57

Purpose of author, 1; of Mysteries, 24-26

Pyramid, "proper steps" open doors in, 26; calculations in, 25-26, 75; ceremonies held in, 26; symbolism of, 67, 75; the great, 16, 25, 31

Pyramids, 16

Pylon, 18

Pythagoras, 96-98; proposition of, 100

Pythagorean school, 96-100

Qebsennuf, 21

Qualities of Deity, Angels channels of, 20; symbolized by animals, 19-20

Quattuor Coronati, No. 2076, 2

Quest for Word, 168

R.W.M. reflects 33°, 49

Raising, ceremony of, 69-70

Raising, Solomon responsible for, 70-71; of Mizraim rite, 70

Ramsay, oration of, 181-82

Ravello, Masonic signs at, 129

Real History of the Rosicrucians, 171

Reception of a Templar, The, 163

Records akashic, 8-9

Records, Masonic of partial value, 3; occult Masonic, 8; of speculative Masonry, 3

Red Masonry, 39

Reformation, the, 140, 142

Rehoboam and 3° ceremony, 70

Reincarnation, 7, 37, 191; and legend of Osiris, 37-38; taught in Druidical Mysteries, 121; taught in Pythagorean school, 98

Religious barriers and Masonry, 149

Renaissance, 140; and Reformation, 141

Resurrection of Osiris, 34, 36, 37, 38

Revelation, Four Beasts in, 21

Revival of Masonry 1717, 3

Revolution, the French, 184, 186

Richter, Sigmund, 172

Ritual, calls down spiritual power, 10; Egyptian and Christian teachings, 47; handed down orally, 150-51; no trace of,

before 1717, 154; of Fourth Initiation, 47; old rhymed, 168; purpose of, 10; rubric of Fourth Initiation, 47

Rituals, origin of, 149; Gould and, 150; Manningham Letters and, 150; no trace of before 1717, 149; Stukely and, 149-50

Roman Collegia, 72, 106, 107; Numa founded, 107; succession of, from Egypt, 108; transition to speculative Masonry and, 108

Roman Emperors and Mysteries, 95

Romanesque architecture, 127-28; due to Comacine Masters, 127

Rose-Croix, a degree of Christhood, 176; analogies in Egypt, 39, 40; Angels of, 40; antiquity of, 5; few passed beyond, in Egypt, 41; M.W.S. of, 41; Mithraic supper transmitted to, 72; ritual of the, 175, 177, 185; ritual of Co-Masons, 176

Rosenkreutz, C., book M. of, 174; death of, 174; initiation of, 171; tomb of, 174; traditional life of, 169, 172; true life of, 174-75; visited Egyptian Lodge, 175

Rosicrucian Brotherhood, and Masonry, 143; attacked and defended, 171; founding of, 174; literature, 169-74; philosophy, glamour of, 169; philosophy resembles Neo-Platonism, 172

Rosicrucian Manifestos, The, 143

Rosicrucians, 10

Rosy Cross earliest reference to, 143; Brothers of, 169; degree of, 168; history of Order of, 174-77; Order of, exists in secret, 175

Round Table, 18, 122

Royal Arch, analogy to, in Egypt, 39; and 3° of Jewish Mysteries, 72; and Zerubbabel, 72; and King Josiah, 72; and King Solomon, 72; associated with 3°, 156; at York, 156; degrees, 11; Egyptian ceremony corresponding to, 40; first mention of, 153-54; of Enoch, 72

Royal Order of Scotland, 124, 168-69, 182

Rubric of Fourth Initiation, 47

Rulers Four, of Elements, 21

Ruta and Daitya, 16

Sacral knot, 55

Sacramental power, 10; introduced into Masonic degrees, 11; of 33°, 45; outpoured by officers, 38; received by Jews from Egypt, 64-65; of Masonic ceremonies, 6, 10

Sais, Temple of Isis at, 18; burial place of Osiris, 34

Saints, Patron, of Freemasonry, 23; and fertility cult, 69

Salt strewn in east, 38

Schaw Statues, 143

Schliemann, 54

Scheffer, Baron C. 183

School, the authentic, 2-3; the anthropological, 3-5; the mystical, 5-6; the occult, 6-7

Schools of Masonic thought, four, 2

Science of The Sacraments, The, 10

Scientific discoveries used for destruction, 31; methods applied to study of Masonry, 2

Scotland, Royal Order of, 124, 168-69, 182

Scots degrees, and Royal Order, 168; development of, 181; rituals of, 182

Scots Lodges claimed extra-ordinary powers, 183

Scott-Elliot, 16

Scottish Rite benefits of the, 190; little value in intermediate degrees of, 12; origin of the, 118

Second or Sacred Lodge, 71

Secrecy, effects of, 178

Secret language of Masonry, 162; of Egyptian Mysteries, 30-31

Secret Tradition in Freemasonry, 74

Secret Sects of Syria and Lebanon, 4

Secret Tradition in Israel, 74

Secrets of Mysteries guarded, 28; Masonic in Southern India, 4

Sepher Yetzirah, 74

Sepher ha Zohar, 74

Serapis, Mysteries of, 32-33

Set or Typhon, 33,37

Sheba, Queen of, 69

Shekinah, 75

Shemsu Heru, 16

Shin, 76

Shri Krishna, 20

Siculus, Diodorus, 26

Signs Masonic, universality of, 3-4

Sisyphus, 87

Solemn Act of Union, 3

Solomon, 1, 26, 66; and ceremony of raising, 70; and

Jewish Mysteries, 67; Song of, 69; sons of, 130-31; Symbolism of temple of, 75; temple of, 66-67

Sophocles, 78; *Les Mystere d'Eleusis* by, 78

Soubise Maitre, 132

South, The, 13

Sovereign, Grand Inspector-General, 43, 44; Angels linked with, 43-44; Pharaoh held position of, 42

Sovereign Prince of Rose-Croix, 40

Speculative Masonry, 107, 141-57, 160

Speth, G.W., 2

Spiritual illumination, Egypt centre of, 25

Spiritual King of World, 43

Spiritual power conferred varies, 11; outpoured, 10, 13, 24; sometimes withdrawn, 11

Springett, Bernard H., 4

Spurious Masonry, 3,48

Star of Initiation, 43; of Horus, 43, 46; of the Sea, 84; of 33°, 43

Steele's Essays, 146

Steinmetzen, 132

Steps, proper, opened doors in pyramid, 26

St. Leger, Elizabeth, 147

Stonemasons of Germany, 132-33

Story of Atlantis, 16

Strict Observance, Rite of the, 179, 180

Substituted secrets, 76

Succession, Masonic, 11, 13, 38-39; and Royal Arch, 39; of higher degrees, 39; of I.M.s, 13-14, 39; types of, 13

Superman, evolution of, 48

Supreme, Aspects of, 20

Sun-God, Osiris the, 37, 44

Sweden, Masonry in, 158

Swinburne, 83

Sword and Trowel, 168, 182-83

Symbolical interpretation of Freemasonry, 5-6

Symbolism, Egyptian, 45

Symbolism, Masonic, antedates 1717, 3; immense antiquity of, 4

Symbolism, Masonic, found on wall paintings, 3-4; existed in Ancient Mysteries, 4; found in Africa, etc., 4; of Deity, animal, 19

Syria, source of Masonry, 4

Syrian descent of 3°, 69-70; s...of g...and d..., 38; in Mysteries of Osiris, 38

s...s..., of Mysteries of Osiris, 38; common origin of Mysteries shown by, 50; of 30°, 41

s...n, of Mysteries of Serapis, 33

T.G.A.O.T.U., 10; consciousness of, symbolized, 10

Table, Round, 18

Tammuz myth, 68-70; Mysteries of, 102

Tantalus, 87

Tatler, The, refers to Masonry, 146

Tauler, Johann, 161

Taverns and Masonry, 148, 151, 185

Tehuti or Thoth, 17

Templars, Knights, 69, 161-67; and Syrian story of 3°, 69; French, settled in Scotland, 124

Temple, King Solomon's, 66-67;

mystic building of, 67, 75;
  rebuilding of, 75; symbolical
  interpretation of, 75
Teresa S., 161
Terra cotta Minoan models, 57,
  59
Test of initiation, 28-29, 31-32,
  46; Eleusinian, 88; of
  clairvoyance, 32
Tetragrammaton, 76-77
Theodoric the great, 127
Theodosius, 116; edict of, against
  Mysteries, 116
Theosophical Society, 162
Thirtieth degree linked with ruling
  Ray, 42; karma studied in,
  41-42; reflects Manu, 48-49;
  reflects W.S.W., 49; vengence
  elements of, explained, 41;
  s...s of, 41
Thirty-first degree, 41-42
Thirty-third degree, and power of
  King, 43, 49, 185-86; awakens
  triple spirit, 43; formed in
  America, 186-87; great white
  Angels of, 43, 44; powers
  conferred in, 44, 185-86; power
  of, almost equals Initiation, 44;
  reflects R.W.M., 49
Third Lodge, 71
Thought-form in inner worlds, 10;
  Masonic, and Craft degrees,
  106-07
Three Degrees, Grand Lodge
  acknowledges, 3
Throne room at Knossos, 56-57;
  and temple of the Mysteries, 57
Thoth or Thuti, 17; The Hidden
  Light taught by, 79-80
Thyrsus or caduceus, 93-94; Ida
  and pingala symbolized in, 94;
  Kundalini and, 94

Timaeus, The, 53
Titus, 72
Tityus, 87
Toys of Bacchus, 94-95
Traces of a Hidden Tradition, 160
Tradition, Articles of Union fixed,
  157; associated with religious
  worship, 4; Chaldaean, 68;
  crossing of lines of, 116;
  Culdees and, 118
Tradition, differences of, of Mark
  Degree, 157; Egyptian, 67-68;
  French, and de Molay, 167;
  French, diverged, 157-58; great
  antiquity of, 5; H.O.A.T.F. and
  Templars, 167; higher degrees
  and, 118; Intentional confusion
  of, 107, 111, 160; Irish, allied
  to York, 155; line of, adopted
  by Anderson, 156-57; many
  lines of, 13; Memphis-Mizraim,
  12; methods of carrying on,
  160; modern Templars and,
  167; of Blue Degrees, 158; of
  I.M. derived from Egypt, 158;
  of Royal Arch, 156; of
  Tammuz myth, 68-69; oral, and
  Roman Collegia, 150; Royal
  Order of Scotland and Templar,
  168; Scottish, and Knights
  Templars, 167; secret Societies
  and Masonic, 161-63; Templar,
  and 18°, 165; Templar and
  Masonic, 164-65; 30°, and
  Templar, 167; three lines of,
  68; two lines of descent of,
  117-18; union of two lines of,
  157; vengeance, and Templars,
  167; York, and "Ancients",
  155
Traditional history, 71; Masonic,
  5, 14, 68; York and, 153

Transactions of Q.C., No. 2076, 2

Transition from operative to speculative, 147

Transfiguration symbolizes Third Initiation, 46

Transitional stage, Masonry in, 12

Transmission of Jewish rites, 71, 72; of Mysteries to Essenes, 72-73

Travelling Freemasons, 126

Tree, the sacred, 51, 55

Trials, preliminary for Mysteries, 28

Triple spirit awakened in 33°, 43

Trinity, idea of, introduced into Egypt, 18

Troubadours, 161-62

Troy, 54

Troyes, Chretien de, 122

Truth, Isis Queen of, 20

Tuamutef, 21

Tuatha De Danaan, 121

Tubal Cain, 70

Typhon or Set, 35, 37; and darkness or winter, 37

T... o... g... r..., 31

Uma, corresponds to Demeter, 83

Union, solemn Act of, 3

Universal language, legend of, in Masonry, 30

Universe, constitution of, symbolized in Masonry, 10; Lodge builds, in miniature, 23

Vaughan, Thomas, 143, 172; and Eugenius Philalethes, 143

Vault, hidden, 39-40

Veils in Royal Arch ceremony, 39-40

Vespasian, 72

Virgil, 102

Virgin-Mother, Isis the, 46

W.J.W. reflects 18°, 49

W.S.W. reflects 30°, 49

Waite, Bro. A.E., 5, 74, 144, 153, 171

Wall-paintings, depict Masonic signs, 4; secret language in, 30-31

Ward, J.S.M., 4, 68-69, 101, 110, 129

Wedgwood, Bro. J.I., on Co-Masonry, 192

Western school of occultism, 175

Wheat in consecration, 24

White Lodge, inspired Mysteries, 25, 42-43, 45

White Masonry, 39, 42-45; great Angels of, 43-44; power ourpoured in, 44

Who was Hiram Abiff?, 4, 68-70

"Widow's son", 162

Wilmshurst, Bro. W.L., 6

Wine used at consecration, 23; poured in south, 23

Wisdom, strength and beauty, 7-8

Women admitted to Mysteries, 54, 85, 191; admitted to Masonry, 191; hierophants, 85; Priestesses of Eleusis, 85

Word, Mason, 143; lost, 39, 75, 182; of power, 32; Omnific, 76; quest for, 168; revealed under oath, 143; symbolism of lost, 76; Zohar refers to, 75

Worker, celestial, in metals, 20

World, King of, 43

World-Teacher, coming of, 195; Tehuti or Toth, 17

Wren, Sir Christopher, 145;

Lodge Antiquity and, 145

York Ancient workings, 153;
"Ancients" and, 153, 155-56;
Athelstan and, 123; City, Lodge
at, 145-46; Culdees of, 123;
Edwin and Assembly at, 139;
Grand Lodge of, 153; guardian
centre of Mysteries, 153;
"Grand Lodge", 146

Zerubbabel, 71-72
Zohar, 74-75